AGAINST GREAT ODDS

AGAINST GREAT ODDS

THE HISTORY OF
ALCORN STATE UNIVERSITY

by

Josephine McCann Posey

UNIVERSITY PRESS OF MISSISSIPPI   JACKSON

Copyright © 1994 by the University Press of Mississippi
All rights reserved
Manufactured in the United States of America

The paper in this book meets the guidelines for permanence and durability of the Committee on Production Guidelines for Book Longevity of the Council on Library Resources.

Library of Congress Cataloging-in-Publication Data

Posey, Josephine McCann.
    Against great odds : the history of Alcorn State University / by Josephine McCann Posey.
    p.   cm.
    Includes bibliographical references (p.) and index.
    ISBN 978-1-61703-194-6
    1. Alcorn State University—History. I. Title.
LD131.A24P67 1994
378.762'285—dc20   93-38375
                                                                                           CIP

British Library Cataloging-in-Publication data available

DEDICATED TO THE ALCORN FAMILY

THE ALCORN ODE

Beneath the shade of giant trees,
Fanned by a balmy southern breeze
Thy classic walls have dared to stand
A giant thou art in learning's band;
O, Alcorn dear, our mother, hear
Thy name, we praise, thy name we sing.

Thy name thy sons have honored far;
A crown of gems thy daughters are;
When country called her flag to bear,
The Gold and Purple answered, "Here"
O, Alcorn dear, our mother, hear
Thy name, we praise, thy name we sing.

Far as our race thy clan shall need—
So far to progress thou shalt lead
Thy sons with clashing arms of trade;
In useful arts full garbed thy maids;
O, Alcorn dear, we proudly bear
Thy standard on to victory.

—Mrs. J. S. Himes

CONTENTS

PREFACE ix

ACKNOWLEDGMENTS xv

1. THE FIRST DECADE 3
2. THE STRUGGLE TO SURVIVE 14
3. INTO THE TWENTIETH CENTURY 21
4. TURBULENT TIMES 28
5. A NEW ERA 37
6. SERVING THE PEOPLE
   Administration, Faculty, and Staff 43
7. A GROWING VARIETY OF CHOICES
   Academics 52
8. HOW TO MAKE A LIVING AND HOW TO LIVE
   Support Services 72
9. BALANCING WORK AND PLAY
   Students and Student Services 82
10. EFFICIENCY AND ACCOUNTABILITY
    Fiscal Affairs 89
11. DETERMINING THE MISSION
    Institutional Advancement, Planning, and Research 94

12. FROM GREEK REVIVAL TO MODERN
    Physical Facilities   99

13. PREPARING TO WIN
    Athletics   104

14. THE ALCORN SPIRIT
    Alumni Relations   110

15. A LOOK TO THE FUTURE   140

EPILOGUE   145

APPENDIXES   147

A NOTE ON SOURCES   207

INDEX   209

PREFACE

Alcorn State University, the oldest historically black land-grant institution in the United States and the second-oldest state-supported institution of higher learning in the state of Mississippi, is the work of black men and women struggling against enormous odds to educate themselves and their children. Named in honor of a white man, Mississippi Governor James L. Alcorn, it was founded on the site originally occupied by Oakland College, a school for white youth established by Presbyterians in 1828. Early on, the issue of race intruded on the quiet isolated campus. Oakland's first president, Dr. Jeremiah Chamberlain, was assassinated at the gate of the president's home as the result of a dispute over slavery. Today, he and members of his family lie buried in the cemetery located on the Alcorn campus.

The Civil War closed the white institution, and in 1871 the state of Misssissippi purchased the abandoned campus for forty thousand dollars, named it after the governor, and designated it for the education of black youth. John R. Lynch, a leading black politician and speaker of the Mississippi House of Representatives, signed the bill that created the new school. Alcorn is predated only by the University of Mississippi in Oxford. To serve the land-grant mission, Alcorn received three-fifths of the allocations, with two-fifths going to the white college. Alcorn's first president was Hiram R. Revels, who resigned his seat as the first black senator in American history to assume the post. The state legislature provided fifty thousand dollars in cash for ten successive years for the school's establishment and overall operations. The state also granted Alcorn three-fifths of the proceeds earned from the sale of thirty thousand acres of land scrip for agricultural colleges. The land was sold for $188,928; Alcorn's share was $113,400. This money, to be used only for the agricultural and mechanical components of the college, was invested, and the 8 percent interest went toward expanding the college's income. In 1878 Alcorn University became Alcorn Agricultural and Mechanical College and was named a land-grant college on the basis of the federal government's 1862 Morrill Act. (The state's original purchase of 225 acres of land has grown to become a 1700-acre campus.)

The school's three major components in 1871 were: (1) the college course of four years, (2) the preparatory course of two years, and (3) the graded course of three years. The departments of study were English, Latin, mathematics, and the industrial department, which included agriculture, carpentry, blacksmithing, shoemaking, printing, painting, nurse training, sewing, domestic science, and laundering. The students spent the mornings from seven o'clock until noon in classes. After noon they worked in the various shops for a rate of eight cents per hour. Room and board, including laundry, was five dollars a month. The institution, like other black schools during these years, was less a college than a trade school.

The goals for the institution set by the Mississippi legislature clearly emphasized training rather than education:

> Chapter XIX, Section 1. Be it enacted by the Legislature of the State of Mississippi, that the institution known as Alcorn University is hereby established as, and declared to be an agricultural college for the education of the Negro youth of the state and to be hereafter known as the Alcorn Agricultural and Mechanical College of the State of Mississippi.
> Section 9. Be it further enacted, that each of the said Boards of Trustees shall possess all the power necessary and proper for the accomplishment of the trusts reposed in them viz: The establishment and maintenance of a first class institution at which the youth of the State of Mississippi may acquire a common school education and a scientific and practical knowledge of agriculture, horticulture, and the mechanical arts, also in the proper growth and care of stock, without, however, excluding scientific and classic studies, including military tactics.

At first the school was exclusively for black males, but in 1895 women were admitted. A women's dormitory, however, was not built until 1902. In 1993, women outnumber men at the university eighteen hundred to twelve hundred.

In 1974 Alcorn Agricultural and Mechanical College became Alcorn State University. Governor William L. Waller signed House Bill 298, granting university status to Alcorn and to the other state-supported colleges. In truth, this law created a change of name rather than of purpose. Alcorn remained the school it had always been.

By adopting continually expanding goals and objectives, Alcorn has survived the difficulties of being a black school in a society that emphasizes white supremacy. At first the emphasis was on preparing youth for service in both general and applied knowledge areas such as agriculture, home economics, mechanical industries, general education and sciences, and teacher education; developing generic leadership skills in addition to those that were peculiar to various areas; and performing functions and services that were specific to land-grant colleges, such as incorporating adult programs necessary to provide citizens basic education on a short-term basis. All these goals were accomplished despite lukewarm support from state officials.

By the early 1990s, however, Alcorn had grown from this limited emphasis to become a more diversified university. It has branched out in its educational services to meet the varied needs of the community at large. It provides an undergraduate education that enables students to continue their work in graduate and professional schools, engage in teaching, and enter other professions. Graduate programs equip students for further training in specialized fields while they contribute to the advancement of knowledge through scholarly research and inquiry. There are also opportunities for students to develop as responsible citizens and scholars in a democratic society. In the post-civil rights world as Mississippi has come to recognize the importance of educating all its citizens, Alcorn has grown in status and importance.

Alcorn's location in rural southwest Mississippi has also been an important determinant of its character. Situated in Claiborne County, approximately four and a half miles northeast of the Mississippi River, it is seven miles west of tiny Lorman, Mississippi; eighty miles south of the capital city of Jackson; forty-five miles south of Vicksburg; and forty miles north of historic Natchez. The school is set apart from heavily populated areas, and its geography symbolically expresses its separation for most of its history from the rest of the state. Although the isolation has helped the college survive, unfortunately at times it also means a distance from the crucial nurture of the outside world.

Alcorn began with eight faculty members in 1871. In 1993 there are more than five hundred faculty and staff. The student body has grown from one hundred seventy-nine mostly local male students to more than three thousand students from all over the world, 60 percent of whom are female. More than 50 percent of the faculty possess doctoral degrees. While early graduates of Alcorn had limited horizons, more recent alumni are successful doctors, lawyers, dentists, teachers, principals, ministers, administrators, managers, and owners of their own businesses. Alcorn State University has had fifteen presidents. Of these, Dr. Walter Washington, who assumed the presidency in 1969, is in 1993 the longest-tenured president not only in Alcorn's history but of any other institution in American academic history.

Over the decades, then, the school that was once a struggling institution has become one of the leading black universities in the nation. Alcorn State University is now fully accredited with seven divisions and degree programs in more than fifty areas. The first graduating class consisted of three members, Lafayette Murphy, A. J. Gossin, and A. D. Snodgrass; in 1993 the total is more than three hundred. Alumni throughout the world have, because of their successes, heightened the school's reputation, demonstrating that graduates leave the university qualified to perform responsibly as citizens of Mississippi and the United States. Alcorn is now a true university, its trade school status and image having been long discarded.

The struggles to keep Alcorn alive have not been in vain. Alcorn has a history so special that even non-Alcornites through the years have made themselves a part of its tradition. Listening to graduates tell of their days at Alcorn, especially in the early years, is to realize how far Alcorn has come since 1871. At the annual alumni banquet in 1974, one 1914 graduate remembered that her father had come to campus as a cook so that his family could be near a school. She recalled how, as a student at Alcorn, she lined up three times a day to march to the cafeteria to eat. Breakfast was served at 6:00 A.M. Other alumni told how they used to have to get permission slips in and out of the dormitories, had to be in at 6:00 P.M., and how they received grades on their rooms for cleanliness.

Alumni often talk about the crooked roads from Highway 61 to the campus and how they thought they would never get to Alcorn. The school was at times in its history almost inaccessible, especially if it rained, because there was only a dirt road leading to the campus. At one time individuals on the way to the campus had to pass through a cattle gap, a crossing that kept cattle from escaping. That was an Alcorn landmark. Crossing it, people felt they had really made a journey.

Alcorn has been described as homelike, where the sweet perfume from the honeysuckle kissed by Mississippi dews pervades a spacious lawn surrounded by modern buildings as well as by antebellum architecture. Many parents have viewed Alcorn as a place where their children will be removed from the contaminating influences of city life.

Alumni who moved away to big cities talk about the advantage of getting youth into an environment conducive to good behavior and concentrated study. The opportunities at Alcorn for self-help have always been greater than at most other schools in the country.

Through the years Alcorn has been called a place where dreams can come true. The administration, faculty, staff, and students appear to share a common belief that the American dream is not dead, that an individual can make it even though life is not easy and getting a college education may not be either. Since its inception, Alcorn has taken strong and positive actions to ensure that black people have a chance at survival. Alumni express immense pride in Alcorn, pride in their degrees and in Alcorn's reputation for excellence. "If I had my life to live over," one alumnus said, "I would choose Alcorn again and would hope the same instructors and students would be there. It is my desire that my children will attend Alcorn and every generation after them." Another wrote: "I must thank those individuals on the faculty who urged me to stick it out when my shoes had no soles and cardboard paper had to be placed in the bottom of them.... Whatever I am today, Alcorn is responsible." Alumni over the years have agreed with former president Levi Rowan when he said that "the state might easily build another college elsewhere and name it Alcorn but nothing would ever carry away and wipe out the triumphant history of the institution."

Throughout the university's history, Alcorn has followed a carefully structured plan to retain and enhance the image and potential of students who passed through, a plan that was designed to attract young people whose intent was to receive a quality education. The student body, formerly all black, now includes whites, Orientals, Africans, and West Indians; the current faculty is a culturally diverse group of men and women; the student population, which once drew on only thirteen counties, now consists of residents of all eighty-two counties in the state, more than thirty other states, and at least eighteen foreign countries. The college has grown from a liberal arts college to a multifaceted state university with numerous degree offerings including a nursing program in Natchez. The facilities have increased from three historic buildings to approximately eighty modern structures. The athletic program, once composed of football, basketball, and baseball, now includes track, tennis, volleyball, and golf. The alumni membership has grown from three to more than twenty thousand.

In 1939, Milan Davis wrote a brief history of Alcorn's first sixty-seven years entitled *Pushing Forward*. In 1971 *The Centennial History of Alcorn A&M College* by Melerson Guy Dunham was published. That book traced the history of the university from 1871 to 1971, from the administration of Hiram Rhodes Revels to the early years of Walter Washington. The present book, while encompassing the story of the first hundred years, focuses for the most part on the last twenty-five, a period of great change and growth for Alcorn.

The "new Alcorn," as President Washington labeled the university in 1993, will continue to serve the generations to come. Its distinct heritage must never be lost, and the preservation of that heritage is the responsibility of all concerned Alcornites and friends. It is my hope that this history of the university will help inspire the determination to preserve all that is good from the past and to continue improvements into the future.

ACKNOWLEDGMENTS

Researching and writing the history of Alcorn has been a challenge and a learning experience. I am grateful to President Walter Washington for the faith and confidence he placed in me for the undertaking of such a major task. To his secretary, Erma Hawkins, who supplied me with any information I requested about his tenure at Alcorn, I am also grateful. I am indebted as well to those individuals, near and far, who responded to my many requests for historical data. I am convinced that there is much more information that has not yet surfaced, and I shall continue to solicit material for the Alcorn archives for use in future editions of the university's history.

I also extend special appreciation to Vice President Rudolph Waters and his secretary, Mary Irving, for their continuous support during this endeavor. As for Doreacer Turner, this project's secretary and research assistant, words cannot express my thanks for all the services she has rendered as well as the work study student, Cheryl Hughes. I wish also to acknowledge with gratitude the guidance and criticism of Dr. John F. Marszalek, professor of history at Mississippi State University and a renowned author, who served as a consultant throughout the project. Special thanks go to Mary Harris, who guided me in the Alcorn Room in the library as I researched, and to Dr. Newtie Boyd, Donna Hayden, Bobby Shaw, Alexsa Mims, Valerie Thompson, and Vander Breland, who rescued us from so many computer and printer traps.

My thanks to all Alcorn employees, friends, and alumni who took time out of their busy schedules to let me interview them in order to obtain additional information or to validate existing data. I am also grateful to those who stopped me on campus to offer documents or pictures that might prove helpful or just to ask how the research was going and to wish me well. Special appreciation goes to Dr. Robert L.

Smith, the acting chairman of the Health, Physical Education, and Recreation Department, for his untiring support from the beginning to the completion of the research. He was most instrumental in my efforts to collect historical data. Special appreciation also goes to Ralph Payne and Henry Houze for their assistance in the securing of pictures. I wish also to acknowledge Karen Roundtree Shadwick, Lola Brown, and Annette Guyton Raper for their assistance in this project. I further acknowledge Dr. Richard M. Abel, Seetha A-Srinivasan, Ginger Tucker, Anne Stascavage and the rest of the staff of the University Press of Mississippi for guiding this book through to publication. I owe special thanks to copyeditor Carol Cox for her careful and thorough work on the manuscript.

For their moral support throughout this writing, I wish to thank my parents, Mr. and Mrs. Calvin McCann; my sisters, Helen and Connie, and their families; my brother, John, and his family; and all of my in-laws. Kristin, my niece and goddaughter, wrote the first paragraph for this book and then lost it, but I thank her anyway. My husband, Curtis, and my son, Carlos, were wonderfully supportive during the long months in which I wrote well into the night, surrounded by books, papers, pencils, pens, pictures, articles, and newspapers. I thank them for their patience.

In my research I realized that there were so many illustrious individuals who are a part of Alcorn's history that it was impossible to try to recognize everyone, especially in the alumni section. I hope to write a history of the Alcorn State University National Alumni Association, in which I will be able to highlight contributing alumni throughout the world in a more detailed way.

AGAINST GREAT ODDS

ONE

The First Decade

In 1871, upon the recommendation of Governor James Lusk Alcorn, the state of Mississippi purchased the site where Oakland College had stood, so that a school for the education of black males could be built. The governor desired equality in the state's educational system, yet he wanted blacks and whites to be kept separate. In his message to the legislature that year, he said:

> Colored boys may be expected to present themselves, within four or five years, at the level of the curriculum of the high school, if not the university. We ought not be unprepared to discharge our obligation to them, as we discharge it to white boys, by the time that they have made the coming demand for a collegiate education.
> ... I am anxious that steps be taken to initiate the realization of that purpose so as to throw out to the emulation of the colored boys of our public schools the same generous system of free and half-free scholarships superior to all clashes of party or race, a perpetual glory of the Mississippians of my own blood ...
> I myself was a slaveholder, and apprehensive that the restraints of reason would have been insufficient in the case of a people who had been held under lifelong restraints of force, I did not accept the facts of reconstruction without some lingering doubts. Evil prophecies in certain quarters fell upon my ear, as no doubt they have fallen on yours, with more or less misgivings. To set at rest that form of opposition to the great work on which the happiness of our fellow-citizens of all classes depends, and

to assure you my judgment and conscience as to the wisdom of reconstruction, I have instituted investigations referred to above into the evidence already given in Mississippi of the capacity of the colored people for well-ordered freedom. I now place the results of my inquiries before you in order to deepen your conviction, as they have already deepened mine, that reconstruction goes forward to the sure consummation of moral and material triumph.

Soon afterwards, the state legislature established the first black land-grant college founded in the United States and named it Alcorn University in honor of the governor. From its inception, though, the new institution was a product both of its environment and of the individuals who peopled it. It was clearly the child of the state in which it resides.

Mississippi is a small state. In 1993 thirty-second in size, it has approximately 47,716 square miles of forest and rich soil, which is its most valuable natural resource. Before the coming of the Europeans, Indian tribes here created an intricate culture and civilization that the white men found substantially different from their own. The Spanish, the English, and the French resolutely pushed the Indians aside, insisting all the way that this action was bringing civilization to a barbarous land.

In 1798 Mississippi finally passed from Spanish to American hands. Many problems persisted, however. There was trouble over the new territory's boundaries. Roads were poor. Traveling, in general, was difficult. For example, it took one governor forty-five days to get from Nashville to Natchez by boat. In 1806 Congress appropriated funds to improve the Natchez Trace, a long-established Indian avenue for hunting and war parties. This slash through the forest was very narrow (twenty feet wide), however, so that travel over it was difficult. Still, the improved road now enabled a mail rider to make the trip from Nashville to Natchez within a week. The Natchez Trace helped tie the Mississippi Territory to the rest of the nation.

One of the earliest railroads in the United States was built in Mississippi, costing around twenty-one thousand dollars per mile. Building roads and railroads was expensive and required increasingly large sums of money, which led to the establishment of more banks in order to finance the ambitious construction.

Under American rule, the Mississippi Territory grew rapidly. White settlers quickly became interested in organizing a state government so they might have more control over their own destinies. In 1817 Congress decided that the Mississippi Territory had a population large enough to be organized into a state. There were fourteen counties in the territory. Adams, Jefferson, Warren, Wilkinson, and Claiborne, where Alcorn is located, had the largest populations and were also the oldest and wealthiest. Natchez, just forty miles from the site where Alcorn would be built, was the new state's leading city. The town of Washington, adjacent to Natchez, became the capital of the territory. Washington surfaced as a possible name for the state. A majority, however, preferred the name Mississippi.

Drawing up a constitution was the next important task. A leading politician, George Poindexter, played a major role. The constitution allowed all white men over twenty-one years of age the right to vote if they paid a tax, served in the militia, and had lived in the territory for at least one year. The governor had to be at least thirty years old and own at least six hundred acres of land or have property valued at a minimum of two thousand dollars. A senate member had to be at least twenty-six years of age, own at least three hundred acres of land, and have property worth one thousand dollars. Representatives had to be at least twenty-two years of age and own at least one hundred fifty acres of land and property valued at five hundred dollars. At the beginning, then, the financial elite clearly governed the state.

With Mississippi a state rather than a territory, a new capital was established and named in honor of Andrew Jackson. Indians owned two-thirds of Mississippi's land in 1817, but white Mississippians believed that this land should be opened for white settlement. This became a major goal for the new state leaders. Pressure to have the Indians moved increased, with whites arguing that progress was being hindered, though in reality they simply coveted the land.

In 1829 Andrew Jackson became president of the United States, representing the wider democracy spreading across the nation. Jackson did not believe citizens should own property in order to be office holders or voters. He also insisted that office holders should be elected by the people and have limited terms. Mississippians shared these and other Jacksonian attitudes and decided to change the state constitution to include them. The result was a system of elections in almost all offices including judgeships. The new constitution, though it applied only to white males, would be the most democratic instrument of government ever to exist in Mississippi.

In 1828 Rev. Jeremiah Chamberlain, a Presbyterian preacher born in Gettysburg, Pennsylvania, decided that he wanted to establish a college under the auspices of his church in Lorman, Mississippi. He submitted his plan to his church's committee on resolutions, and they agreed to set up an institution of learning that would focus on the usual branches of science and literature, combined with a preparatory grammar school and a theological professorship. The committee consisted of men from three Louisiana parishes and eight Mississippi counties. At that time there was no institution in Mississippi, Louisiana, or Arkansas prepared to provide a collegiate course. The college was chartered in 1830 as the "Institution of Higher Learning under the care of the Mississippi Presbyter," and the name was changed to Oakland College in 1832.

The new school opened its doors on May 14, 1830. The college was controlled by the Synod of Mississippi. An unknown donor contributed twenty-five thousand dollars for the purpose of endowing a theological professorship, and over two thousand acres of land were donated. The college also acquired a president's home, a professor's house, a steward's house, and fifteen cottages for students. The majority of the students became planters, physicians, and lawyers, but some did prepare for the ministry. The first baccalaureate degree to be conferred in the state of Mississippi was granted by Oakland College.

During the first year, Chamberlain, who was president of the school, and his brother John were the only faculty members, but by the early 1850s the faculty had grown and courses were offered in such areas as rhetoric, moral and mental philosophy, Christianity, chemistry, astronomy, political economy, ancient languages, mathematics, English, and literature.

By 1851–1852 almost one thousand white males had been educated. There were now thirty cottages for students, halls for the literary societies, and a college library with about four thousand volumes. Most of the construction work was done by slaves. On September 5, 1851, Chamberlain was stabbed and killed by a community resident as a result of a dispute over slavery.

During the presidency of R. L. Stanton, several professors were added and at least seventy thousand dollars was expended in 1853–1854 for the construction of buildings and for the liquidation of accumulated debts. Stanton resigned as president, however, because all salaries other than the president's were dependent on monies from tuition, and he found it difficult to obtain and hold competent faculty members.

Rev. James Purviance replaced Stanton as president and also took over his duties as professor of mental and moral sciences and evidences of Christianity. The curriculum included the teaching of arithmetic, English grammar, Greek, French, Spanish, reading, and writing. Tuition was advertised as twenty dollars for the summer terms and thirty dollars for the winter terms, plus twelve dollars a month for boarding, washing, and similar necessities. Students furnished their own beds, bedding, and furniture.

The college closed because of the Civil War. Afterwards, an attempt was made to revive it. Rev. Joseph Calvin was elected president but died early in his administration and the school was closed for good. In 1871, the synod sold the college to the state of Mississippi, which made it the site of Alcorn University. The price was forty thousand dollars and, after all debts were paid, the remaining funds were used to build Chamberlain Hunt Academy located in Port Gibson, Mississippi.

The state experienced tremendous change between 1830 and 1840. Andrew Jackson's removal of the Indians meant that large areas of new land could be opened for settlement. Land, therefore, became cheaper and more available. Approximately seven and a half million acres of land were sold over a period of ten years, and the 1834 cotton crop was as large as that of any other state. Mississippi's wealth grew dramatically.

In 1837 a panic hit the United States, and Mississippi suffered. The price of cotton dropped from around seventeen cents a pound to around eight cents a pound and the worth of a black slave field hand from one thousand dollars to two hundred fifty dollars. The value of cotton land dropped from approximately twenty-five dollars per acre to two to three dollars. These changes in the economy brought economic hardship and property loss. By the mid-1840s however, the state seemed to be back on its feet.

Cotton reigned as king in Mississippi, and cotton cultures meant slavery. By 1840 there were more blacks in Mississippi than there were whites. The state's demand for black slaves was so voracious that they had to be brought from other areas within the United States. Most slaves worked in the fields, but some were household slaves. Whatever they did, they were viewed as inferior people whose very natures suited them only for slavery. The seed of racial prejudice found welcoming soil in Mississippi, and Alcorn would later be affected by the flourishing plant.

Higher education began early in Mississippi with the establishment of Jefferson College at Washington. In 1869 collegiate education for blacks in Mississippi started with the establishment of private Tougaloo College, though the school did not receive its charter until 1871. In 1866, Shaw College (later Rust College) in Holly Springs was established. Other black institutions were established in the postwar era including Jackson College, which began in Natchez in 1877 and moved to Jackson in 1883. Alcorn, however, was the only fully state-supported college for African-Americans to be organized at that time. State-funded Mississippi A.&M. College (later Mississippi State University), the University of Mississippi, and the private Mississippi College were not open to blacks. A separate board of trustees governed each institution. Members of the boards of the public colleges were appointed by the governor, and he was the link between the board and the college.

By 1860, of the 791,305 people in Mississippi, 436,631 were of African descent. Slavery was more entrenched than ever, but a rising tide of national opposition increasingly frightened the slaveholders. The dispute over slavery grew ever hotter. The pro-slavery South was appalled when the Republican Party came into existence in 1854 espousing a policy of ending expansion of slavery into the territories. The resulting split brought on the Civil War.

Mississippi was the site of some of the war's fiercest fighting, with Vicksburg a particular area of contention. Armies marched and fought all around what is today Alcorn State University. The seat of state government was moved several times during the war because leaders felt unsafe in Jackson; Columbus, Enterprise, Macon, and Meridian all served as Mississippi's capital at different times during this period. Problems included clothing and food shortages, inflation, limited medicine, and the closing of schools. Most of all, whites worried about the effect of the conflict on their slaves.

After the war it was not easy to restore government or even normal life. Property had been destroyed and slaves emancipated. The system of slavery was dead, though the exact status of the freed slaves was uncertain, and conflict revolved around their future. Republicans gained control of the state government, but their own internal disputes and their inability to overcome their own racism as well as the state's made the postwar years turbulent. James L. Alcorn, a native Mississippian, was elected governor, but when he sought a second term, Adelbert Ames, a white northern army officer, defeated him. By 1875, the Republicans were driven out of office, and the old-line white leadership was back.

It was during these turbulent times that Alcorn University came into existence. Governor Alcorn favored separate but equal schooling for blacks, but many white Mississippians opposed any education for the former slaves. They wondered whether the state could justify higher education for a group of people many of whom lacked even the basic rudiments of reading and writing, but the legislature, which for one of the few times in its history contained black members, pushed ahead under Governor Alcorn's leadership. Thus Alcorn University was founded in an effort to keep from integrating the University of Mississippi.

The first president was Hiram Rhodes Revels, a native of Fayetteville, North Carolina, and a descendant of free blacks. Born on September 22, 1822, he attended Knox Academy, a preparatory school, but he never went on to gain a college degree. Concerning his early education, Revels said: "Two fine colored schools existed in Fayetteville, one taught by a colored lady and the other by a white lady. I attended the former, and together with other colored youths was fully and successfully instructed by our able and accomplished teacher in all branches of learning embraced in the curriculum of that school."

In 1845 he was ordained as a Methodist minister and served as pastor of the African Methodist Episcopal (A.M.E.) Church in Baltimore, Maryland, where in 1861 he organized two so-called colored or Negro regiments for the war. In 1863 he founded a school for freed blacks in St. Louis. He emphasized the importance of education and stressed to his students that they had to be prepared twice as well as white students. He later worked with the Freedmen's Bureau in Vicksburg. Settling in Natchez in 1866, he married Phoeba Bass, a native of Zanesville, Ohio, and the couple produced six daughters. Revels served as pastor of Zion A.M.E. Church on Pine Street in Natchez. In 1868 he became city alderman and in 1869 state senator from Adams County. Revels had quickly become one of the most significant Mississippi blacks of the Reconstruction Era.

A key moment in his political career occurred on the very first day of his service in the Mississippi senate. The impressive prayer he rendered when that body met in January 1870 convinced many who heard him that he was truly a man of great standing. White Republicans were particularly convinced that he would be a "suitable colored man," as the term was then, for the United States Senate. The state senate elected him United States senator in 1870. As a minister, he had always had ambivalent feelings about politics, but he came to believe that he could be of more service to blacks in public office than in the pulpit.

When Revels arrived in Washington, the Senate debated what to do about him. Should a black man be seated in the United States Senate? Several weeks of argument followed, focusing on the moral and legal implications of a black man holding a seat in a body where such as John C. Calhoun, Henry Clay, and Daniel Webster had sat. Revels was elected, however, by a vote of forty-eight to eight and took the oath of office on February 25, 1870.

He served in Washington only a short time, from February 1870 to March 1871, before he resigned to become president of a new school for blacks in Mississippi. Governor James Lusk Alcorn succeeded him for the full senatorial term. Once more Revels's desire to be of service to his race and state pushed him in this direction. There was talk in the legislature of naming the new school Revels University, but the new president insisted it be named after Governor Alcorn. Both men actually played major roles in the founding of the school, working together to prepare the bill that established it. The legislation was later signed by John R. Lynch, the black speaker of the state house of representatives. The management and control of Alcorn are both under the governance of the Board of Trustees of State Institutions of Higher Learning.

In the college's first year President Revels supervised eight faculty members, in addition to serving as professor of moral and intellectual philosophy. The faculty members were John G. Mitchell, A.M., professor of agricultural chemistry and mineralogy; Lawrence W. Minor, A.M., professor of Greek and Latin; John R. Blackburn, A.M., professor of mathematics and natural philosophy; Isaiah Mitchell, instructor in English and geography; Milton Coates and Patrick F. Williams, assistant instructors; Hon. George F. Brown, lecturer on political economy and constitutional law; and Samuel J. Ireland, superintendent.

The curriculum included one course of study for all students at either the secondary or college level. The emphasis areas were agricultural science, industrial arts, teacher training, and classical collegiate; it was also possible to study Latin for five years and Greek for four years. In 1871 four-year scholarships were awarded to one student from each district on a competitive basis. Each one also received a hundred-dollar stipend from the school fund. This stipend, however, was discontinued in 1878.

Few records remain from these early years. One of the most detailed descriptions of the school appeared as an advertisement in the July 23, 1874, issue of Frederick Douglass's *The New National Era:*

> The University, occupying the site of the institution, formerly known as Oakland College is situated in Claiborne County, four and one-half miles northeast from Rodney on the Mississippi River.

The location, far removed from the contaminating influences of city life, is high and healthful; and the surroundings are agreeable and attractive in an eminent degree.

Its commodious buildings all erected and furnished for academic purposes, are situated in a beautiful oak grove, gently undulating and clothed in a perennial dress of verdue pleasing to the eye and quietude.

No discrimination is recognized by the institution on account of color, caste or other class distinctions.

The ample endowment of the University enables it to offer the facilities at a very low rate. Board, fuel and lights are furnished to each student at the rate of ten dollars per month, payable in advance; and for tuition, which is free to students from Mississippi. A matriculation fee of fifteen dollars is required from students coming from other states.

A competent corps of teachers are employed to give thorough instruction in branches usually embraced in the curriculum of American Colleges.

For further information address W. H. Furniss, Dean of the Faculty or Rev. H. R. Revels, D. D., President.

Despite such public relations bravado, the early years were difficult ones. In 1873, the annual audit indicated mismanagement of funds. Because of the supposed condition of the school, especially in the area of finance, the legislature removed some officials and requested that the governor reconstruct the institution: "Be it resolved by the legislature of the State of Mississippi that the auditor of public accounts use $250 from funds belonging to Alcorn University to investigate the conditions of affairs of said university."

After a board of trustees investigation, however, the school was given a favorable financial bill of health and a pledge of continued support. Revels, however, resigned his presidency when Adelbert Ames defeated Alcorn for the governorship. He knew that his close political relationship with Alcorn would cause him and the school problems with Ames. Revels had tried to remain neutral in the election, but Ames suspected that Revels secretly still supported Alcorn. He tried to remove Revels from his post, but Revels resigned instead. Republican politics was putting the new school in a terrible bind.

Ames now had to name a successor to Revels. He offered the post to Frederick Douglass, who declined, citing a lack of formal education. In 1875, Revels abandoned the Republicans to become a Democrat. When the Democrats took control of state government that year, he was reinstated as Alcorn's president. It was under his leadership that, in 1878, the state legislature reorganized the institution, changing its name to Alcorn Agricultural and Mechanical College in order to conform to the requirements mandated in the 1862 federal Morrill Land-Grant Act.

The law reads: "Be it enacted by the legislature of the State of Mississippi that the institution known as Alcorn University is hereby established as and declared to be an agricultural college for the education of the colored youth of the state, and to be hereafter known as the Alcorn Agricultural and Mechanical College of the State of Mississippi." This reorganization enabled the school to become officially the first college for black people established under the 1862 federal legislation, an achievement that became known beyond the state's boundaries. The appropriation for 1878 was six thousand dollars, including interest on the agricultural land scrip. The enrollment in 1882 was 160.

In order to meet the requirements of a true land-grant school, however, Alcorn had to change. The curriculum had to include at least one agriculture course, although students did not have to present any specific credentials in order to pursue its study. The offerings were already as follows:

Academic Department
Mathematics—Mental, Higher and University Arithmetic, Algebra and Geometry.
English Language—Reading, Writing, Grammar, English and American Literature, History and Elocution.
Miscellaneous—Geography, Natural Philosophy, Chemistry, and Natural History.

College Preparatory Department
Freshman—Latin, Greek, Algebra, Geometry, English.
Sophomore—Latin, Greek, Trigonometry.
Junior—Latin, Greek, Botany, Astronomy, Natural Philosophy.
Senior—Chemistry, Rhetoric, Human Intellect, Zoology, Geology, Political Economy, Anatomy, Physiology, Constitutional Law, Evidences of Christianity.

The study of agriculture and military tactics became a requirement for all students, as mandated by the state. By that time, there were approximately 170 males enrolled at the school.

Revels sought to make Alcorn into the leading college in the state. He wanted it to mean to black citizens what Oakland College had meant to whites. In 1882, after nearly ten years of service, he resigned as president due to failing health. Regaining his strength, he felt strong enough to serve as a professor at Rust College in Holly Springs, Mississippi. In 1884 poor health once more caused him to resign. He died in 1901 of a stroke that he suffered while attending an annual religious conference in Aberdeen, Mississippi. He was serving as superintendent of the Holly Springs District of the African Methodist Episcopal

Church at the time. He is buried in the city cemetery in Holly Springs, Mississippi.

The first decade of Alcorn's existence was full of struggles, both internal and external, but there was hope and faith that Alcorn would overcome the barriers and serve the race.

TWO

THE STRUGGLE TO SURVIVE

Upon the resignation of Hiram Revels in 1882, John Burrus, the son of a slave woman and a white man, became the second president of Alcorn A.&M. College. He was born in 1848 in Tennessee, somewhere between Nashville and Murfreesboro. The middle of three sons, he and one brother entered Fisk University at the same time during the fall of 1867 along with two young women. They became the first graduates of Fisk in 1875. Burrus's motivation to go to school came from an alleged statement made by John C. Calhoun: "Show me a Negro who can solve a problem in algebra or conjugate a Greek verb and I will show you a Negro with a soul." Burrus said to his brother, "You take the mathematics and I'll take the Greek." This was the challenge that led them to success. They proved that a black person could easily solve a problem in mathematics and conjugate a Greek verb. In 1879 Burrus received a master's degree from Fisk, then studied law, and in 1881 was admitted to the Nashville bar. When he became president of Alcorn, he employed his brother James and other Fisk graduates.

In addition to being president, Burrus was professor of mental and moral science and constitutional law. He struggled with a state board of trustees in which half of the members were opposed to higher education for blacks. He refused to bend to the pressure, however, continuing to push for needed funds for the college. In 1884, a bill was passed requiring all schools funded by the legislature to file biennial reports reflecting detailed accounts of all expenditures. He used the periodic reports that he had to make to the legislature concerning the progress of the college as an avenue for soliciting funds and other needed assistance. Enrollment was better than ever. The 1885 president's report showed an average enrollment of 216 students with the 1887 graduating class consisting of 9 members. In 1890, the total enrollment was 248; in 1900 it increased to 339. There were 7 graduates and 16 teachers.

Burrus was greatly concerned about the agricultural and mechanical components of the college because the curriculum had not changed much, and he wanted to be sure that the college was fulfilling its mandate under the land-grant charter. It was obvious to him that the agricultural and mechanical program was in need of much improvement. He wanted to see more congruency between agricultural theory and practice.

During this time the best farm products and the best written examination papers from the college were recognized, being put on display at a state fair in Vicksburg, Mississippi, in 1886.

The Second Morrill Act (1890) was passed during Burrus's administration. No funds were available in the legislation for buildings, so Burrus warned the state legislature that, unless such funds were provided on the state level, Alcorn would be receiving less than its proper share of benefits from the new Morrill Act. Since the congressional act took care of some of the other expenses, the state had to provide the buildings. Alcorn's enrollment had increased to the point that students were being denied admission because existing dormitories could not accommodate them. Even Belles Lettres Hall, which had been built in 1830, was converted to a dormitory. Burrus's efforts led to special appropriations for buildings and repairs in 1890 that resulted in a hospital and a combination dormitory and classroom building. It was during this decade, too, that a college brass band and a literary society were established. The Young Men's Christian Association was organized in 1885. The college Lyceum Association had already been established at some previous time. Alcorn's graduates, having increased from three in 1882 to sixty-two, became successfully employed in the marketplace.

Burrus had a strong commitment to industrial (mechanical) education, which developed at a slow pace between the school's founding in 1871 and World War I. When he became president in 1882, he was instrumental in establishing the first trade department, which had a significant impact on the college. Burrus advocated a system of students doing repair work on the campus buildings as a way to save the college money. From 1885 to 1887 all maintenance was done by students. The tasks involved work in carpentry, masonry, plastering, painting, plumbing, tinnery, and glazing. Burrus said that "although we have no shops where the trades can be taught systematically, still we try to teach them as far as we can." The new Morrill Act of 1890 aided considerably in the development of industrial education at the college. In January 1891, a letter from the federal commissioner of education emphasized the limitations in the act on the use of federal funds. The letter, addressed to the presidents of state colleges of agriculture and the mechanic arts, stated:

> In this connection, your attention is respectfully invited to the limitations placed by the Act upon the use of the money received, which is to be applied only to instruction in agriculture, the mechanic arts, the English language, and the various branches of mathematical physical, natural, and economic science, with special reference to their application in the industries of life and the facilities of such instruction.

Burrus felt that all Alcorn students should indeed be required to study some type of trade. The mechanic arts program and the agriculture program were established at different times, but the Revels administration did not view them as being different in purpose even though the Morrill Act provided for both. There was not enough emphasis on separate curricula until Burrus's presidency.

At the beginning of the third decade in Alcorn's history, Burrus was still at the helm. The departments of blacksmithing and carpentry were initiated in 1893, both being taught by white men because black instructors could not be found. Few blacks had training in the mechanical arts area.

In 1893, one of Alcorn's graduates became president of Gibsland College in Louisiana. Another was given a professorship of agriculture at Prairie View Normal School in Texas. Still others chose to become successful farmers and to take on leadership roles in various black elementary and secondary schools all over the state. In 1893 Burrus established the first professional organization for black teachers in Mississippi.

In spite of President Burrus's successes, he and his brother James resigned from Alcorn after they were charged with violations relating to the financial affairs of the school. Burrus cited health problems as the reason for his resignation; his brother James said he was leaving to

President Hiram Rhodes Revels,
1871-1882

President John Houston Burrus,
1882-1893

President Wilson H. Reynolds,
1893-1894 (Unfinished term
completed by Andrew Howard whose
picture is not available)

President Thomas J. Calloway,
1894-1896

President Edward H. Triplett,
1896-1899

President William H. Lanier,
1899-1905

President Levi John Rowan,
1905-1911, 1915-1934

Isiah S. Sanders, acting president,
June 29, 1934-August 24, 1934

President John Adams Martin,
1911-1915

President William Harrison Bell,
1934-1944

President Preston Sewell Bowles,
1944-1945

President William Harrison Pipes,
1945-1949

President Jesse R. Otis,
1949-1957

President John Dewey Boyd,
1957-1969

President Walter Washington,
1969-1994

Oakland Chapel, 1830

President's Home, 1830

Left: Dormitory III, 1830; *below:* Belle Lettres, 1830.

Cleopatra D. Thompson Women's Tower, 1972

W. S. Demby Men's Tower, 1972

Dormitory II, 1830

John Dewey Boyd Library, 1969

E. Albert Dumas Hall (Library and Science Building), 1960

Administration Building, 1928

Administration Building, 1977

Above: Jesse A. Morris, Sr./W. C. Boykin Agricultural Science Building, 1974; *right:* Mechanical Arts Building, 1961.

Left: Industrial Technology Building, 1981;
above: Dairy Plant, 1972.

Eunice D. Powell Hall (Home Economics Building), 1955

Dorothy Gordon Gray Home Management House, 1956

Gymnasium/Auditorium, 1959

Above: Alcorn State University Nursing School, 1984; *below:* Davey L. Whitney Health, Physical Education and Recreation Complex, 1975.

The First "Miss Alcorn,"
Henriene Simpkins Knaives, 1926-1927

This page: Academic Life

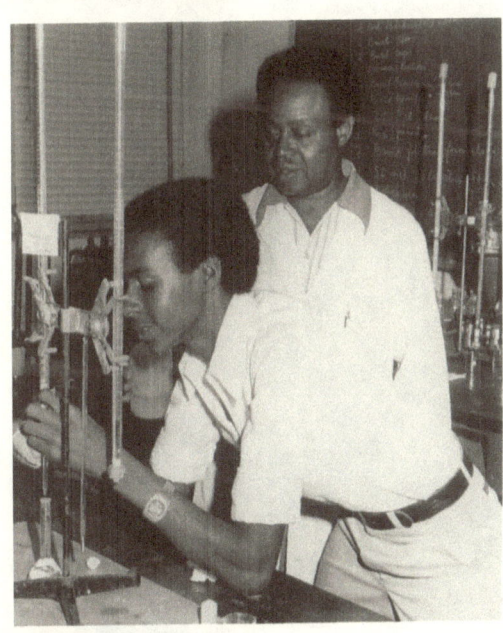

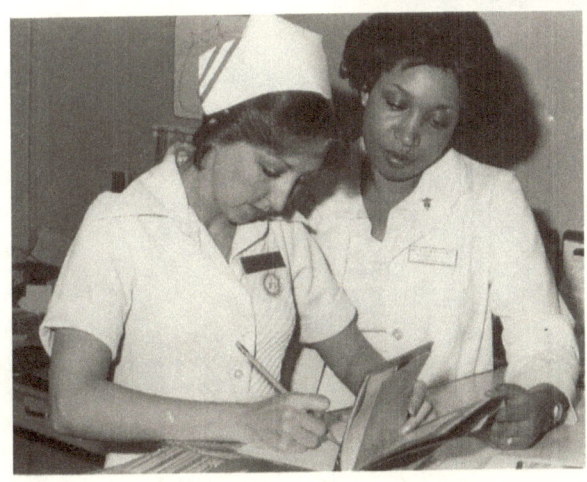

Student Union, 1964

go to Fisk University. A legislative investigation, however, revealed that the allegations were false. Governor John M. Stone stated in his 1894 biennial message that Burrus's problems with the university were due to personality conflicts with the trustees rather than to any lack of efficiency. The faculty and students supported Burrus, but he did not return. After his resignation he spent a year practicing law in Vicksburg, Mississippi. He later returned to Nashville, Tennessee, where he died on March 27, 1917.

The board of trustees selected Wilson H. Reynolds to become the new Alcorn president. Reynolds was a public school teacher in Vicksburg and was considered a man of high educational standing. One of his first priorities as president was to make the college a graded school in order to catch up with modern education. He was also concerned with uniformity in studies so that student classification could be determined. He believed that the college needed better publicity and that a college newspaper would help the local public admire and appreciate Alcorn's activities. After serving only four months, he suffered an influenza attack in December and died suddenly. Andrew J. Howard, a mathematics teacher, was asked by the board of trustees to complete the school term while the search for a replacement took place.

Alcorn was now very attractive to black educators across the nation, individuals who were anxious to become part of a great educational setting. After reviewing many applications, the board chose Thomas J. Calloway, another Fisk graduate, as the fourth president. Calloway was recommended by Booker T. Washington, who described him as having great executive ability and the talent of seeing to the heart of all issues. Calloway was born in Cleveland, Tennessee, in 1866 and graduated from Fisk University in 1889. Before becoming Alcorn's president, he had served as assistant high school principal in Evansville, Indiana, and as a clerk in the War Department in Washington, D.C. Calloway, as hard driving as Reynolds had been, was determined to ensure that people know about the college. While Reynolds had emphasized local publicity, President Calloway was chiefly concerned with the school's statewide reputation. Students were challenged to sell subscriptions to the college paper, thus carrying the story of Alcorn and its benefits to every corner of the state.

Calloway wanted to institute industrial education at Alcorn, and in 1899 this wish became a reality. Calloway's first aim was to secure the thinking mind, followed by training in righteousness. He said that he would rather graduate honest fools than wise devils. The industrial department grew, with considerable work done for off-campus residents. A firm in Atlanta, Georgia, purchased iron beds from the department; merchants purchased shoes made there; and the college printing office did most of the printing for the Alcorn community. A two-horse wagon made in the blacksmith shop was awarded a medal; a dozen shoes received honorable mention at the 1895 Atlanta Cotton States and International Exposition. The shoe department, which had been added in 1894, was well organized and equipped with the latest tools. Twenty-seven young men were trained, and 107 pairs of shoes were made in the first year.

Calloway wanted to admit females to the college and appealed to the board of trustees, but that male body did not act on his suggestion. In his report to the trustees in 1895, he said:

> In my report to you May 23, last, I stated that I had visited all the leading schools for colored people in Virginia, North and South Carolina, Georgia, Alabama, Tennessee and Kentucky, Arkansas and Missouri. Alcorn College is the only one strictly speaking that is for boys only. Comparing the educational work of other schools with ours, I am satisfied that boys are better trained in the presence of girls.

Pointing out that it was strange for this to be a debatable question in Mississippi when all other states in the union already favored coeducation, Calloway appealed to the legislature to act favorably on this matter. Unfortunately, President Calloway's tenure lasted only two years, the end coming after a misunderstanding with the local secretary-treasurer over the financial management of the school. Existing records do not indicate the exact nature of the problem.

Rev. Edward H. Triplett, a renowned Baptist minister, became Calloway's replacement. He was not college trained, and his administrative style did not gain faculty support. He was not viewed as being of presidential quality, and the faculty felt that he had become president through favoritism rather than qualification. Faculty unrest resulted in the board of trustees releasing the entire faculty charging the president to hire a completely new staff. The board began to think highly of Alcorn's industrial education program (though there was evidence of previous success) and put more funds into it.

Despite Rev. Triplett's popularity with the board, however, friction increased between him and other school personnel. In 1897 during the Christmas holidays, he was shot, the suspect being the secretary-treasurer of the college. Triplett lived, but when he recovered he remained at Alcorn only as a professor of history. The board dropped him as president. Triplett's administration was a difficult time for Alcorn, full of internal struggles and changes in leadership. He was not always as tactful as he should have been; a self-made man and nonintellectual, he was completely out of step with his faculty members.

William H. Lanier of Jackson, Mississippi, became the seventh president. Though a Tougaloo College graduate, like most of the previous presidents he had also studied at Fisk University. He too was a fan of Booker T. Washington and his nonpolitical vocational training ideas. He started his administration by concentrating on the industrial education program. He felt that Alcorn was offering insufficient training in agriculture, carpentry, dairying, and stock raising. He also wanted to add harnessing and tailoring. He believed, like Booker T. Washington, that the special mission of black colleges was in the realm of industrial training.

In 1900, the governor of Mississippi, Anselm McLaurin, commented on the improved harmonious tone at Alcorn. The Board of Trustees Report to the Governor in 1899 indicated that the college was enjoying the most prosperous year in its history and was a well-organized and efficient institution of learning. The report stated:

> In presenting the reports of the president and the heads of departments of Alcorn A.&M. College, we have the qualification to add that the college is enjoying the most prosperous year in its history. All the departments are working harmoniously and satisfactorily. The friction and inharmoniousness which have been obtained for several years have been removed. We now have the pleasure to report a well-organized and efficient institution of learning working toward the high and wise ideals which inspired and controlled its timely establishment.
>
> Believing that the future of the Negro in this country is almost entirely an industrial future, we have sought to enlarge facilities for improving efficiency and increasing the productive capacity as a skilled agriculturalist and mechanic. The property of the institution already very valuable, has been improved and several much needed buildings have been erected at comparatively small cost. But additional dormitory and other accommodations are imperatively demanded since more than one hundred additional students have applied for admission for the second half term. Their coming will overtax the capacity of the college.

Lanier made some changes in the college system. The printing department was abolished to make way for a painting department; thus the only college publication, *The Alcorn Lever*, ceased to exist. The new paper, to be edited by the president, was called *The Alcorn Agricultural and Mechanical College Informer*.

President Calloway's earlier plea for women students was heeded in 1902 under Lanier's administration. Women were finally admitted in 1903 when Truly Hall, a dormitory for females, was constructed. Applications were received from over five hundred women during the first year of coeducational status.

The mechanical and industrial areas of the college were expanding, and new teachers were being hired, increasing the faculty to sixteen. The enrollment by 1900 was three hundred thirty-nine students. Governors, the legislature, and the Board of Trustees of State Institutions of Higher Learning began to take notice. Alcorn was being seen as a college that produced useful graduates in the state, the South, and the nation. Lanier was definitely a man of sound educational ideas, possessing unusual resourcefulness and originality. His administration reflected a well-managed institution. He served as president until 1905, and after his administration for the first time an Alcorn alumnus, Levi J. Rowan, was named to the presidency. The event was symbolic. The school now had enough talented alumni so that one of its own could be chosen as its leader.

THREE

INTO THE TWENTIETH CENTURY

Born in nearby Rodney, Mississippi, in 1871, the year of Alcorn's founding, Levi J. Rowan could not have realized when he graduated from the school in 1893 that he would go on to become its president. He married Mattie Foote of Yazoo City in 1897. She was a famous musician, and their four daughters also became great musical artists. Rowan, a brilliant man who would prove to be successful in anything he tried, began teaching English at Alcorn in 1898 and became the department chairman in 1901. He was appointed president in 1905 and served two separate terms totaling more than twenty-five years. Each time, he did well. Mississippi Hall, a dormitory for males, was built in 1907 during his first short term in the presidency.

In 1910 there were 170 females and 445 males enrolled, and the faculty numbered 21. By then all Alcorn students were required to learn some type of trade. Enrollment had expanded to include students not only from neighboring states but from British Guiana and the British West Indies as well. Although there were many successes, harmony on the campus did not last. In 1911, President Rowan recommended the reappointment of some faculty members that the board was displeased with for reasons now unknown. Consequently the board fired him. The faculty and students protested the board's action, and Rowan remained at Alcorn but only as chairman of the English Department.

John Adams Martin, another Alcorn alumnus, became the next president. He had attended elementary school, high school, and college at Alcorn and had taught there for several years as a professor of mathematics. He later resigned to become principal in Jackson and Yazoo City schools. (Martin Elementary School in Jackson is named in his honor.) As Alcorn's president, he gained recognition for reorganizing the association for black educators that had been initiated by President Burrus, naming it the Mississippi Association of Teachers in Colored Schools. He served as the association's president from 1906 to 1912, being the first Alcornite to do so. During his second year as president, his health began to fail, and he was forced to give up his duties. Rowan took over again. When Martin's health improved, he resumed full duties as president.

Martin's tenure saw the establishment of the Manual Training Department, in which students of any grade could study. At first, the board did not accept the president's proposal for such a department. Martin wrote in his letter:

> I do not know that we should be justified in asking the great intelligent public to make much of it, or to give support to it. But it has been proven over and over again by those who have witnessed manual training and its processes that it is not merely a training of the senses alone, but it is the training of the mind, of the character; and anyone who doubts it has only to go into the first good kindergarten and he will discover that even at that early age the training of the mind and character is begun through the training of the hand, eye, and ear.

The letter must have been effective, because, in 1913, the board yielded to Martin's request. Physical education was promoted, and a professor was chosen to work with the students in athletics. Most significant of all, during Martin's administration specific requirements for graduation were mandated. All graduates had to spend the entire academic year at the college; orations for graduation had to be prepared by the students themselves and graded by a special committee; seniors had to take their final and third exam before graduating; and students who failed to comply with established rules were not permitted to graduate. President Martin died suddenly in December 1915 during his fourth year as president, and Levi J. Rowan was again named president.

The fiftieth anniversary of the college was observed during this period. Many exciting activities were scheduled in connection with the commencement that year. An electric clock for the tower of the chapel was dedicated, along with a system of electric bells. A program clock to give signals for systematizing the daily schedule was also instituted. Funds for this project came from faculty, current students, and former students. The most significant event of the day, however, was the homecoming of graduates, who shared their life stories and told how Alcorn had prepared them for what they were doing. In the mid-1920s, 98 percent of all black county extension agents in Mississippi were alumni of Alcorn.

Rowan had several major goals for his second term: to increase the length of the school year, to select better prepared teachers, and to increase faculty salaries. He was also continuously concerned about improving the physical plant of the college. Each year that he was president, he made sure that some type of improvement took place. He supervised the construction of many buildings. In addition to Mississippi Hall, which was built during his first term, he was responsible for the erection of Academic Hall, the steam laundry, a trades building for the mechanical arts, a hospital, a dining hall, and livestock barns to house farm animals. He also put Alcorn in communication with the outside world through a telephone line to Port Gibson. The engineering department began operating during the 1933–34 academic term, but the program had little success as a result of low funding.

In 1928, the legislature appropriated $200,000 to match $100,000 given by the General Education Board. These funds ensured a building program for Alcorn and resulted in the Rowan Administration Building, the Bowles Industrial Hall, the Teachers Training Department, the expansion of the library, and other needed improvements.

A 1932 statute consolidated the separate boards of trustees at state colleges and universities into one board that would govern all of the state institutions. College presidents had to prepare detailed budgets, and appropriations were made to each school. In 1934, Alcorn was given the authority to add new programs and expand those that were ongoing.

Rowan was appointed to President Herbert Hoover's White House Conference in 1930 to discuss better race relations. He served Alcorn well both on campus and off. When he died in June 1934, just two years before the end of the sixth decade of Alcorn's existence, the school lost a major leader.

The board of trustees interviewed fifteen applicants to fill the vacancy. The choice was William H. Bell, who became the tenth president of the college. A native of Sumter County, Alabama, who had grown up in Meridian, Mississippi, Bell was then serving as dean at South Carolina State College. He was a Rust College graduate and had received advanced degrees from Northwestern University and the University of Chicago. He too was concerned with increasing teacher salaries and improving the physical plant. He pushed through an improvement in academic standards, and the enrollment became higher than ever in the history of the school. The college also qualified for a rating of "B" from the Southern Association of Colleges and Schools, the first time in the history of Alcorn that the college was rated by a regional accrediting team.

In the early 1940s, Bell presented a list of Alcorn's urgent needs to the legislature. Included were a home economics building and equipment, a men's dormitory, a health center with an auditorium, a stock barn, a dairy barn and equipment, a vocational trade building, five teachers' cottages, fire protection equipment, fire trucks and equipment, a library building, home management houses, and improved roads, all totaling $1,277,753. Because of World War II, war industry courses were organized in blacksmithing, marine pipefitting, applied electricity, and auto mechanics. Civilian defense training was conducted in first aid, fire fighting, and air raid warden service. The college cooperated with the teacher training division of the state department of education. Business courses became a part of the curriculum. There was an effort to improve instruction in Negro rural schools and to cooperate with the state board of health in ensuring health consciousness in the schools. Following the war, the demand for physical education teachers and coaches was even higher, so the physical education department was organized in the late 1940s.

Physical activity had been a part of the school's program since its founding. Two activity courses had long been in the curriculum, and all students were required to take them. Recreation during this period included hunting, fishing, group singing, and group games. The B.S. degree was not offered in health and physical education until 1946, but the school actually fielded its first baseball team in 1875 and participated on an intercollegiate level from about 1890. Baseball was discontinued in 1937 but came back after some seventeen years. Football first came on the scene in 1922. Alcorn became a charter member of the South Central Athletic Conference in 1923. From this period until

1969 the college had championship teams in baseball four times; in football, sixteen times; in track and field, seven times; and in basketball, twenty-four times. Athletes who were considered to be all-time greats during these years included (in football) Johnny Spinks, Samuel Crump, Franklin Purnell, Clayton Love, Willie McGowan, Smith Reed, Robert Hall, Craig Walker, Oscar Martin, David Hadley, Lawrence Watkins, Willie Banks, Robert Brown, and Marvin Weeks; (in baseball) Bill Foster, Melvin Powell, A. D. Clark, and Percy Bailey; (in basketball) Willie Norwood, Julius Keys, Riley Williams, John Cooley, George Morris, Lee (Chick) Garner, Vernon Purnell, and William Price; (in tennis) Clay Thacker; (in golf) Ivan Womack; (in track) Mildrette Netter, Samuel Crump, Willie McCoy, Willie Magee, Jerry Sims, Mollie Hence, and Helen Williams.

The college also began to serve more off-campus groups, but housing facilities restricted this expansion to teachers, farmers, ministers, and vocational and extension workers. Bell felt that, after the war, there would be more demand in this area than could be met without additional dormitories. During Bell's term, the college was faced with the problem of how to contribute to the war effort while at the same time preserving the fundamentals of its varied educational programs.

Bell's first priority was to make the college more accessible to the people whom it served and to maintain contact with them. He felt that this could be done by improving the road from the campus to Highway 61. Alcorn was the only state institution of higher learning that did not have a surfaced road to its campus. House Bill #519 provided for such a road, but the law had never been applied to Alcorn. House Bill #358, passed during the regular 1942 session of the Mississippi legislature, authorized and empowered the highway commission to construct and pave a road leading from or by Alcorn to U.S. Highway 61, but no appropriation was made to put the law into effect. Bell protested that the common complaint that the college was too far down in the woods to serve blacks efficiently had to be eliminated.

Even though Bell appeared to have the good of the college at heart, alumni condemned his administration as being too concerned with liberal arts and not enough with the functions of a land-grant college. They said he neglected agricultural and mechanical training. Alumni and friends of the college suggested programs of training, including some for cooks and maids. A portion of the letter from an alumni committee criticizing Bell clearly showed its concerns:

Jackson, Mississippi
May 8th, 1944

To The Board of Trustees of
Institutions of Higher Learning
Jackson, Mississippi

Honorable Board Members:

In accordance with the request of the Board of Trustees, we the members of the Alumni Committee for the Advancement of Alcorn College do respectfully submit the following recommendations as being the improvements which will enable the college to more nearly meet the educational needs of Negroes in Mississippi.

Item one: Training Program

The college should immediately develop a program which will function in fact as well as in theory.

1. Train workers in agriculture to become proficient in: (a) production of food and feeds, (b) soil conservation, (c) food preservation, (d) farm mechanics, (e) care of live stock and poultry, (f) forestry, and (g) farm carpentry.

2. Train workers in mechanic arts in the following: (a) farm electricity, (b) ground hog saw mill operation, (c) bricklaying, (d) building construction and blue print reading, (e) cement finishing, (f) painting, (g) plastering and (h) shoe repairing.

3. Train workers in home economics along the following lines: (a) food and nutrition, (b) clothing, (c) handicraft, (d) dietetics, (e) food preservation, (f) health and sanitation and (g) child care.

4. It is the committee's conviction after taking stock of the employment opportunities in the state the college should (a) maintain, what for lack of a better name, we shall call a two year terminal course in general agriculture for those boys and young men who desire technical training in one or more phases of agriculture for the purpose of entering the farming occupation either as owners, operators, or plantation managers, but who would not be interested in securing a degree or in teaching agriculture. The requirement for entrance in such a course would probably be no more than a grammar school education (b) maintain a two year terminal course in Homemaking for those girls who would be interested only.

Bell felt that the function of the college in a postwar world would depend on the nature of that world. There would be a greater need for well-trained individuals in all areas. He stressed that Mississippi was one of the few remaining southern states that did not give black youth the opportunity to be trained in a first-class "A"-grade college. But he resigned under the pressure, feeling that the work of the college had been successful and the faculty and students had accomplished a great deal under his leadership. The board of trustees thought the school was in a shambles and needed a new president.

Bell's administration had taken place in the midst of World War II, when the college had to adjust its activities to support the war effort in keeping with the pattern of participation that had been set by state and federal authorities. War industry courses were organized, students bought war stamps, teachers participated in the 10 percent plan for purchasing war bonds, civilian defense training was conducted, and there were many students who joined every branch of the armed services. President Bell's tenure as president ended in 1944, one year before the war was over. Alcorn would have new leadership as it entered the important postwar years.

FOUR

TURBULENT TIMES

ANOTHER ALCORN ALUMNUS, Preston Sewell Bowles, became president in 1944. He served for only one year, becoming at the age of seventy-five the only person in the history of the school to be named President Emeritus.

A Claiborne countian born in 1869, Bowles had received his B.S. degree from Alcorn in 1895. He had taught high school before coming to Alcorn as an assistant professor of English. The English Department had traditionally emphasized formal grammar, and Bowles was instrumental in having literature added to the curriculum. As president he encouraged vocational education. When he made an appeal to the state board of trustees, it transferred him to the Department of Agriculture, and under the auspices of the National Vocational Education Act, vocational education finally became a reality. Bowles chaired the department.

Dr. William H. Pipes then became president, the first such official at Alcorn to hold a Ph.D. He took over in 1945 but the inauguration was on May 5, 1947, an occasion that was attended by representatives from many religious, school, and civic organizations. Pipes was born in Sunflower County near Inverness, Mississippi, to parents who were sharecroppers. He received his education in the Clarksdale, Indianola, and Inverness schools. He received a B.S. at Tuskegee Institute where he completed courses in banking and mechanics; his master's from Atlanta University; and the Ph.D. degree from the University of Michigan. He had had various university-level teaching experiences, including one at Southern University in Baton Rouge, Louisiana. He was the first black Michigan State University professor and the first American black to earn a Ph.D. in speech. He was also Professor Emeritus of American Thought and Language at Michigan State, the first black to earn a full professorship there.

Pipes was determined to direct Alcorn according to its land-grant status. Though he believed that blacks should secure equal training to that afforded whites in all fields, he did not feel that Alcorn had actually conformed to the intent of the legislature when it had become an agricultural and mechanical college in 1878. He sought cooperation from the school's administration, faculty, and students, and from the legislature. His philosophy was that "we are all Mississippians and as Mississippians, we will prosper when we learn how to live and work together, dignifying and magnifying Mississippi."

The early years of Pipes's life had involved farming, religion, and poverty. His people dating back to slavery had all been poor farmers, and his mother had promised the Lord that if He gave her a son she would dedicate this son to His service. Booker T. Washington was a great inspiration to the family. When Pipes was a child, his mother had become fascinated by Washington's philosophy of education when Washington delivered a speech in Mound Bayou, Mississippi. Washington had encouraged blacks to lift themselves from low economic conditions by getting an education and acquiring skills such as those being taught at Tuskegee Institute where he worked. Washington had been offered a job at Alcorn in 1896, but he had refused it, replying that, even though the salary offered to him by Alcorn was larger than his salary at Tuskegee, he preferred to remain where he was because he felt that, for some years to come, he could do more good there than anywhere else. Additionally, he said, there were many individuals throughout the North who had given large sums of money to his work and he did not want to disappoint them nor Alabama officials by leaving. He felt that, if he left Tuskegee, some of the problems that were being worked out would intensify again. He further responded that since Tuskegee was largely his own creation, he could not very well leave.

Booker T. Washington's influence led Pipes's mother to help him go to Tuskegee despite their poverty and the fact that his father was an Alcornite. During high school, Pipes developed inflammatory rheumatism, which kept him confined for months, and he also received a cut and a broken wrist that almost caused him to lose his right hand. This injury kept him from ever being able to close his hand all the way. Refusing to let this handicap hinder him, he learned to perform tasks with his left hand. The episode taught him to face difficult situations and overcome them.

Pipes believed, as President Bell had, that either a paved road had to be built from Highway 61 to the college or that the school needed to move to a more central location on a good highway. He also stressed the need for a better physical plant with the equipment necessary to carry out the mission of a land-grant college. It was important to get back to the function and first principles of the land-grant mission. Pipes's aim was to receive an "A" accreditation rating from the Southern Association of Colleges and Schools. His effort to gain accreditation for Alcorn was frustrated when Jackson State was assigned the role of providing general education courses for black college students in Mississippi.

Slowly, the school began to look like a land-grant college, with a focus on agriculture, home economics, and trades. During Pipes's tenure, the main highway was hard-surfaced at last, and faculty salaries finally increased. President Pipes served as president for only four years; in July of 1949 he resigned. The college had not progressed as quickly as he had desired, so he decided it needed new leadership.

Dr. Jesse R. Otis took over the presidency. He was a native Mississippian born in Jefferson Davis County. His early education was obtained at Piney Woods Country Life School. He received a B.S. degree from Iowa State and later the master's and Ph.D. from Cornell University. Several buildings were constructed during his tenure as president: Pritchard Hall, Eunice Powell Home Economics Building, and a home management house where home economics students live and practice home management skills.

The school's new buildings did not secure for it the long-sought "A" rating, because it failed to qualify in seven of the twenty-one mandated standards of the Southern Association of Colleges and Schools. Since instruction was one of the areas of failure, Dr. Otis set out to secure a better-trained faculty. He employed the first full-time faculty in forestry. He considered the functions of a land-grant college to be instruction, research, and extension. Instruction had long been the dominant concern, and Otis wanted more emphasis on the other two areas as well. As a result, for the first time research became a part of the college faculty's function, most of it, of course, related to agriculture. The Baptist Student Union was organized. The first teaching fellowship ever given to a black at Cornell University went to an Alcorn graduate in 1954.

In 1951, Otis issued a ten-year development plan. He stressed that educational objectives grew out of the needs of the people being served. The program that he developed was based upon the needs of black youth at a land-grant college. He believed that it was the quality of the students and the teachers that made an institution, not the buildings, as important as these were. He highlighted the position and status of the college by pointing out that its location had many advantages. Its wealth of resources included valuable land, potential or actual mineral holdings, and a group of excellent students who could become top-level citizens and leaders with the right training. Enrollment had increased to 644, and there were many successes. Otis proposed other major areas of concentration leading to the B.S. degree; these fell under the auspices of the agriculture, education, general science, and home economics departments. Otis recommended that no graduate-level work be offered so that the focus could be on undergraduates.

As for the administration necessary for his proposed program, he suggested only one new position, that of a dean for the lower division. The existing administrative structure during this period included a president; an administrative secretary; a recording secretary; deans of the college, the lower division, and of agriculture, education, engineering, general science, and home economics; a comptroller; a registrar; a dean of students, dean of men and chaplain, and dean of women; a superintendent of buildings and grounds; a director of public relations; a librarian; and a director of health service and college physician.

The building expansion program, as proposed by Otis, included approximately twenty-five new buildings, both instructional and noninstructional, some of which became a reality, if not within ten years, at some later point in the history of Alcorn. The proposed building plan totalled $5,388,000.

In 1957, serious trouble occurred during Otis's administration. Students boycotted classes in protest against newspaper articles written by history professor Clennon King, a black faculty member. The articles attacked the National Association for the Advancement of Colored People (NAACP), accusing it of negatively affecting race relations in the South.

In one article King said, "Perhaps the NAACP is the National Association for the Agitation of Colored People after all." King maintained that the NAACP was hurting the black cause in the South and represented only a small minority of the black population. He felt that the NAACP had become almost sacred among blacks and that those who questioned it were vilified, especially if they were themselves black.

The students demanded that King be fired for writing such articles. President Otis said he would not attempt to deal with the demands until the students returned to classes. Clennon King accused other teachers of pushing the students to protest. He told the press that he would leave the school but felt that he should be paid for the remainder of the year.

Many blacks on and off the campus called King an "Uncle Tom," considering him disloyal to his race. Otis would not discuss the matter with King. He felt that it was up to the college board of trustees to decide whether King should be fired or not, insisting that it was not college policy to deal with controversial matters. The college had not had any trouble before, and Otis felt that it had the best student government to be found anywhere.

College board members supported Otis and said no negotiations would take place until the students returned to classes. The board threatened to close the school if they did not. The students were given until that Friday to return. If they did not, the cafeteria was to be closed at noon. If they did not return by Monday, a prorated share of their tuition would be given back to them, and the school would be closed. After a series of meetings, Otis recommended that King be fired for involving the school in such controversy. King said that he would not protest his firing.

The students did not appear for eight o'clock classes on Friday. Instead, they met in the chapel for prayer. The striking students were expelled that Saturday. The others, approximately ninety-five at the time, were allowed to attend classes. The board then accused Otis of approving of the walkout and discharged him of his duties as president of the college. He was required to remove himself immediately from the premises. Governor J. P. Coleman commented that the whole chain of events was childish. The students continued to insist that their complaint was not a protest of King's right of expression, but of his drawing the college into a racial controversy.

After the dismissal of Otis, the board immediately appointed John Dewey Boyd, the president of Utica Institute, to be in charge. Although Boyd indicated that he could not be released from his job at Utica until after the board met that Monday, he was given a free hand in running the college immediately. The board felt that faculty and administration had allowed the students to take over. Boyd, however, anticipating that the Clennon King situation could destroy his effectiveness, planned to release King as soon as he took over. Matters now became even more complicated. The chairman of the board of trustees ruled that King could keep his job at Alcorn, but King told newsmen that he did not plan to return at that time. Students seeking readmission had to be individually screened by the new president. Boyd quickly reinstated about 100 of the boycotting 549 students, but put all of them on probation.

As the result of a request from the president of the Mississippi Regional Council of Negro Leadership, who was in Mound Bayou, at least nine of the country's leading newspapers agreed to spearhead a nationwide drive to assist students who were ousted from the college. They pledged to help pay the difference between the cost of attending a private college and a state-owned college such as Alcorn. In the meantime, King asked for a leave from the college for a brief rest. Boyd agreed.

In the final analysis, 539 of the 549 boycotting students returned to the college. None of them was penalized, but they had to agree not to strike again and to follow the rules of the college and the board. Boyd reported, in May 1957, that Alcorn was operating smoothly and effectively again. He praised the student body and faculty for cooperating and permitting the campus to return to normal as quickly as it had. Clennon King was given a new contract by the Board of Trustees of State Institutions of Higher Learning, but he apparently never returned to the campus to work. He was given "make work" off campus so he could complete his one-year contract. He is alleged to have attempted to be admitted to a doctoral program at the University of Mississippi but was sent to Whitfield instead as the result of unusual behavior.

Dr. John Dewey Boyd, who took over the helm after Otis's dismissal, was a native of Wilkinson County, Mississippi, the fourth alumnus of the college to hold the position of president. He had received his master's degree from the University of Illinois and had done further study at Harvard. His work experience from 1931 to 1947 included teaching agriculture and being principal in Sunflower (Moorhead Colored School) and Marion (Lampton Colored School) counties. In 1947 he was a professor of agronomy and manager of the college farm at Alcorn. He left in 1951 to become the president of Utica Institute in Utica, Mississippi. The school became a junior college under his leadership. He had learned firsthand as a youth the value of hard work.

In 1957 when he became Alcorn's fourteenth president, he had a great challenge ahead of him, including an $85,000 deficit. He changed that to a $50,000 surplus in a short period of time. In addition, the number of faculty members holding doctorates was increased, the curriculum became more varied and organized, the enrollment increased to its highest point ever, and the physical plant continued to improve. During Boyd's administration, there were three divisions in the college: (1) the Division of Arts and Sciences, which housed humanities, mathematics, science, and social science; (2) the Division of Education, which housed elementary education, business, health and physical education, and secondary education; and (3) the Division of Vocational Education, which housed agriculture, home economics, and industrial education. These divisions were created as part of Alcorn's effort to become a full member of the Southern Association of Colleges and Schools (SACS), which had begun admitting historically black schools in 1957. Alcorn became a member in 1961.

In addition to Boyd's administrative successes at the college, he still found time to paint. His paintings, which now hang in selected places on campus, were an inspiration to the entire Alcorn family. He was married to Cleopatra Carter, also from Wilkinson County, and they had one daughter, Katie.

As the college entered its ninth decade, Dr. Boyd's major aim, as it had been with several former presidents, was to receive an "A" rating for the college from the Southern Association of Colleges and Schools. Several buildings were renovated and refurnished, including Oakland Chapel, the president's home, and Bowles Hall. New buildings constructed included the fine arts building, Burrus Hall, Robinson Hall, gymnasium, New Women's, Revels, a housing complex for faculty consisting of thirty-three buildings, the science library building, the dairy, the infirmary, and a million-dollar building, the John D. Boyd Library. The dining hall was expanded; three dormitories for women and two for men were built. A new sewage system was acquired and street and light improvements were made.

Boyd was a true scholar. He believed in quality education and hoped that Alcorn College would develop a group of scholars who would be useful to society. He held many local, state, and national positions. He was a delegate to the White House Conference on Education in 1959 and advised the president of the United States on civil rights problems. During his administration, the college was admitted to full membership in the Southern Association of Colleges and Schools. Alcorn began to focus on workshops and institutes in various areas of curriculum. The enrollment increased by at least 24 percent each year of Boyd's administration, and the number of graduates steadily increased. It was during this period that sports began to become prominent. The basketball team was the champion of the Southwestern Athletic Conference in 1968, and the football team was SWAC co-champion that same year.

In spite of President Boyd's successes, his administration was plagued by marches, strikes, and other forms of student unrest, part of the civil rights and student revolutions of the period. In 1966, mass marches, street rallies, and other types of demonstrations took place at Alcorn. State police came on the campus carrying tear gas and swinging billy clubs. The target of the student protest was John Dewey Boyd. Students were angry over courses, teachers, poor food, and curfews. Boyd responded by suspending eight students and firing the chief campus policeman, all of whom were involved in civil rights activities. Charles Evers, a member of the NAACP, spearheaded a march on the campus. "J. D. Boyd," he shouted at one of the rallies, "has to go. He's only concerned with pleasing the white folks." Evers and his off-campus followers were stopped by a wall of helmeted troopers enforcing a state injunction against demonstrating. Evers told them this fight was among Negroes, and that white folks should stay out of it. Students threw bottles, rocks, and bricks at the troopers' cars, and the troopers responded with tear gas, which broke up the march and stopped the hail of debris. Evers spearheaded another march that night and Governor Paul B. Johnson, Jr., summoned 250 National Guardsmen to be on standby. The next day Evers and his marchers came back again, about one thousand strong. When ordered out of the road, they started to disperse but then came back. A marcher shoved one of the troopers and a policeman clubbed him; then a bottle hit the officer in the face. The troopers charged and threw tear gas into the crowd. The crowd scattered immediately. After about fifteen minutes Evers left and headed for a civil rights meeting in Detroit. Boyd commented, "I am not opposed to civil rights. I have gone about as far as a man in my position could . . . and I was working for better race relations before Mr. Evers even knew what they were."

In 1968, trouble returned. Boyd announced that prior to Thursday night, February 15, 1968, he had never been involved in any questions concerning politics. That night, however, a student gave the security officers an identification card belonging to Charles Evers. On Friday, the 16th, this student and two others forced their way into the president's home during the noon hour to talk with him. After being told that they would need to get an appointment with his secretary and that he did not have conferences during the noon hour with students, they cursed and called him a "handkerchief head nigger" and "an Uncle Tom nigger." When he asked them to leave, they shouted these statements over and over as loudly as they could. They left and went to the dining hall, saying that President Boyd had told them to go to the cafeteria and get their meals before anybody else did. These three then proceeded to get other students involved, and a riot ensued, which patrolmen tried to control by firing their guns. At least three students were injured. Boyd had come into a situation of student unrest and, despite his successes, encountered similar problems near the end of his administration.

On June 30, 1969, Boyd became the first president officially to retire from the college. Every previous president had quit or been fired. After retirement Boyd spent most of his time at his home in Jefferson County, no doubt wondering what it all meant and what the future held for the school he had served so long.

FIVE

A NEW ERA

On July 1, 1969, Dr. Walter Washington became the fifteenth president of Alcorn Agricultural and Mechanical College. It was the beginning of a new era for this historically black land-grant institution. Even the most solid foundation has to be renovated occasionally, and Alcorn was in need of just that kind of refurbishing. "Commitment to excellence" was Washington's philosophy from his first day on campus and throughout the coming years. Forty-six years old when he took the position, Washington was by the time he retired in 1994 the longest-tenured university president in the United States.

Walter Washington was the sixth and last sibling born to Rev. Kemp and Mrs. Mabel Washington. A native of Hazlehurst, Mississippi, he attended the elementary and secondary schools there. He received the A.B. degree from Tougaloo College, where he met his wife, Carolyn, and continued his education at Indiana University, George Peabody College for Teachers (now part of Vanderbilt University), and Yale University. He was the first black person to earn a doctorate at the University of Southern Mississippi, where a building was named for him in 1993. He has received honorary Doctor of Laws degrees from Indiana University and Tougaloo College. Purdue University conferred an honorary Doctor of Science degree upon him. The Association of Vanderbilt Black Alumni named him their 1993 Distinguished Alumnus. He has held memberships in many professional organizations, such as the Board of Entergy Corporation (formerly Middle South Utilities), Mississippi Power and Light Company, Blue Cross and Blue Shield of Mississippi, and the National Commission for Cooperative Education. He served as chair of the President's Council of the State University Presidents and was a member of the College Commission of the Southern Association of Colleges and Schools, the Mississippi Association of Educators, and the National Education Association. He has received many other awards and numerous national recognitions.

When Washington came to Alcorn in 1969 he was not particularly well known; he was merely the promising president of the small nearby black Utica Junior College. He set out as his basic priority the task of making what he believed to be a good institution into a better one, realizing that support would come as a result of success and that success would foster further support. Many of the challenges that he set forth for the school in the beginning became realities as far as possible considering the chronically uncertain status of funding. For example, the lack of proper appropriations meant that the school never had enough money to pay adequate salaries to faculty and staff. Despite this problem, Washington was successful in holding strong faculty members through such efforts as faculty development programs, whereby teachers could go away to earn their doctorates and then return to Alcorn. He also tried to make the school a pleasant place to work. The result has been minimum turnover, even given the low salaries. Washington made a personal commitment that lack of money would not keep Alcorn down, and he successfully spread that message to his coworkers.

Another concern of Washington's from the beginning was the school's graduation rate, and he never felt that there was enough progress in this area. Aware that the problem of black education at lower levels limited Alcorn's success, he nevertheless insisted that the door not be closed on any aspiring student. It particularly disturbed him when students had to be separated from the educational process for any reason, since he believed that such failure only reinforced the historic negatives students carried with them.

Earlier in life Washington's goal had been to become governor of Mississippi. He was inspired as a child by the inaugural speech of Governor Thomas Bailey in 1944. As time passed, however, his commitment to education moved him in a different direction. Also, he knew that as a black man there was no chance for him to pursue so lofty a political goal in Mississippi.

Prior to becoming a college president, Washington had served his apprenticeship in various other educational arenas. Upon graduating from Tougaloo College, he taught in Crystal Springs, then Hazlehurst, Mississippi. In 1952 he became principal of Hinds County Agricultural High School and in 1954 he was named dean of Utica Junior College where he served in this capacity for one year before becoming principal of Sumner High School in Clinton, Mississippi. He returned to Utica Junior College in 1957 as president, a post he held for twelve years.

In all these positions he gained important experience that prepared him for the Alcorn presidency. Washington began his term of office by holding a retreat with student leaders and administrative personnel to discuss any possible problem areas. He decided not to make hasty changes in existing administrative personnel, but to study the needs of the college first. He involved members of the Board of Trustees of State Institutions of Higher Learning, of the legislature, and of the state building commission, as well as other prominent citizens in his study of the campus to determine what the college needed most to move forward. He carefully weighed the ideas from faculty, staff, students, and off-campus individuals.

By the beginning of the 1970 calendar year, Washington had already broken precedent by appointing two assistants for buildings and grounds, one to be responsible for maintenance and the other for plant operation. He realized that the campus's appearance and smooth operation would have a tremendous influence on how outsiders perceived it and how Alcornites perceived themselves. He saw an attractive campus as a foundation for progress in every other area of the school's functioning.

Washington realized, upon his arrival, that the school had the best-trained faculty in its history, with more teachers than ever before holding degrees beyond the master's. A program of professional development was already in place, and he sought to build on it. He also inherited the largest student body in the school's history. Having become known in areas outside its immediate vicinity, Alcorn was now attracting young people from all over the state.

So, Washington had some advantages when he began the task of building a new Alcorn. He wanted a college with an environment that would ensure that students would gain the knowledge and skills necessary for achieving excellence in a complex society. He wanted the school's graduates to be able to cope with the changes they would encounter in their future lives. Assuming the presidency with cautious optimism, he emphasized involving the faculty in all areas of the school's administration.

In addition to appointing two assistants for buildings and grounds, he created a new administrative post, the office of vice president. He also wanted strong directors of the campus's academic programs. He was instrumental in revitalizing the alumni office, hoping to improve Alcorn's relations with its alumni and to increase the flow of information to the public about the college's achievements.

Washington also began working to secure adequate funds for the school. Though the capital outlay effort got off to a very good start during his first year as president, he immediately began trying to secure further funds from the 1971 legislature. He remained concerned with upgrading existing facilities and had as a major goal the establishing of a branch experiment station for the school.

Washington's style of fiscal management was conservative. He believed in strict accountability for all monies spent, insisting that it was only through such a policy that a university could operate successfully. He kept a tight rein on expenditures because funding was behind all university operations. He viewed the prompt payment of bills to be of equal importance with an attractive campus, a competent faculty, and hard-working students.

Washington's concern about improving Alcorn's image led him to take on many local, state, and national appointments. In the first year of his presidency he was elected vice chairman of the Commission on Secondary Schools of the Southern Association of Colleges and Schools, the first black to hold such a position. The commission's task was accrediting secondary schools in the region. Having previously served as chairman of the Mississippi Accrediting Commission and being a member of the state committee of the Southern Association of Colleges and Schools, Washington had a long history of experience in accreditation. Because of such expertise he was also appointed to serve on the State Advisory Commission of Title VI-A of the Higher Education Act of 1965. He also served on the advisory committee of the American Council on Education's Institute for College and University Administrators.

Washington's goal of having an agricultural experiment station at Alcorn became a reality in 1971. Governor John Bell Williams's efforts in this behalf earned him a vote of thanks from Mississippi blacks. Williams had a record of opposing civil rights, but he was favorable towards Washington's presidency. He helped to obtain appropriations for Alcorn from the state legislature in 1970, including a million dollars for the renovation of the present structures. Williams helped obtain funding for four buildings at Alcorn, with eight going up on the campus

A New Era

in four years (women's tower, men's tower, the new administration building, faculty garden apartments, the agricultural science building, the campus union, the biology research lab, and the health physical education complex). Even more significantly Williams had included Alcorn in his earlier inaugural address.

Washington gave many speeches at high schools in an effort to encourage young people to be the best they could be, and he frequently challenged Alcorn faculty and students in the same way. When he first came, he congratulated everyone for the good spirit evident on the campus. He demanded excellence from faculty, staff, and students in everything they did. The major mission of the college was teaching and learning, he said, and every resource had to be used toward that end. He challenged the faculty to "chew up the books in the library," to keep abreast of current trends and developments in their disciplines and to upgrade themselves through continuous study. He further urged the faculty to make the students their number one priority. He challenged students to take on freedom with responsibility; to study until their brains hurt; to make the faculty stay up all night preparing lectures; and to aspire for the highest position and best jobs in the land. He felt that if students studied diligently and were taught properly, they would be able to escape academic and financial poverty. Washington, among other black college presidents, had agreed in 1977 to make no more apologies for the existence of black institutions. Martin Luther King, Jr., had gone to Morehouse College, a black school, and found there his role and mission to lift a people who had been left in America's basement. Black students could do the same at Alcorn and other black colleges. Black schools needed no defense.

Walter Washington's long-time partner in his enterprise was Dr. Carolyn Carter Washington, the First Lady of Alcorn State University and for many years a faculty member. The two met as freshmen at Tougaloo College in 1944 and were married in 1949.

After graduating from Tougaloo in 1948, Carolyn Washington taught at the Choctaw County Training School in Ackerman and at Parish High School in Hazelhurst. From 1951 to 1955 she was a home demonstration agent with the Mississippi Cooperative Extension Service in Lincoln County. After that, she taught school at Sumner Hill, and in 1957 she joined the faculty at Utica Junior College where she taught family living. She began teaching in the social science department at Alcorn in 1969. Dr. Washington, who retired in 1988, received a master's degree from the University of Wisconsin and a specialist certificate from the University of Illinois; she did additional study at Mississippi State University and earned the doctorate from the University of Southern Mississippi in 1976. She was a member of the National Education Association, the American Home Economics Association, the Mississippi Teachers Association, the District Teachers Association, Phi Delta Kappa, and Delta Kappa Pi (two honorary organizations at U.S.M.). In 1961 and 1962 she served as president of the Negro Section of the Mississippi Home Economics Association. A talented soprano, she sang in the concert choir in college and performed at the first convocation held at Alcorn under her husband's presidency. She has always been a gracious hostess and in her role as first lady put everyone around her at ease. Her contributions during her husband's tenure were many and varied.

Over the years, Walter Washington traveled extensively to many countries in Europe, Africa, and Asia, including China, Liberia Ethiopia, Kenya, Taiwan, Italy, Great Britain, Morocco, and Chad. His travels enabled him to learn more about what individuals need to succeed in a complex world. He once said that the difference between working at a university and selling a product in a corporation is "the satisfaction of knowing you are helping people." Although Alcorn competed in the marketplace, he maintained, the primary product was service. His administrative style with his administrative council, faculty, staff, and students indicated his desire to be of service, and under his leadership the new Alcorn was on the move.

SIX

SERVING THE PEOPLE

Administration, Faculty, and Staff

THE ALCORN ADMINISTRATION IS STRUCTURED so that institutional goals can be met in academic affairs, athletics, fiscal affairs, institutional advancement, planning, and research. President Washington relies on members of the Administrative Council and of a standing committee, the Planning, Management, and Evaluation (PME) Committee, to assist him in major decisions. The PME committee coordinates any revisions of the school's mission and goals and develops and implements systems of evaluation. The Administrative Council is a policy and decision-making body that oversees university planning, approves budget allocations, and establishes institutional priorities.

Administrative Council members are key people in the forward movement of the new Alcorn. In 1993 they were Vice President, Dr. Rudolph Waters; Dean of Academic Affairs, Dr. Malvin Williams; Director of Agriculture, Research, Extension and Applied Sciences, Dr. Samuel Donald; Business Manager, Wiley Jones; Dean of Student Affairs, Emanuel Barnes; Director of Institutional Advancement, Dr. Franklin Jackson; Director of the Nursing School, Dr. Frances Henderson; and Director of the Graduate School, Dr. Norris Edney. These council members also serve on the PME committee with President

Washington as chairman: Vice President, Rudolph Waters; Athletic Director, Cardell Jones; Director of Institutional Research and Assessment, Dr. Sidney McLaurin; Director of the Division of Business, Dr. Robert Williams; Director of the Division of the General College for Excellence, Dr. Newtie Boyd; Director of the Division of Education and Psychology, Dr. John Hendricks; Director of Admissions and Recruiting, Albert Johnson; Director of Financial Aid, Laura Shelvy; Director of the University Library, Dr. Epsy Hendricks; all department chairpersons; the Registrar, Dr. Alice Gill, assisted by Charles Davis; chairman of the Faculty Senate, Dr. Levie Robinson; two at-large faculty members; president of the Student Government Association; president of the National Alumni Association, John Walls; Director of Personnel, Oliver Taylor; Director of Public Relations, Ralph Payne; and Superintendent of the Physical Plant, James Martin. The large membership of this committee ensures representation from all areas of the university.

The administrator who reports most directly to the president is the vice president, Dr. Rudolph Waters. He serves as a major advisor to Washington and to other administrative officers. A native Mississippian, Waters has been in the field of education for thirty-nine years. His experience includes being registrar, dean, and acting president at Utica Junior College and dean of students, dean of instruction, and coordinator of Title III programs at Alcorn. He has been vice president at Alcorn since 1970.

Dr. Waters's many professional affiliations include the American Association for Higher Education, National Education Association, Southern College Personnel Association, and National Association of Collegiate Deans and Registrars, the National Society for the Study of Education; he has coordinated or chaired more than fifty secondary school evaluations for the Southern Association of Colleges and Schools and has served on many other visitation teams for various accreditation agencies. He has also been a member of the governor's Private Sector Council in the state of Mississippi and has served on evaluation teams for federal programs in several states and on the board of directors of Andrew Jackson Council, Boy Scouts. A graduate of De Paul University, Boston University, and Kansas State University, Waters was a participant in the Institute of Academic Deans at Harvard University in 1964 and has done further study at Southern Illinois University.

Waters has demonstrated throughout his long tenure that he is willing to get behind whatever effort is necessary for the growth of the school. He has lobbied the legislature on a continuous basis in order to ensure that Alcorn never be forgotten. He has instilled in students the idea that a university is great because of its alumni and has supported Washington's view of the importance of learning for success in whatever endeavors an individual pursues.

Erma Hawkins, the only executive secretary/administrative assistant during Washington's tenure, is a native of Meridian, Mississippi. She received a B.S. degree from Rust College, an M.Ed. in business from University of Southern Mississippi, and an M.S. in guidance and counseling from Alcorn. She has studied at Mississippi College and completed course work in school administration at Alcorn. She was secretary to the academic dean at Rust prior to coming to Utica Junior College as secretary to then President Walter Washington.

Hawkins was the first secretary in the state of Mississippi to hold two honor certificates from the National Association of Educational Secretaries. She served as service editor of the *National Educational Secretary* from 1971 to 1973 and was a member of the publication committee in 1977. She is a life member of the Mississippi Association of Educational Secretaries, having served as secretary and member of the executive board, and was named Secretary of the Year by the Higher Education Division in 1985. She is also a charter member of the Alcorn State University Association of Educational Office Personnel and served as president in 1982 and 1983. She was a contributing editor to the National Association of Educational Secretaries' publication *Take Time to Plan* and has contributed to and been featured in *National Educational Secretary*.

Erma Hawkins is a planner, an organizer, a committed individual, and a strong believer in doing a task well or not doing it at all. Her attitude and work habits made her an invaluable assistant to President Washington.

Alcorn's faculty and staff have been described by Vice President Waters as the soul, spirit, and conscience of the university. In 1993 the faculty included members of many nationalities and races, though the largest percentage was African-American, some 66 percent. In that year, more than 50 percent of the faculty held the doctorate degree, approximately 30 percent were tenured, and more than 10 percent held the rank of full professor. The faculty is international and cosmopolitan, having studied in leading colleges and universities throughout the world.

The Dean of Academic Affairs, the chief academic officer at Alcorn, has the responsibility of orienting faculty and staff to the organizational and administrative processes of the university, as well as to the procedures of the business office. This task is traditionally accomplished in a special session held during the annual fall faculty/staff conference. Dean I. H. Sanders, the first academic dean at Alcorn, served from 1914 to 1935 and was responsible for ensuring the integrity of academics and academic support programs. Malvin Williams, the dean in 1993, acquired all his education, from elementary school through college, at Alcorn. He insists that Alcorn is the best place in the world to work if employees do their job, though doing it may overwork them. In describing Alcorn academics, Williams points out that the curriculum had changed from being very rigid to being nonstructured and that, by 1993, structure had returned. The recent concept of students' rights led to experimentation with a less formal approach, with students later realizing that structure was indeed needed. Williams is a great advocate of faculty members doing whatever is necessary to move students forward and encourages heavy use of office or conference hours.

One member of the administrative council whose work is especially scrutinized by the faculty is the business manager, the individual who is directly responsible for managing the fiscal affairs of Alcorn. Wiley Jones, the business manager in 1993, was often labeled as "tight with the money," but his record of keeping the university in the black speaks for itself. When asked for the secret of his success, Jones pointed to being trained and familiar with the concepts of fund accounting and financial resources management, having competent people around him, following procedures to the letter, and understanding what auditors expect. Jones worked his way up the ladder at Alcorn, having worked with the past business manager, O. W. Moses, who put many years into the job before he retired and who trained Jones well.

The Dean of Student Affairs is directly responsible for the well-being of the students. Emanuel Barnes, the 1993 dean, always has the students' needs at heart and is fair in dealing with them. The students respect him and support his view that student affairs is the university office which, more than any other, determines how successful a student will be at the university, whether he or she will achieve a degree or not. Like many other Alcorn administrators, Barnes began work at the school immediately after his graduation, holding the post of dormitory dean before he became Dean of Students. James Bolden and Fred Harris, who preceded Barnes, had the same type of concern for students. They were strong believers in following the rules.

The Director of the Division of Agriculture, Research, Extension, and Applied Sciences is another administrator who reports directly to the president. Dr. Samuel Donald took over the position following the demise of Dr. Jessie Morris in 1980. Donald has overseen the division's growth in personnel, funding, and facilities. He worries that, in some areas, the division has fallen short because of the lack of financial resources but, he says, "As with all areas composing Alcorn, we've done a wonderful job with what we have." Bringing in external monies has been his top priority. He has been able to get faculty and staff involved in those efforts. "We all realize," he goes on, "that we don't get the state support that our sister institutions get."

The Director of Athletics advises the president on intercollegiate athletics and coordinates Alcorn's athletic program. Cardell Jones, the athletic director in 1993 and also the head football coach, strives to build successful programs in all sports at the university. An alumnus of Alcorn, he came back to the school after having served as an assistant football coach at Jackson State University.

The Director of Institutional Advancement, Planning, and Research coordinates the development, implementation, and monitoring of Alcorn's long-range plan. He also assists in efforts to acquire external funds. He oversees admissions and recruiting, alumni relations, development, institutional research and assessment, placement services, planning, public information services, and strengthening of the institution's programs. Dr. Franklin Jackson, the director in 1993, is also the special assistant to Walter Washington and the academic cochairman of the University Cluster which was established in 1972 to improve the development of the university. When Jackson came to Alcorn, his first impression was that it would be conducive to serious learning. He liked the location, the beauty of the campus, and the family atmosphere.

Dr. Norris Edney, an administrative council member, reports directly to the president on matters governing the graduate school, directs the Division of Arts and Sciences, and is the faculty athletic representative. He serves on many boards and has directed the graduate program since its inception.

Dr. Frances Henderson, also a member of the council, reports directly to the president on the affairs of the nursing school, of which she is director. She chairs the Mississippi Council of Deans and Directors of Schools of Nursing, which oversees the nursing education and accreditation process and ensures that high standards are always maintained in Mississippi. She was instrumental in securing funds from the Kellogg Foundation for more than one million dollars to establish a program at the nursing school to improve access to health services for adolescents and their families in sections of rural and urban Mississippi.

During 1989–1990, Alcorn initiated a Faculty/Staff Mini-Grants program. Proposals for research grants of up to five thousand dollars are submitted yearly by faculty members, who are also encouraged to attend professional meetings. Some faculty members enroll in campus courses, receiving the benefit of a fee waiver. Such incentives assist faculty in receiving additional degrees or endorsements that enhance them professionally and enable them to be better teachers as a result of continuous training and professional development.

Faculty participation in university affairs takes place through the Faculty Assembly, of which all faculty are automatically members. The Faculty Senate is composed of a group of elected representatives; its 1993 chairman is Levie Robinson. These two groups allow the faculty's concerns to be communicated to the administration. Recommendations that come through these bodies are presented to the president and the Administrative Council for consideration. The senate meets monthly, and the assembly meets twice per year, once during the spring and once during the fall.

Students view the university faculty primarily as classroom teachers. A faculty member's effectiveness is measured by that person's knowledge of subject matter and his or her ability to organize and present oral and written course work clearly. Faculty members must be able to motivate student interest and participation; they must show interest in scholarly pursuits as demonstrated through publications, professional papers, artistic performance, and other undertakings; and they must participate in service activities both within and outside the university.

The Higher Education Appreciation Day Working for Academic Excellence (HEADWAE) was established in 1988 by the Mississippi legislature to honor students and faculty members who have made outstanding contributions in promoting academic excellence. Alcorn State University faculty members who have received this honor are: 1989, Dr. Kenneth Simmons; 1990, Dr. Josephine McCann Posey; 1991, Dr. Frances Henderson; 1992, Dr. Ella Anderson; and 1993, Dr. Alpha Morris.

Faculty rank ranges from instructor to full professor. An instructor usually holds the master's degree only, whereas a terminal degree is normally required for an assistant professorship. The associate professor must have a terminal degree with a minimum of nine years of teaching, service, and research experience, with at least five of those years at the university level. A professor must have fifteen years of teaching, research, and service, ten of which must be at the college level. One major concern of the Alcorn faculty is that a new member is sometimes employed at a rank equivalent to or higher than faculty already on board. Some teachers have also felt that promotion is too slow. The administration admits that sometimes new faculty members are employed at an equal or higher rank because of the market value and the demand at the time of employment, and that the promotion process is sometimes slow because there is no salary incentive to accommodate any promotion.

Tenure is the means by which a faculty member may obtain security in his or her position. It is granted on the basis of demonstrated capabilities and continuing intellectual development, not simply because of length of employment. If a faculty member has a grievance in any matter other than dismissal, he or she has to seek a solution to the problem through the proper channels. If the issue is not thereby solved, the academic dean selects a committee to look into the complaint as set out in written grievance procedures.

Annual evaluations of all faculty and staff are made so as to establish a basis for administrative recommendations (salary, merit pay, rank, promotion, and tenure) and to encourage improvement of individual performance. The employee has an opportunity to discuss the evaluation with his or her immediate supervisor. The evaluation scale ranges from poor (unsatisfactory) to very good (outstanding), the latter warranting consideration for merit pay. The exact amount of merit pay is based on individual performance in teaching, research, and public service. Some faculty members dislike the merit pay concept, expressing doubts about the fairness of the assessment procedure.

Faculty members have academic freedom, which means that they are to pursue the truth without any untoward influences, either from outside or inside the Alcorn community. The following statements demonstrate the university's concept of academic freedom:

> 1. Faculty members are entitled to full freedom in research and in the publication of the results when the above does not conflict with the adequate performance of their other academic duties, but research for pecuniary returns should be based upon an understanding with the authorities or the administration of the university.

2. Faculty members are entitled to freedom in the classroom in discussion of their subject, but they should be careful not to introduce into their teaching controversial matters which have no relation to their subject. Limitations of academic freedom because of religious or other aims of the institution should be clearly stated at the time of appointment.

3. The college or university teacher is a citizen, a member of a learned profession, and an officer of an educational institution. When teachers speak or write as citizens, they should be free from institutional censorship or discipline; but their special position in the community imposes special obligations. As a person of learning and an educational officer, a teacher should remember that the public may judge a teacher's profession and institution by said teacher's utterances. Hence, they should at all times be accurate, should exercise appropriate restraint, should show respect for the opinions of others and should make every effort to indicate that they are not institutional spokespersons.

The land-grant purpose of "serving the people" at Alcorn is as important today as it was in 1871. Faculty members are expected to meet all classes on time, attend faculty meetings, maintain conference and academic advisement office hours, maintain the roll book and call roll at each class meeting, fulfill commitments to research and public service projects, attend commencement and other special university functions, serve on various assigned committees, and administer examinations as scheduled by the dean of academic affairs.

Even though Alcorn is primarily teaching-oriented, its faculty conducts a considerable amount of research, especially in agriculture and related areas. Alcorn's policy is to encourage faculty involvement in any research that contributes to the improvement of instructional activities, to the acquiring of advanced knowledge, and to professional growth. While faculty and staff are encouraged to seek external funding as a means of supplementing institutional funds, they are prohibited from getting so involved in such efforts that their responsibilities to Alcorn are neglected. During the summer, faculty members may be released from all teaching responsibilities to do research full-time.

Alcorn provides fringe benefits to faculty and staff through a program of group life, accidental, death, and dismemberment insurance benefits. A voluntary health insurance program is also available. A full-time faculty or staff member must become a member of the Public Employee's Retirement System. Additionally, Alcorn maintains standard workers' compensation insurance coverage in accordance with Mississippi state laws providing for hospitalization, medical care, and weekly compensation for disability.

Faculty members may be granted a sabbatical leave for the purpose of professional development in research, writing, studying, acquisition of advanced degrees, or other creative efforts. Sabbaticals are not vacations or rest periods but are available to increase the usefulness, effectiveness, and productivity of faculty. Since 1975, Alcorn has granted approximately thirty such leaves. A plan of activities during the sabbatical period must accompany the application, which goes through normal channels to Walter Washington and then to the Board of Trustees of State Institutions of Higher Learning for final approval. Requests must be submitted at least six months in advance. A faculty member who is granted leave must agree to remain as a full-time regular faculty member an additional semester for each semester of leave. If the faculty member does not return, the repayment of salary paid during the leave is required.

Collaborative efforts on the part of the administration, faculty, and staff have contributed to the success of the new Alcorn. There is a sense of dedication and commitment that causes each entity to go beyond the minimum and demonstrate all of those qualities necessary to reach the maximum in achieving goals.

SEVEN

A Growing Variety of Choices

Academics

ALCORN IS COMMITTED TO ACCESS AND QUALITY in all its academic programs and services in an effort to facilitate the optimum success of each student. After 1975, it became possible for students to pursue degrees at the graduate as well as undergraduate level.

By 1975 undergraduate offerings were available in forty-eight different areas: accounting, agriculture economics, agricultural education, agronomy, allied health, animal science, biology (teaching), business education, chemistry, chemistry (teaching), computer science and applied mathematics, early childhood education, economics, elementary education, English (communication), English (teaching), food/nutrition, general agriculture, health and physical education, health science, history, home economics (education), home economics (general), industrial arts education, industrial technology, institutional management, mathematics, mathematics (teaching), medical technology, music education, nursing (associate), nursing (baccalaureate), political science, pre-dentistry, pre-engineering, pre-forestry, pre-law, premedicine, medical records administration, pre-nursing, pre-optometry, pre-pharmacy, pre-veterinarian medicine, psychology, recreation, secretarial science, social science education, sociology and social services, and special education.

With the establishment of graduate studies, students were able to gain graduate credits in approximately twenty different areas. In 1993 Alcorn offered graduate degrees in elementary education and secondary education. By that year there were seven academic divisions, with about fifty-three major areas. The seven divisions were Arts and Sciences, Education and Psychology, Business, Agriculture and Applied Science, Graduate Studies, Nursing, and the General College for Excellence. Each division is composed of academic departments that offer one or more courses of study. Proficiency examinations are required for successful completion of any program.

Alcorn is accredited by the Commission on Colleges of the Southern Association of Colleges and Schools (SACS) to offer the associate, baccalaureate, master's, and educational specialist degrees. The education specialist degree is offered in elementary education only. Specific programs are accredited by the appropriate agencies. The food and nutrition and institution management programs, for example, are approved by the American Dietetic Association (ADA).

In 1983, the General College for Excellence was established. This college coordinates lower-division advising, counseling and testing, and special programs. It maximizes a student's chances for succeeding, whether the problems be academic or personal in nature. The General College provides many services to students at all levels.

Advising is a continuing process of communication and is an essential part of Alcorn's commitment to the higher education of its students. The advisement system is designed to motivate students toward successful degree completion and career preparation. The General College is the initial academic advisement area for individuals who are beginning freshmen, readmitted students, or transfer students who are not yet eligible to be assigned to a major academic department. An advisement record is kept on each student detailing strengths and weaknesses. This record is prepared by the Counseling and Testing Center and passed on to the student's academic advisor. While in the General College, students also receive instructional experiences that will ensure a much greater degree of success in higher education than would be possible otherwise.

The General College for Excellence fulfills the university's goals of providing students with general knowledge in the areas of English and writing, creative arts, social science, natural science, and mathematics. It further provides diversification of effective educational programs, activities, and services to accommodate students with varying levels of potential for achievement. It is also the responsibility of this division to provide students with an orientation to the university (its rules and regulations), to monitor the progress of each student on a continuous basis, and to recommend when students should begin studying in their major departments.

This division is very concerned with augmenting student retention in the institution. The number of students identified in the division increased from 730 in 1983 to approximately 950 in 1993. More than 6,000 students have passed through the General College, and the retention rate increased from 58 percent in 1983 to more than 66 percent in 1993. The enrollment of the entire university has increased from 2,500 to more than 3,000 since the establishment of the General College. No Alcorn student is permitted to register in a regular college course in an area in which there is a demonstrated deficiency until that deficiency is corrected. Dr. Newtie Boyd, the only director in the history of the General College, is assisted by Dr. Frederick Harris and ensures efficient coordination of all programs, activities, and services sponsored by this unit.

The Learning Laboratory is a component of the General College and is operated by a coordinator and general college staff members. Students also serve as tutors and laboratory assistants. Available to those students needing assistance in meeting the requirements of the General College, the laboratory incorporates computer-assisted instruction and is designed to support students with weaknesses as well as those who just want to expand their knowledge in a particular area. Students are also encouraged to develop self-reliance, self-confidence, and a strong desire to complete their education.

The Special Services Program seeks and assists those students who have demonstrated academic potential but lack the secondary school preparation needed to succeed in an institution of higher learning. The goal is to increase the achievement, retention, and graduation rate through the special services of instructing, tutoring, and counseling. The special services program offers developmental reading designed to increase vocabulary, comprehension and creative thinking skills. Tutorial service is also given in English and mathematics. The intent is to help special services students develop self-confidence and be motivated to proceed and complete their education. J. W. Fortenberry was responsible for the effective implementation of this component of the General College until his death.

Tutorial assistance is provided for students who need help in achieving the necessary requirements for mastery of course content and individual academic skills. This assistance is also available when they enroll in their regular courses. The tutorial program is supervised, monitored, evaluated, and revised as needed.

Counseling services are provided for General College students. The Counseling and Testing Service includes developmental workshops in communication skill building, leadership training, assertiveness training, and life planning; crisis intervention counseling and personal and social adjustment counseling; vocational education; psychological testing of interests and aptitudes; referral service; and peer counselor training. The Office of Counseling and Testing coordinates all university-wide testing programs, including: English Proficiency for undergraduate and graduate students, National Teacher Examinations (NTE), American College Test (ACT), Graduate Record Examination (GRE), Graduate Management Admission Test (GMAT), Law School Admission Test (LSAT), Miller Analogies Test (MAT), General Education Development Test (GED), New Medical College Admission Test, Descriptive Tests of Mathematics Skills, Descriptive Tests of Language Skills, Sophomore Competency Examinations, and the National Engineering Aptitude Search Test. Individual testing in ability, aptitude, and interest are also available through this office. The Counseling and Testing Center offers assistance to students in individual and group settings in the areas of social development, personal development, educational development, and career planning. This service is rendered by staff qualified in the area of human behavior. The counseling and testing services fall under the auspices of the General College. The Director of Counseling and Testing, LaPlose Jackson, is responsible for the effective implementation of this component of the General College. Each student is assigned to a counselor who offers counseling services in college orientation, academic achievement, personal and social development, personal survival, and planning. Mr. Jackson attended Alcorn in the 1950s when he worked for twenty-five cents per hour, went on to become Director of Financial Aid for more then twenty years, and then was made Director of Counseling and Testing.

For approximately eight years, the Stanford Test of Academic Skills was used as the placement test for entering students. In 1993, ACT results were used for this purpose. When tests place students into developmental classes, the services mentioned are available to help them progress to regular classes. To do so, students must have completed at least forty-seven hours of course work and demonstrated a 12.5 grade level for any subject area requiring developmental education as evidenced by the American College Tests. They must also maintain a GPA of 2.00.

Since 1983, the General College for Excellence has developed two computer-assisted instructional laboratories and funded four student-support service programs, ESTP-ROTC programs, the Upward Bound program, and English and mathematics programs, as well as developing an interresidential hall counseling program.

Having once served on the Committee on Educational Opportunities for Minorities sponsored by the National Association of State Universities and Land-Grant Colleges, Walter Washington knew that the concept of the General College was an important means of upgrading educational programs for minority groups in land-grant colleges and universities. Students who leave the General College for Excellence feel prepared to enter regular classes.

The establishment of the nursing division at Alcorn in 1977 was much more controversial than the creation of the General College for Excellence. The University of Southern Mississippi had its nursing program located in Natchez. The chairman of the medical affairs committee of the state board of trustees, Dr. Verner Holmes of McComb, said that it was not fair for Southern Mississippi to run a nursing school in Natchez with Alcorn right next door. President Washington insisted that his school did not want to drive Southern out of the field of nursing; he simply wanted a nursing program for Alcorn. Prominent officials criticized the proposed move, with Natchez mayor Tony Byrne saying it would be detrimental to the Natchez community.

City leaders and officials in Natchez went to great effort to stop the change. Complaints included the assertion that a quality program of nursing instruction was in danger of being destroyed in an effort to quiet criticism resulting from inadequate support of Alcorn State University in the past and present, thus keeping officials from having to focus on building a statewide system of equal opportunity in higher education. Opponents claimed that the transfer would not do much to strengthen and balance the curriculum at Alcorn, while it would reduce the effectiveness of the higher education curriculum already offered in Natchez. The argument was that both Alcorn and the University of Southern Mississippi would be losers, and that the people of southwest Mississippi would be denied quality, equality, and availability of tax-supported higher education. Alcorn State University proved these perceptions to be incorrect. Five years later Tony Byrne spoke of the good working relationship with Alcorn. The Alcorn nursing division was working well.

It has had three directors in its history. Dr. Frances Henderson, the director in 1993, was preceded by Dr. Cora Balmat, for whom the school was named, and by Dr. Rose Mary Tyndall, the first director. Upon establishing the nursing school Alcorn had three goals: to strengthen and reorganize the curriculum, to achieve national accreditation, and to establish a baccalaureate degree program. Dr. Eva D. Smith was the first chairperson of the baccalaureate degree nursing program, followed by Drs. Nancy Dodge, Ruth Stevens, Frances Henderson, and Joyce McManus. All three of the goals have been achieved. The size of the faculty has increased from three to seven, and clinical hours increased from twelve to fifteen. Within five years, seventy-seven students had graduated, with sixty-four gaining nursing licenses.

But there were further problems. In 1981 the completion of the building for the Alcorn State University Division of Nursing was in economic limbo. The state building commission placed a hold on the one million dollar appropriation because of a projected state sixty-eight million dollar budget deficit. The building was not completed until 1984. The division had already received the National League for Nursing accreditation for the associate degree in 1981 and for the bachelor's degree in 1982. The baccalaureate program was designed to enable graduates to make intellectual decisions needed to deal with complex and varied nursing problems. They are further enabled to function professionally by being accountable to self, clients, and the nursing profession. The associate program was designed to enable the students to develop technical competence in nursing through encountering sufficient learning experience. Initially, the nursing division fell under the Arts and Sciences, spearheaded by Dr. Norris Edney, but later, because of its comprehensiveness, it became a separate division.

The 1984 facility reflects the latest in educational technology. The curriculum combines course requirements with planned and guided learning experiences in clinical nursing in cooperating hospitals and community agencies. The Division of Nursing has been very successful in receiving grants, including $1.2 million from the Kellogg Foundation. It has also achieved the 100 percent pass rate on the registered nurse licensure examination in both the associate degree nursing program (chaired in 1993 by Dr. Jo Pierce) and the bachelor science nursing program (chaired in 1993 by Dr. Joyce McManus). It was cited as having one of ten exemplary nursing centers by the National League of Nursing in 1992. The center has contributed to the success experienced by Alcorn professionally in race relations.

The Division of Graduate Studies, directed by Dr. Norris Edney, was established in 1975 following authorization by the Board of Trustees of State Institutions of Higher Learning. It is designed to meet the needs of elementary, secondary, and/or junior college teachers and administrators. Emphasis is placed on the in-service needs of individuals employed in agribusiness, industry, and/or other educational or governmental agencies such as Cooperative Extension Service, Soil Conservation Service, Farmers Home Administration, the Agriculture Stabilization and Conservation Service, Public Welfare, Public Health Service, and Headstart programs. Students enrolled in the division may work toward a master of science degree in education, an educational specialist degree in elementary education, and the master of science degree in agriculture.

In addition to providing for the advanced training of individuals, the graduate division seeks to promote research in an effort to contribute to knowledge in an environment of inquiry and freedom. The involved scholars are encouraged to seek new truths and demonstrate the ability to apply acquired knowledge to the improvement of the conditions of mankind.

The division seeks to provide a well-rounded program by offering research opportunities through formal training and related experiences. Emphasis is placed on developing competencies in the students that result in upgrading professional certification and encouraging as well as promoting scholarship and scholarly activities among students and faculty members.

The Graduate Council is the governing body responsible for the development, formulation, and approval of policy relative to the graduate program. The council is composed of representatives from each of the areas at the university offering graduate degrees or a graduate concentration, a library representative, selected division directors, the Director of Institutional Planning, Development, and Assessment, and public school superintendents. The division's director, Dr. Edney, also serves as chairman of the council. The council determines policies of admission and retention, as well as readmission. It approves the graduate curriculum and recommends policies having to do with its structure, academic standards, and anything else related to degree requirements. The council is also responsible for hearing any appeals that may come from students or faculty concerning policies that apply to them. The graduate faculty of the division is selected by the respective departments and approved by the council.

Students are admitted into an unconditional, special, or non-degree status and have the option of a thesis or non-thesis plan. They have to maintain a 3.00 (B) average and successfully pass a core comprehensive examination and an area comprehensive examination prior to graduation. Graduate elementary education programs of study are: elementary education with endorsements in early childhood education and reading; secondary education with endorsements in agriculture, biology, business education, chemistry, English, general science, home economics, industrial education, mathematics, and social science; special subject fields and administration composed of administration and supervision (elementary and secondary), athletic administration and supervision, guidance and counseling, health and physical education, and special education; agriculture with endorsements in agricultural economics, agronomy, and animal science; and the educational specialist degree in elementary education only.

The division has maintained the accreditation of the National Council for Accreditation of Teacher Education (NCATE), and the graduate enrollment has increased from approximately one hundred to three hundred graduate students. The master's degrees in biology and agriculture were added to the curriculum in 1990, the educational specialist degree was approved in elementary education in 1990, and in 1993 graduate courses existed in several off-campus areas including Natchez and Vicksburg. The graduate division is also a part of the Vicksburg Consortium in Collaboration with Mississippi State University. The division's name changed in 1990 to the Division of Graduate Studies, Research, and Continuing Education. The success of its graduates indicates that the division is making a significant contribution to the university and the state. For example, Carolyn Gamblin, a 1975 graduate of Alcorn, was the first black female to graduate from the University of Mississippi School of Dentistry. In 1980, five 1974 graduates of Alcorn received the M.D. degree from the University of Mississippi School of Medicine.

The Division of Arts and Sciences, under the direction of Dr. Norris Edney, offers programs of study leading to the bachelor of science and bachelor of arts degrees in biology, chemistry, English, mathematics, social studies, and music education. The division is committed to producing life-oriented individuals with the knowledge to succeed in a variety of careers. The primary objectives of the division are to offer a broad program of general education, to promote constructive and critical thinking capability in students, and to lay a strong foundation for advanced learning. In addition, it tries to help students develop an appreciation for civilization and accountability. Particular emphasis is placed on applying the scientific method.

The Department of Biological Sciences, with Dr. Willie Humphrey as acting chairman in 1993, provides students with knowledge essential to understanding the basis of life from a biological perspective. Students are trained in this department to enter professional studies such as allied health, dentistry, medicine, pharmacy, optometry, physical therapy, and physio-therapy, as well as to teach in the secondary schools. There are six basic curricula in this department: biology (pre-professional), pre-nursing, biology (teaching), health-related professions, health science, and medical technology. The department has succeeded in establishing a master's program and gaining monies for renovating classrooms, labs, and offices. It has received approximately $1,518,600 in grant money over the last few years.

The Department of Chemistry and Physics, chaired in 1993 by Dr. Joseph Russell, who is assisted by Dr. Troy Stewart, provides students with knowledge essential to understanding the physical sciences and their relationship to today's scientific and technological society. Courses of study are offered to prepare students who are going on to graduate school in five different curricular options: the pre-professional curriculum (medical or dental); the non-professional curriculum for those planning careers in a related area but not leading to advanced study; the secondary teaching curriculum for those planning to teach; and the chemistry technology curriculum for those who wish to pursue a course of study between chemistry and technology. By 1992 the department had purchased $800,000 worth of advanced lab equipment and succeeded in establishing a media and learning center.

The Department of Communications, under the leadership of Dr. David Crosby, trains students in techniques of modern communication through the use of print, radio, and television. It enhances the university's educational process through instructional and information programming by linking the university with the rest of the state. Students have opportunities to work part-time and do internships in both radio and television. The course offerings lead to the B.A. degree with emphasis in either print or broadcast journalism. This degree was first approved in 1990. Since then the department has been successful in acquiring all of the prerequisites needed for an effective program including the installation of a darkroom, a television production studio, a radio station, and an electronic newsroom. In 1993 the department had about 122 majors. The programs vary from religion to jazz. Local and world news and weather reports are aired on WPRL, the campus radio station.

The Department of English and Foreign Languages (formerly the Department of English) provides courses leading to the B.A. degree in English with a concentration in literature and teaching. With Paul Broome in 1993 as acting chairman, students learn to appreciate, understand, and interpret the human experience in verbal and written expression. The curriculum prepares majors to enter various occupations including teaching, writing and editing, business and sales, public relations, and government services (local, state, and federal). Students are also prepared for graduate study and have the option of pursuing graduate studies in English at Alcorn leading to the master of science degree in secondary education. A teaching endorsement may also be pursued in French and Spanish. The department has a communication skills center and a computerized composition writing laboratory. It has recently developed a standardized grading system for freshmen English essays and a comprehensive testing plan for all English majors. Faculty members have viewed the standardized system as being advantageous because it put more validity into the process.

The Department of Fine Arts (formerly the Department of Humanities) was established in 1973. It includes the areas of art, humanities, speech, and theater. Students are provided with the opportunity to acquire a broad cultural background. They are trained for success in graduate studies or a career as an artist or music teacher at both the elementary and secondary levels. They work to interpret, maintain, and create the highest level in individual and group performance as well as to enhance the cultural and aesthetic life of Alcorn. The department is accredited by the National Association of Schools of Music (NASM) where its 1993 department chairperson, Dr. Joyce Bolden, serves as associate chair. The department has a computer-assisted instruction music laboratory and a music library. Bands (concert and jazz ensemble) and choirs often perform locally, statewide, and nationally. The three choirs, each with a different director, are the Concert Choir, the Gospel Choir, and the Interfaith Choir. The band, under the direction of Mr. Samuel Griffin, assisted by Mr. Timothy Chambers, has style, grace, talent, and pride. Griffin, who came to Alcorn in 1966, started off with a band of approximately 35 to 40 members; in 1993, he had 188 members with 144 instruments, 4 drum majors, 16 flag girls, and 12 golden girls. In 1975 the group became the first college band to perform in the New Orleans Superdome, and it has performed before large crowds in other cities such as Chicago, Los Angeles, and Philadelphia. Previous directors of the band at Alcorn include William Smiley, Kenneth Sampson, V. G. Dalton, and William Hamlin.

Student musical recitals are held regularly. In 1990, the department acquired approval to offer the bachelor of music in performance degree, and in 1993, it had a degree-granting program that afforded the students the opportunity to specialize in instrumental, piano, or vocal performance. One faculty member, Mrs. Clarence Carter Smith, has presented "A Night with Clarence Carter Smith" since 1972. She plays and sings various types of songs and involves faculty, staff and students as participants in games and other related activities.

The Department of Social Sciences, chaired in 1993 by Dr. Alpha L. Morris, who succeeded Dr. Bernard Cotton, provides a broad education for students preparing to teach and engage in research. Students are exposed to the history of great issues and institutions, past and present, with special attention to socio-cultural, economic, and political problems facing society. They are prepared to teach in elementary and secondary schools, to pursue graduate studies, or to demonstrate competencies necessary for employment in other fields. The department's six major curricular areas are criminal justice, economics, history (teaching), political science, pre-law, and sociology/social work. Internship programs are offered through the department for interested students in federal, state, and local government agencies or the private sector. In 1993 the department had a Social Science Learning Resource Center supervised by Artie Smith and funded by a three-year Lilly Endowment Grant, a Mental Health Enrichment Program, and two projects funded by the United States Department of Agriculture (USDA).

The Department of Mathematical Sciences, with Dr. Joseph Smith as acting department chairman upon the retirement of Bettye Allen, offers basic college instruction in mathematical concepts and computational skills including the utilization of computers. Majors are available in mathematics, computer science and applied mathematics, and mathematics teaching at the secondary level. The department emphasizes a broad knowledge of industry, graduate schools, mathematics teaching, and preparation for other employment. Computer usage is emphasized. The mathematics program, formerly a part of the chemistry and mathematics department, was renamed the Department of Mathematical Sciences. Students may pursue a master of science in education degree in secondary education with an endorsement in mathematics. The department has a personal computer lab and conferred its first computer science and applied mathematics degree in the 1980s. The computer accommodations are equipped to network with the supercomputer at the University of Mississippi and other universities, a system that has benefited faculty, staff, and students.

The Department of Military Science (Army ROTC), with Captain Thomas J. Bartak as acting head in 1993, increases the opportunities for students who choose either a civilian or military career. Emphasis is on selecting individuals for positions as officers in the United States Army, the Army National Guard, and the United States Army Reserves. The Army ROTC is a four-year program (two years basic and two years advanced). The basic component, normally taken during the freshman and sophomore years, covers areas of management principles, national defense, military history, leadership development, military courtesy, discipline, and customs. The advanced component is generally taken during the junior and senior years. Students who have demonstrated the potential for becoming effective officers are selected for enrollment. This component provides additional instruction in leadership development, organization and management, and tactics and administration. The advanced cadets attend a six-week camp where they put principles and theories into practice. All expenses are paid. In order to enroll in the basic phase course, the student must be a U.S. citizen, at least seventeen years old, physically qualified and enrolled as a full-time student. Professional military training is required of all students who aspire to become commissioned officers. The department also has enhanced skill training with courses designed to assist ROTC cadets with reading, writing, and mathematics. Students enrolled in the basic component have no military obligation. They may withdraw at any time up to the end of the school year.

The Division of Education and Psychology, in 1993 headed by Dr. John I. Hendricks, houses the Department of Education and the Department of Health, Physical Education, and Recreation. Opportunities are available for students to pursue the Bachelor of Science degree and the master's degree in both departments, as well as the educational specialist degree in elementary education.

The division, which has as its primary concern the preparation of highly qualified elementary and secondary school teachers and other educational personnel, endeavors to attract highly intellectual individuals with moral integrity. It strives to prepare students through specialized courses and experiences and through promoting a broad understanding of the learner and the teaching-learning process, to provide opportunities for professional laboratory experiences, and to enable students to develop a meaningful philosophy of education.

Student teaching is the culmination of the teacher preparation program at Alcorn. In order to be permitted to student teach, the student must have been fully admitted to teacher education as certified by the Advisor for Admission to Teacher Education, recommended by his or her department chairman, completed all general education requirements, maintained a 2.50 on all work, completed all professional education requirements with no grade less than C and completed at least 95 percent of the major field requirements. The applicant must also have successfully passed the general knowledge and communication skills portion of the National Teacher Examinations, passed the English Proficiency Examination, and been recommended by two faculty members. The student teaching experience is based on structured observation and evaluation of instructional plans, instructional settings, and classroom performance. The university faculty supervisors and cooperating teachers jointly supervise and monitor the student's field experiences.

The Mississippi Teacher Assessment Instrument (MTAI) is the state-mandated evaluation tool for beginning teachers. In keeping with the professional education unit's theme, Alcorn labels it as Alcorn's Proficient and Effective Teacher Assessment Instrument (APETAI). Student teachers are evaluated on the competencies identified in APETAI that are congruent with the competencies identified in MTAI. They must demonstrate the ability to be a scholar, a facilitator, a manager, and to be proactive. Student teaching includes a pre-seminar, a mid-point seminar, and a post-seminar. Students are expected to perform student teaching services daily for a period of twelve weeks. The division is also responsible for the Beginning Teacher Support Program (BTSP), a service given to first-year teachers after graduation to assist them in being successful teachers. Special sessions are scheduled on Saturdays for the convenience of the teachers who are not available during the work day.

In addition to supervising student teaching, the division is responsible for clinical and field-based experiences. Teacher education students are provided with early professional involvement in the elementary and secondary school environment. They move gradually from observation to more direct teaching experiences where they are involved in designing instructional plans, microteaching, and other classroom activities. Such experiences occur before student teaching, taking place in surrounding school districts as early as the student's sophomore year.

Course offerings are well-planned and sequenced. The teacher education program supports independent thinking, effective communication, relevant judgments, professional collaboration, effective participation in the educational system, discrimination of values in the educational arena, and professional ethics. Multicultural education and global perspectives are emphasized as an integral part of the selected studies. All teacher-education programs at the undergraduate and graduate levels are accredited by the National Council for Accreditation of Teacher Education (NCATE).

Within the Division of Education and Psychology, the Department of Education, with Dr. Levie Robinson as acting chairman in 1993, concerns itself with the preparation of all prospective teachers by providing professional education courses. The department administers a curriculum for elementary education majors and provides courses in secondary education as well. The aim is to familiarize students with the behavioral and learning characteristics of pupils enrolled in the elementary and secondary schools, to provide strategies for effective teaching, and to enable them to meet state requirements for certification. A student majoring in elementary education may obtain a concentration in math, social studies, language arts, or reading by completing additional requirements. For students majoring in special education, emphasis is placed on the mildly and moderately handicapped (including children with learning disabilities), mildly emotionally disturbed, mentally retarded, and the severely and profoundly handicapped. A non-teaching degree is also available in the department for students who plan to pursue advanced studies in psychology focusing on the application of psychological principles to behavior, learning, and personality. The department provides psychology service courses for all teacher education and some other majors.

The department has a Curriculum Resource Center (CRC), directed by Doris McGowan, a computer center coordinated by Dr. Gerald Ritter and Dr. John Lee, and psychology laboratory, coordinated by Dr. Gerald Ritter and open on a daily basis to pre-service and in-service students. Workshops, seminars, and mini-courses are sponsored in designated areas throughout the academic year and summer months to provide in-service personnel with simulated opportunities to observe, examine, and study teaching/learning situations and discuss solutions to classroom-related learning problems. In 1983 there was only one psychology graduate, but by 1992 graduation, the number had increased to more than twenty. The college board granted permission to offer the educational specialist degree in elementary education in 1990. Its first graduate will complete the program in 1994. The master's degree in elementary education has been offered since 1975.

The Department of Health, Physical Education, and Recreation, under the leadership of Dr. Robert L. Smith, who serves as acting chairman, aids the student in personal growth and commitment by promoting suitable physical qualifications, intellectual competency, and desirable personality and character traits. The department focuses on four basic components: service classes for the development of neuromuscular skills, understanding, and attitudes through selected activities with emphasis in carry-over or lifetime sports; teacher-education curriculum to prepare students for positions as health and physical educators and/or coaches on the elementary and secondary levels; the recreation major for students who seek employment as recreation professionals in public, private, or voluntary agencies; and a graduate program that provides opportunities for advanced study in health and physical education, athletic administration, coaching, and scholarly research and inquiry. Hygiene courses are offered to help students develop desirable health habits, attitudes, and knowledge.

The physical education curriculum is organized so that the student will have the opportunity to develop proficiencies and understandings in subject matter and experiences in major and minor sports. The recreation curriculum provides the student with in-depth experiences in various aspects of the total recreational scene and develops competencies essential for professional growth and maturity. The department makes every effort to promote in the student the fundamental capacities for human leadership, scholarship, service, and professional skills and focuses on meeting the educational needs of the students statewide, nationally, and internationally. It is vitally concerned with the special needs of the diverse population the university serves. The emphasis is on field-based delivery.

The Division of Business, in 1993 under the leadership of Dr. Robert Williams as division director and Leon Crawford as acting department chairman, came into being in 1977, although business courses had first been offered during President Bell's administration. It offers majors in accounting, business administration, and office management for the bachelor of science degree. Students in this department may select a concentration in management or finance. The division strives to develop economic and occupational competence in its students; to create wise consumers of resources, goals, and services; and to teach positive interpersonal and leadership skills. Emphasis is placed on a plan for accommodating personal and technological changes to prepare students for entry-level positions, but they are equipped as well with the tools to strive for higher levels of responsibility in business, government, and education. An adequate foundation in the professional business world is provided so that students may pursue advanced studies. The curriculum stresses problem-solving techniques, analytical skills development, and application integrated with computer usage.

The business division provides courses leading to an endorsement in business education under vocational education. The degree is offered via the industrial technology department. Students are involved in the Black Executive Exchange Program (BEEP), the result of President Walter Washington's participation in a BEEP seminar emphasizing its advantage for youth. Students also participate in a wide variety of co-op programs and internships. The division has a Center for the Study and Development of Entrepreneurship and a computer facility.

The program of study in business education focuses on preparing individuals for careers as teachers. The goal is to prepare students to teach business courses offered on the secondary and post-secondary levels. The business education curriculum prepares students to serve as teachers, secretaries, administrative assistants, supervisors, clerks, bookkeepers, and data processors. Students may also pursue graduate-level course work in business education.

The Division of Agriculture, Research, Extension and Applied Sciences (AREAS) houses the departments of agriculture, home economics, industrial technology, cooperative extension and research. Primarily it is responsible for the land-grant function as it relates to teaching and research and the dissemination of information to the public. The division seeks to carry out a program that prepares students to be successful in their careers, to conduct a research program that will assist students in discovering new knowledge in order to better utilize existing knowledge, and to be of service to rural and urban people in the various disciplines. The curriculum in the division leads to the bachelor of science degree in agricultural education, agricultural economics, agronomy, animal science, agri-business management, general agriculture, home economics, food and nutrition, industrial technology, and technology education. The curriculum leads to the master's degree in education with teaching endorsements in each department. There are also endorsements in agricultural economics, agronomy, and animal science. If a student is not interested in a degree program, he or she may enroll as a special student in forestry, agriculture, or industrial technology.

The Department of Agriculture, in 1993 chaired by Dr. Charles Tillman, who succeeded Dr. Willie Fred Jackson, prepares students for employment in agricultural extension, teaching vocational agriculture, practical farm operation and management, and industry and government agencies. The department focuses on multiple research productivity and service activities. The Cooperative Extension Program within the department represents the outreach service function of the department. The pre-forestry program is a collaboration between Alcorn and Mississippi State University and involves other universities that have professional forestry programs. The program has a two-year curriculum at Alcorn with an additional two years at a cooperating university. The department established the Branch Experiment Station in 1971 as one of Walter Washington's early wishes to acquire new buildings and laboratory facilities for dairy, beef, swine, and poultry. Research is ongoing in fruits. A new agribusiness management program was approved in 1988, and the department received capacity building grants in 1989 that allowed the curriculum to include international development, dairy curriculum development, vetiver grass, and funding of a community college recruitment project. For the past seven years, the department has hosted international students from Honduras, Bolivia, South Africa, Pakistan, and other Third World countries.

The Department of Home Economics, in 1993 chaired by Dr. Eula Masingale, prepares students for degrees in home economics and food and nutrition. The programs prepare men and women for professional careers and advanced study. Course offerings with emphasis on family living include child development, consumer education, family relationships, merchandising, clothing, textiles, equipment, home furnishings, and food and nutrition. The curriculum provides opportunities for internship and clinical or field-based experience to promote leadership skills and good decision-making qualities. Through its land-grant function of teaching, research, and public service, the department seeks to foster citizenship through personal and cultural enrichment, scholarly creativity, and professional development. The department is sensitive to the needs of the handicapped and culturally deprived individuals as well. One of the special features of the department is the Nursery-Kindergarten Center, which is licensed by the Mississippi State Board of Health to accommodate twenty-five children. The center supports varied instructional programs in a laboratory setting that allows for observation and interaction with youth during the formative developmental years. The department offers an advanced program in food and nutrition and sponsors a recruitment and retention project.

The Department of Industrial Technology, chaired by Dr. Napoleon Moses in 1993, who succeeded Dr. Kenneth Simmons, provides curriculum in general education, a technical specialty, science, mathematics, and industrial management with four-year concentration areas for students interested in business, government, and industry-related professions. The basic core program focuses on specific technical outcomes including researching, designing, and testing technical projects; terminology, purpose, and historical developments of industrial technology; computer systems; and ways to gain and progress through meaningful employment. The program also concentrates on specific management outcomes including the classifying and analyzing of manufacturing processes; the demonstration of techniques of effective technical communication (oral and written); the analysis and evaluation of various production methods; the mastery of knowledge and skills in the supervisory management and industrial management processes; and the issue of how to work cooperatively in culturally diverse settings. The entry-level positions for which graduates are prepared include production, communication, transportation, energy, distribution, industrial planning, management, supervision, and technical sales. Students are also prepared for teaching positions in industrial technology at the secondary or post-secondary educational level. The department, which is accredited by the National Association of Industrial Technology (NAIT), also hosts the university's summer computer camp for students from southwest Mississippi and elsewhere. The camp, in which participants receive an introduction to computers, was begun by Dr. Napoleon Moses in the summer of 1991.

The university has made significant academic advances since 1969. The undergraduate enrollment has remained above 2,500 for each year except 1980. Graduate enrollment was steadily increasing. The enrollment in the nursing school located in Natchez increased from 77 in 1977, the first year, to 132 in 1992. Since 1977, approximately 527 students have graduated from the Division of Nursing and all but ten have received their licenses.

Many of Alcorn's academic programs are professionally accredited. Alcorn seeks to ensure that all its programs gain such professional accreditation, and it has been remarkably successful in doing so during Walter Washington's presidency. In December 1991, the Southern Association of Colleges and Schools (SACS) reaffirmed the university's accreditation. In 1992, the National Council for the Accreditation of Teacher Education (NCATE) reaffirmed all teacher education programs at both the basic and advanced levels. The associate degree in nursing has been accredited since 1982 by the National League of Nursing, the music in education program since 1981 by the National Association of Schools of Music, and the industrial technology program reaffirmed in 1992, having received initial accreditation in 1988.

Alcorn has shown a steady increase in faculty with terminal degrees, with the largest gain being in the agriculture, education, and social science departments. In 1969 only 17 percent of the faculty had terminal degrees; in 1992 that figure stood at 50 percent. Some fifty faculty and staff members have found assistance in Alcorn's faculty development program for doctoral study, mini-grants, travel to professional meetings, and similar activities.

During these years, approximately seventeen new programs have been implemented, with the largest number of new degrees being offered in the Division of Arts and Sciences. The student body at the university has also become more diverse. Though in 1993, the majority was still African-American, the number of other nationalities had increased. Sixty-four percent of the students at the campus branch in Natchez are not black.

The academic programs at Alcorn have done an excellent job of preparing youth for the outside world. The gradual addition of programs over the decades indicates Alcorn's willingness to meet the needs of a changing society.

EIGHT

How to Make a Living and How to Live

Support Services

In an effort to help students make the most of their talents and to prepare them for service to their race and nation, Alcorn has attempted to provide quality education. Walter Washington has solicited involvement from the community as well. Alcorn's outreach and commitment to students have attracted young people from all over the United States. During their four years in Lorman students are taught not just how to make a living but how to live, how to get along with others, and how to work harmoniously within a system. Young men and women who come to Alcorn frightened and insecure are often able to leave four years later standing tall with confidence in themselves and their future. This miraculous change takes place because the faculty has worked with them, guided them, and motivated them. In addition, the university's strong academic support services offer a further bulwark against discouragement and failure.

In 1970, the J. D. Boyd Library, named in honor of the former Alcorn president, was occupied. Built with a capacity for more than 175,000 volumes, the building also contains an audio-visual center and a map collection, and it serves as a depository for state documents and selected United States Government Publications. In 1991 the library had 199,472 volumes (an increase of 25,000 over 1970), 228,362 government documents, 4,577 titles in audio-visual materials, 37,652 volumes in micrographies, and 764 periodical subscriptions. In 1977 reading space was converted to stack space that could house new books and journals. In 1993 space continued to be a problem, as the continuous increase in library holdings strained the building's capacity to contain them.

The library's seating capacity is approximately nine hundred. There are three levels, with reading areas on each floor. The building also contains an archives room, a computer room, a seminar room, four study rooms, forty-seven faculty carrels, individual study carrels, and tables that seat from four to six students. Online cataloging was initiated in 1985 through the Southeastern Library Network, Inc. (Solinet). Online searching of computerized databases such as Infotrac is also available through the reference office. Alcorn has a connection with the largest libraries in the area through the Tri-cooperative Reference Resource Network (a Library Source Exchange).

Library services play a significant part in a student's educational experience, whether he or she is involved at the undergraduate or graduate level. Interlibrary loan services are particularly important at the graduate level. In 1981, the library spent a total of $473,511.56 for operation and materials. In 1992, the total was $770,808.

Library services, including an orientation for new users, provide students with the opportunity to learn how to continue lifelong study. In 1993 the library's experienced personnel included the director, Dr. Epsy Hendricks, who chaired the state's University Library Directors Council in 1989. She was succeeded as director in 1993 by Jessie Arnold as a result of retirement.

The Honors Curriculum Program was established in 1970 for students who have exceptional intellectual ability. Honors work, however, was offered as early as 1960. In 1993 the program was directed by Dr. Donzell Lee, who was assisted by Dr. Larry Konecky, and was coordinated by the Honors Program Council. Entering freshmen are selected according to results on admission and placement tests. Full admission requires a 21 on the ACT and provisional admission a 19 or 20 ACT score. Those who complete at least twenty-four hours of honors course work while maintaining a cumulative grade point average of

3.25 or above graduate as Honors Curriculum Scholars. If a student enters the honors program after the first semester of the freshman year, the selection is based on cumulative average plus faculty recommendations. The aim is to bring together students and teachers, with the teacher assuming a mentor's role. Students also have the opportunity to participate in extracurricular activities providing exposure to cultural and intellectual opportunities beyond those that are traditional in a college program. In 1992, 610 students made the dean's list.

Honors students are also provided the opportunity to become a part of the Honors Student Organization and to represent the university at regional and national honors conferences. Alcorn's honors organization won second place in the Campus All-Star Challenge College Bowl Competition held in Washington, D.C., during the spring of 1990 and received twenty thousand dollars that was given to the Alcorn Foundation earmarked for the honors curriculum budget. Alcorn also received an additional one thousand dollars because one of the team members, Shayla Thomas, was named to the West All-Star Team. In 1992 they gained third place and in 1993 fourth place in the regional, receiving five thousand dollars each year. In 1991, they received twenty-five hundred dollars for participating. Alcorn has been involved in the Challenge Bowl contest for four years, with the team being coached by Dr. Konecky.

The Cooperative Education Program engages students in alternating periods of off-campus work and on-campus study. Students are thus enriched and strengthened in education, personal development, and avocational preparation as they integrate theory and practice. They are afforded an opportunity to be employed in jobs closely related to their major area of study and are able to work full-time and earn a regular salary. Students explore their career interests, encountering a real workplace setting before making a final occupational commitment. The university, in this way, extends classroom and laboratory facilities to include more sophisticated facilities, equipment, and expertise in business, industry and government agencies.

The Office of Admissions and Recruitment, spearheaded by Albert Johnson in 1993, is the first Alcorn office most students encounter. An applicant may apply any time during the calendar year. To be eligible for admission, he or she must be a graduate of a recognized high school, have earned at least a C average and acquired at least 13½ high school units: four in English, three in mathematics, three in the sciences, two and a half in social studies and one in either mathematics, science, or a foreign language. Alcorn does not discriminate on the grounds of race, color, religion, sex, national origin, age, or handicap. A student eighteen years of age or older who has not finished high school must take and successfully pass the GED. A student twenty-one years of age or older may register without meeting these requirements and may take a maximum of twelve hours. Degree student status is acquired when regular admissions standards are met or when a C average or above is maintained in a minimum of twelve semester hours.

State standards were raised during the 1980s for anyone wishing to attend Alcorn or any other university in the state. Alcorn, however, was always ahead of the state's mandates. In 1979, Alcorn's ACT requirement was 11 while the state's standard score was 9. Washington knew that strong steps had to be taken to ensure the survival of black colleges.

Over the past twenty-five years new approaches have been taken to recruit and retain students and to secure alumni support. Initially the university's facilities had to be upgraded. The Charles Stewart Mott Foundation provided funds to Alcorn for an expansion and strengthening of the school's recruitment and public relations programs. This project improved the distribution of information regarding major curricular offerings as well as funded off-campus workshops and tours for approximately 50 percent of the state's high school counselors and approximately 75 percent of its public officials. The recruitment effort embarked upon by the university and involving students, faculty, and alumni was designed to attract young men and women intent on a quality education.

A transfer student must be eligible for readmission to the school from which he or she is transferring in order to be eligible for admission to Alcorn. Former students who left in good standing and have not been enrolled for one or more semesters may also be readmitted. A foreign student must follow regular admission procedures and must give evidence of financial support before arriving on campus, because the university does not assume responsibility for a student who arrives with inadequate resources.

Mature applicants who do not meet all admission requirements may be admitted as special students and may take up to thirty semester hours before meeting regular admission requirements. Veterans must follow regular admission procedures.

A student is placed on academic probation for one semester if he or she does not maintain at least a 2.0 cumulative grade point average. Once a student is placed on such probation, he or she must carry a reduced load and raise that average during this period of time or be suspended for one regular semester. A student enrolled at Alcorn on a full-time basis must complete degree requirements within six years. If a student is seeking a second undergraduate degree, he or she will be allowed an additional two years to satisfy requirements for both degrees.

Incoming students are given a freshmen or transfer student orientation that furnishes them with information concerning all aspects of the university including financial assistance and mandates for maintaining assistance. This orientation is an effort to help students adjust to life at Alcorn. Entrance and placement examinations are given and students are given General College advisors until they leave the General College.

The Office of Career Planning and Placement Services, spearheaded in 1993 by Al Johnson, assists students in career planning by scheduling interviews with employers, securing job listings, counseling, providing occupational literature on career opportunities, consulting with professional staff and employers, and maintaining and reproducing credentials. Prospective employers are able to benefit from having their needs made known to the students and alumni, from visiting and interviewing qualified applicants, and from making contact with professors and other university personnel. Students are informed of changes in educational and degree programs. Students have a source of accurate and timely information on market trends and on the curriculum of specific career areas, while the institution is represented to the public in the professional arena. Students receive help in obtaining permanent employment, cooperative education positions, intern positions, and summer employment. Graduates receive assistance in making career changes. Off-campus recruitment activities for graduate and professional schools are also coordinated by this office. Al Johnson creates opportunities for representatives to come from all over the world to the campus and recruit.

The Industry Cluster, the National Alliance of Businessmen College/Industry Relationship, was established at Alcorn in 1973. Composed of business and industry members, it has increased from approximately twenty agencies in 1974 to approximately fifty in 1993. This program is a cooperative effort in which representatives from the business world work together to strengthen the curriculum of a developing institution. It promotes the Curriculum and Motivation Task Force, the Resource and Educational Task Force, the Membership and Foundation Task Force, and the Placement Task Force, through which business management practices are shared with the university.

"Cluster" was organized in the 1960s because of President Lyndon

B. Johnson's concern about the unemployment rate among minority groups. His hope was that the Cluster would provide a means for black institutions to move toward the American mainstream with the help of the business world.

The Alcorn State Cluster has studied academic departments and made recommendations for improvements, as well as making it possible for students and teachers to take tours. Businesses have donated scientific and professional journals and other instructional materials. A mobile unit was donated for recruiting purposes. Provisions have been made for internships, cooperative education positions, and summer employment as well as full-time employment for Alcorn students.

Through the Cluster, a communication media center was established, and equipment has been donated for academic and institution management requirements. Students benefit from the expertise of management and the use of technological resources to ensure mastery of skills.

Cluster provides jackets to presidential scholars each year. To be named a presidential scholar a student must be registered for at least twelve hours of academic credit and maintain a straight A grade point average. These jackets are provided by Cluster members, Dow Chemical Company and the Miller Brewing Company. Scholarships are also provided for academically superior students. In 1985 the Cluster provided the Presidential Scholarship Award and the Departmental Award Program. In his 1989 commencement speech at Alcorn, George Bush, then president of the United States, praised Alcorn for its good job in preparing productive citizens for the nation, thus taking note of one of the Cluster's goals. The Alcorn State University/Industry Cluster has been an integral part of the modern growth and development of the university. It has helped to project the image of the university far beyond the campus into the boardrooms of leading American corporations.

Dr. Franklin D. Jackson, Director of Institutional Advancement and Planning and Special Assistant to President Walter Washington, serves on the Business Advisory Council of the National Alliance of Business. In 1993 he is the academic cochairman of the Alcorn State University Industry Cluster, while Clinton Hunt of Dow Chemical is the industry cochairman. Dr. Jackson says, "The Alcorn State University/Industry Cluster has played a significant role in opening doors of opportunity to training and employment for students and graduates of Alcorn State University, as well as for students and graduates of other historically black colleges and universities in the nation. Through the work relationships among business, industry, government, and the university, students and graduates have obtained employment at the professional, managerial, and technical levels in Fortune 500 companies. Most of these training and employment opportunities were not available to Alcorn students and graduates prior to the Cluster."

The Alcorn State University Foundation, directed in 1993 by Oliver Taylor, was founded in 1973. Gifts are administered by the foundation in strict compliance with the instructions of the donor. Donations handled by the foundation include stocks, bonds, wills, insurance policies, works of art, real estate, and matching gifts as well as cash. Since 1974, the foundation has distributed $938,318 to 1,289 students. In the 1991–92 academic year alone, it distributed over $138,284 to 140 students. The foundation administers 22 endowed scholarship programs. A $5,000 minimum is required for an endowment and a $1,000,000 minimum is required for an endowed chair.

The Alumni Fund and Campus Campaign Programs have assisted the foundation in obtaining larger contributions as a part of the self-help program. A "Report of Giving" is published annually containing the names of those individuals, alumni chapters, foundations, businesses and/or organizations that have made contributions through the foundation to assist the university in funding its programs. Oliver Taylor is particularly happy about the foundation's sponsoring of the Senior Award for Excellence since 1981 in the amount of one thousand dollars each year. Recipients have been:

YEAR	NAME	MAJOR
1981–82	Linda R. Smith	Agriculture
1982–83	Pamela A. Davis	Biology
1983–84	Donita G. Morgan	Chemistry
1985–86	Clyde E. Glenn	Biology
1985–86	Imogene McGriggs	English
1986–87	Charmaine Edwards	Chemistry/Pre-Med
1987–88	Robert R. Norvel, Jr.	Biology
1988–89	Sharon Pitterson	Animal Science
1989–90	Robert Tatum	Chemistry
1990–91	Nancy R. Palmer	Pre-Med/Chemistry
1991–92	Marcus Reeves	Biology/Pre-Med
1992–93	Trena L. Brown	Elementary Education

In 1968, the Upward Bound project was initiated. This program provides culturally enriching experiences, leadership development training, and practical skills to disadvantaged youth from surrounding communities. It is housed under the auspices of the General College and is authorized under Title II-A of the Economic Opportunity Act, funded by the U.S. Department of Education.

Upward Bound at Alcorn is one of more than three hundred precollege programs in the United States, Guam, Puerto Rico, and the Virgin Islands. All land-grant institutions were given an opportunity to submit proposals for giving children from disadvantaged backgrounds help in school. At Alcorn, Dr. Jessie Morris, Sr., Dr. Calvin White, Dr. Henry Parker, and Mrs. Vivian Tellis worked on the proposal to get Upward Bound funded. A year-round program, it is designed to help high school students help themselves. A 1981 study of the program indicated that more than 90 percent of students participating in Upward Bound programs across the nation further their education at institutions of higher learning.

Students participate in the program during the summers and on Saturdays during the academic year. In 1993 the major subjects and their teachers were English (Emma Waites), reading (Elnora Washington), science (Linda McMurtry), and mathematics (John Turner, Jr.). Extracurricular activities include ceramics, music, art, typing, leathercraft, dramatics, sports, field trips, swimming, and talent programs. The Upward Bound choir won first place at three consecutive Upward Bound state annual retreats where they convened with Upward Bound students from other predominantly black universities and junior colleges in Mississippi. Young people in this program share educational experiences with peers of similar backgrounds, support career planning, and engage in scholarly, social, recreational and athletic activities.

J. W. Fortenberry, the program's director until his death in October 1993, pointed out that it has played a decisive role in the development of hundreds of disadvantaged and first-generation college-bound youth. For many young people it has meant the difference between dropping out or completing high school and then moving on to college. Upward Bound is an integral part of Alcorn and has provided it and other colleges and universities with outstanding students. At Alcorn, students in the 10th, 11th, or 12th grades from Adams, Claiborne, and Jefferson counties are provided with training in academic skills and the attitude necessary to succeed in a complex society. University students who serve as tutors are able to develop leadership skills and to strengthen their commitments to their families and to their communities. Effective working relationships are established with high school principals, faculty, and counselors. Young people are also able to gain a greater appreciation for their ethnic heritage. Edna Lewis, the counselor for

Upward Bound, has watched student participants in this program grow and develop a sense of self-esteem. J. W. Fortenberry said that the program has been successful in giving students needed skills. "Our goal," he says, "is to make the students productive citizens, improve themselves, family, and community."

The Cooperative Extension Program at Alcorn, serves the needs of people in southwest Mississippi who are disadvantaged and have limited resources. Emphasis is placed on home economics, community and youth development, and agriculture and natural resources. Research efforts began in the early 1970s with projects instituted totaling approximately $5 million. In 1980, there was a University and Community Interaction Conference held at Alcorn with community representatives from Adams, Claiborne, Jefferson, Warren, and Wilkinson counties. At this conference, information was provided about services available at Alcorn and about the school's priorities and concerns as they related to community growth. Walter Washington has frequently expressed strong support for outreach services even though the university's lack of adequate funding has long hindered its ability to do all it might.

The Cooperative Extension Program has, however, helped farmers turn weed patches into productive gardens. These farmers value the assistance. One said, "I never got an opportunity to attend college but I feel that I have gotten the experience from being involved in the cooperative extension program. I really love it." Through this program, small landowners have been shown how to improve their diets as well as raise their income through the sale of garden produce. The experiment station provides research information on vegetable plant varieties and cultivation methods necessary to get the best production from available acreage. Farmers in the business of raising cattle or hogs learn how to improve their herds and pastures. The Mississippi Agricultural and Forestry Experiment Station on Alcorn's campus provides such services through research and experimentation. These services help insure improved quality and increased prices of feeder pigs taken to market. The number of gardens in southwest Mississippi has increased about 25 percent because of the extension service. Families are assisted by economists in improving their budgets and also learn about nutrition and health care.

The Cooperative Extension Program has been another component of Walter Washington's vision to move the university to new heights. The annual Field Day at the university for the purpose of bringing small farmers in southwest Mississippi to the campus to keep them abreast of current agricultural research and to introduce them to the various cooperative extension activities has long been a success. More than one thousand participants from thirteen southwest Mississippi counties, along with others from throughout the state, usually attend.

The University Press of Mississippi, founded in 1970 and located in Jackson, Mississippi, serves Alcorn and the state's other universities through the publication of scholarly works. The press is governed by a board of directors consisting of two representatives from each of the eight state universities, a member of the Board of Trustees of State Institutions of Higher Learning, and the director of the press. In 1993 Alcorn's two representatives were Dr. Rudolph Waters and Ralph Payne. In its nearly twenty-five year history, the press has published nearly seven hundred books. Three were written by Alcorn faculty: *The Centennial History of Alcorn A. & M. College*, by Melerson Guy Dunham, *Black Mississippi History Makers* by Dr. George Sewell and *Black Mississippi History Makers* (Revised) by Dr. George Sewell and Dr. Margaret Dwight.

Finally, the Office of Public Relations, directed by Ralph Payne, provides news about the institution. Its major publications include the *Alcorn State University Weekly Bulletin* and the *Alcorn Herald*. This office also develops feature stories, news releases, brochures, and announcements and supervises the production of the student newspaper and the yearbook. Other publications produced in this office are the *Alcorn Report* and the *Alumnus Magazine*, joint publications with the Office of Alumni Affairs.

None of the programs discussed in this chapter is part of a traditional classroom activity, yet each plays an important role in the academic life of Alcorn. These programs allow teachers and students to work more efficiently in the classroom, and they also provide opportunities for students to pay for part or all of their education. Even school students participate in research apprenticeships at Alcorn, working with agriculture researchers and gaining valuable experience not available in ordinary summer jobs. In 1992, approximately 175 Alcorn students worked as co-ops and interns in 28 states and the District of Columbia.

NINE

Balancing Work and Play

Students and Student Services

Alcorn's administration wants to make it clear that the welfare of the students is the university's primary concern. To this end, student retreats are held and student representatives are members of major university committees. The school tries to ensure that, no matter what the problem or need might be, Alcorn students know how to get help outside the classroom. Students are given a handbook explaining services as soon as they arrive on campus. They also quickly learn that the faculty and staff are there to help them in adjusting to the university environment and in leading a life of personal and social enrichment. This effort is intended to reduce the attrition rate as well as to encourage physical, intellectual, and emotional development in students.

Students at Alcorn are encouraged to balance academics with pleasure. Though they enjoy the learning environment, they also welcome the opportunity to be on the "yard," the "green," or the "reservation," as it's sometimes called. They also become involved in more organized activities such as intramural baseball and football; canoeing, tennis and horse shoes; swimming in the olympic-size pool; dancing (indoor and outdoor); concerts, plays, and movies; gymnastics; handball and racquetball; weight lifting; and bowling. The student union, or SUB as it is generally called, directed by Willie Moses, is the center for the recreational side of student life. Here they play games of table tennis, checkers, chess, cards, and pinball, listen to the juke box, and watch television. As they enjoy these activities, they are right at the post office where they can pick up or mail a letter. In the same building they can buy a Coke and chips or just chat in the fast-food section, patronize the barber and beauty salon, or visit the bookstore where they can purchase anything from a textbook to an Alcorn T-shirt.

In spite of all of these attractions, students realize that most of their time must be spent in studying, going to the library, attending classes, preparing for their future career, and keeping their priorities in focus.

On the Mississippi legislature's Appreciation Day, described in chapter 6, the following academically talented students have been recognized: 1989, Antonio Phillip; 1990, Diana Jackson; 1991, Glenda Dannette Day; 1992, Pamela Love; and 1993, Angela Stewart.

Even though students enjoy the balance between academics and recreation, they have been disgruntled at times with aspects of campus life. In 1979, they boycotted classes because action had not been taken by the administration on some complaints they had filed earlier. At least three of the eight dormitories had been without heat for two days. Some individual rooms had had no heat for even longer, so that students were forced to purchase electric heaters. Several dorms lacked hot water. There were also complaints about the lack of adequate medical facilities and the need for trained medical personnel, such as doctors, as well as emergency medical technicians.

In response to the complaints, Walter Washington explained that the primary problem was the university's water system, which was being phased out to make way for a new $500,000 system scheduled for completion within two weeks. (This new system became a reality within the promised time.) Washington also pointed out that he was working with students on a one-to-one basis. He had toured all of the dormitories promising that the new water system would take care of the heat and hot water problems. He also assured students that the delay had not been the university's fault. Initial discussions on this new water plant facility had taken place back in 1969 but lack of state funding had delayed it. As for the meals, Washington said that they were well prepared and nutritionally balanced.

Students were satisfied with the efforts of the administration, and the boycott ended. This was the only time during Washington's administration that students boycotted classes because of what they felt were unmet needs.

Annual retreats, in which student representatives discuss concerns and university issues with university representatives, have resulted in many significant improvements to student life. For example, in the 1990s, students received revised dormitory visitation policies, dormitory telephones, and cable television, all of which had been longstanding requests.

In 1993, the student enrollment was approximately three thousand, which is about the maximum the university can house in comfort. The need for more dormitories is crucial; too many young people have been denied the opportunity to get an Alcorn education because there has been no room for them to live on or near the campus.

One of the essential student services is the Student Health Service, supervised in 1993 by two physicians, Dr. Willie McArthur and Dr. Shanti Pandy, along with two full-time nurses, Betty Johnson, Director of Health Services, and Marvell Spears, and Mary Buie, nurse's aide. The health unit also has an emergency medical technician, Jessie Davis. When services are needed from the county health department or the state health department, they are rendered upon request. Many kinds of health services are available at no cost to students, including counseling, general treatment, temporary hospitalization, general instruction, physical examinations, and follow-ups. Dental services are not available. A minimum fee is charged for special medicines or injections. Students must show evidence of immunizations or exemption from immunizations.

Over the past two decades, health services have been expanded in several ways. Copies of pamphlets and information on sexually transmitted diseases are now distributed, information sessions on health care are held, medical history forms are required, and a medical self-help center provides medicine and health-care materials and new equipment for ambulances. A cardiopulmonary resuscitation class is regularly conducted by certified faculty or staff.

Major revisions have also been made in the area of residential living. All residence halls for male and female students are equipped to make the dormitory experience as enjoyable and comfortable as possible, educationally and socially. Air-conditioned rooms are furnished with study desks, single beds with mattresses, dressers, mirrors, and chairs. The student must furnish items such as blankets and bedspreads, but the university provides curtains and linens. Each residence hall has a head resident director who is responsible for assigning rooms and ensuring that the dormitory runs smoothly. Students may reserve rooms in advance and must pay a fifty dollar refundable breakage fee to ensure that rooms are kept clean and university property is not destroyed or damaged. An inventory is taken of each room before it is officially assigned to students. The signing of the inventory commits a student to being responsible for the room from that point on. Rooms must be neat and clean at all times. The university reserves the right to inspect rooms in the residence halls at any time deemed necessary. Room visitation procedures for applicable students must be adhered to as outlined in visitation guidelines. The visitations take place in upperclass dorms for women only. The hours are Monday and Wednesday (8:00 P.M.–10:00 P.M.); Friday and Saturday (8:00 P.M.–12:00 midnight).

The situation regarding rules in 1993 is somewhat different from that of earlier times. Some of the rules in effect during the 1940s were:

1. It is the aim of the college that students will learn to do right because it is right, and not for fear of punishment.
2. The college has for its object the development of self-respect.
3. The demerit system is designed to take care of minor infractions.
4. Attendance at the college is a privilege and not a right.
5. The possession of firearms is forbidden. They must be deposited at the college office.
6. Smoking on campus or in buildings is prohibited except in rooms designated for that purpose.
7. All communications with the board of trustees by anyone in the service of the college must be with the consent of the president.
8. For Sunday school and all public occasions all young women will be expected to wear solid navy blue suits with plain white blouses.
9. Beginning on Palm Sunday and continuing until the end of the second semester young women will be expected to wear solid white dresses or suits except for travel.
10. Evening dresses should be worn to formal or semi-formal affairs.
11. Students whose bills are in arrears may not register for the succeeding semester; all those whose bills become one month in arrears will be requested to withdraw.

In recent years, the administration has hired additional residence hall directors, increased the janitorial staff, improved the general appearance of the residence halls, coordinated workshops for residence hall directors and janitorial staff, and tightened control in student disciplinary matters. In 1993 these improvements continued to be implemented by the Dean of Student Affairs, Emanuel Barnes, and associate deans James L. Bolden and Herbert Anderson; the Coordinator of Management for Residential Living, Clynell Moses; and each of the head residence directors. Parents and students have always complained about the dorms, but there have been continuous efforts to keep them in good condition, and students are encouraged to help in this endeavor. Yet, dormitory life is exciting to the students. Some types of behavior there have not changed much over the years. Students realize that the dorm is home away from home, and they try to make the best of the situation. Telephone exchange services are available to all students. The 1993 head operator, Marietta Thornton (preceded by Wilmetta Boykin), is assisted by Octavia Odem.

The Alcorn State University Commons, under the direction of Elbert Smith, who is assisted by Bernadine Coleman and Dorothy Hunt, makes every effort to satisfy students' nutritional needs. Three meals are served each day, seven days a week. On holidays, only two meals are served, but students are given a "snack bag" at the second meal. Students are issued a nontransferable meal card that must be presented before they are served. The meals, which are varied, tasty, and well-balanced, are served in semi-buffet style. The setting is expected to promote the students' social graces. Occasionally special meals such as Italian dinners, picnic fare, and soul food are served on the lawn outside the cafeteria. Students have also always frequented Patton's groceries near the campus.

The university provides transportation to students upon request when vehicles are available. Students sometimes want to go shopping, on field trips or tours, or to the local bus station. For travel off-campus, a small fee is required unless the trip is academic in nature. The security office also provides transportation in cases of emergency. Students who have automobiles on campus must register them with campus security along with proof of insurance. The university does not bear liability for students nor does the university approve or accept responsibility for student transportation in private vehicles.

The security force at Alcorn is an integral part of the educational process. It consists of males and females with high school-to-college education. Several of them are veterans of the United States Armed Forces and other university security departments are also on the force. Officers in the department are continuously trained in areas such as traffic problems, firing and care of various weapons, and crowd control.

Instructions on firing are conducted by nationally ranked officers from the police department in the state's capital, Jackson. The Alcorn Security Force investigates automobile accidents that occur on the campus and submits reports to involved individuals and insurance companies. All motor vehicles on the campus (faculty, staff, and students) must be registered and identified with the proper decal. Traffic signs and regulations must be observed and obeyed. There has long been a very effective working relationship with the sheriff's departments of Jefferson and Claiborne counties on such matters as thefts or the need for more security for campus events such as football or basketball games.

The university laundry, supervised by Lettie Williams, includes facilities for dry cleaning. The students have assigned dates to deposit and pick up linen and laundry.

The campus post office, headed by Postmaster Bernard Johnson since 1976, operates an efficient system of communication for faculty, staff, and students. Service includes dissemination of incoming and outgoing mail and packages. Individuals may also purchase money orders. There is no general delivery and a rental fee of $4.50 for a small post office box and $7.50 for a large box is charged per year for all students, faculty, and staff. Johnson, who is assisted by Eleanor Hill, has been able in recent years to attend various seminars on mailroom operations. Approximately five thousand pieces of mail go out on the average per day.

As part of the overall learning experience at Alcorn and in support of the university's effort to provide wholesome cultural entertainment for students, extracurricular participation is highly encouraged. Mary Walls, the 1993 Director of Student Activities, coordinates such events as dances, movies, lyceum attractions, and live entertainment. Students are provided the opportunity to select, organize, and attend varied attractions on the campus. The Student Affairs Office approves the scheduling of all functions. Nationally known entertainers such as comedians and television stars come to the campus for selected events. Students attempt to stay in tune with today's times and select their attractions accordingly.

Students are also encouraged to participate in cocurricular activities such as social and religious organizations, departmental clubs, and recreational activities (athletic and nonathletic). Each organization must have a campus advisor and receive university approval. (For a list of organizations, see Appendix 1.)

Alcorn has always seemed like heaven to some students and isolation to others. Usually, a student who makes it through the first semester falls in love with the university and does not want to leave. Most students over the years have indicated that they loved Alcorn and would choose the school again if they had to start all over.

TEN

EFFICIENCY AND ACCOUNTABILITY

Fiscal Affairs

THE CONTINUED EXISTENCE OF ALCORN would not be possible without the dedicated work of the Office of Fiscal Affairs. This office, directed by Wiley Jones, administers accounting, budgeting, travel reimbursement, payroll, and financial record-keeping and reporting; auxiliary enterprises; buildings and grounds; cashiering; housing; personnel; the post office; property and inventory control; purchasing; bursar; receiving and storage; and student financial aid. The offices work together to ensure stable services including food, laundry, telephone exchange, transportation, and the campus union.

The Office of Fiscal Affairs advises the president and the University Administrative Council on matters pertaining to the fiscal and financial status of the university as well as assisting them, along with faculty and staff, in preparing budgets. This office must keep abreast of federal and state laws, regulations, and board policies governing the handling of funds. The responsibilities of this office include all tasks necessary to foster and promote the growth, development, fiscal stability and integrity of the university.

During recent years, a new and improved financial accounting system has been installed, enabling the business office to prepare reports in a more timely fashion. There is also a new human-resource system, which allows accurate data to be generated immediately when critical management decisions must be made.

The Office of Student Financial Aid was moved to the fiscal affairs unit in 1986 because of the fiscal impact that it had on the entire university. This move made it possible for the business manager, Wiley Jones, and the director of financial aid, Laura Shelvy, to improve the university's services to students and parents. For many years, the financial aid office was handled by the dean of students, James L. Bolden. As enrollment increased, it became necessary to set up a separate office. More than 95 percent of Alcorn students receive some type of financial aid during their college years. This percentage refers to students on university funds and federal funds. The financial aid programs provide assistance to students who need aid to attend the university and acknowledge outstanding and personal achievements of others. The office's major purpose is to assist those students who do not have sufficient resources to attend college but seriously desire an education. Assistance is provided through employment, grants, loans, and scholarships. These monies are made available through the university, private sources, and federally funded programs. Some of the most sought-after student aid programs are the National Direct Student Loan (now Perkins Loan), the Federally Insured Student Loan, a University Loan, the Basic Educational Opportunity Grant, the Supplemental Educational Opportunity Grant, the State Student Incentive Grant Program, the Nursing Student Assistance Program, the Mississippi Guaranteed Student Loan Program, the Plus Grant Program, the Pell Grant Program, Work-Study Program (full-time and part-time), University Scholarship, Army ROTC Scholarship, Athletic Scholarship, Music Scholarship, and the State Assistance Program.

To be considered for financial aid, a student must submit an application for admission to the university. A financial aid form acquired from the guidance counselor at the student's high school must be sent for processing to the College Scholarship Service in Princeton, New Jersey. An application for financial aid must also be submitted to the financial aid office. Since Alcorn has a variety of financial aid programs, students desiring help normally have no difficulty finding the package that meets their needs.

To continue to be eligible for financial assistance, a student must demonstrate satisfactory progress in his or her academic program. All proper forms must be submitted in a timely manner. Without exception, all financial aid materials must be filed and a student must have an awards letter marked "final" before he or she is permitted to live in campus housing. Students receiving less than full aid must pay a hundred dollar nonrefundable deposit before moving into a dormitory. Students not having any aid must pay a two hundred dollar nonrefundable deposit. This deposit serves as payment toward registration. Improvements in the area of financial aid in 1993 have allowed students to mail residence hall deposits as well as to register by mail.

The most pressing problem for the Office of Fiscal Affairs has long been the frequent budget cuts the university has been forced to sustain. In 1992 the university faced a 5 percent state appropriations budget cut in the amount of $452,455, slightly down from 1991 when the recision was $783,213. Each year since 1982, the university has received a clean unqualified favorable audit from the state and federal governments in all areas including capital inventory items in spite of total budget cuts over those years of $4,943,557. In fact, each auxiliary unit including the bookstore, campus union, dining hall, faculty and student housing, and laundry have closed recent years with a profit.

In recent years many changes have been made in the area of fiscal management. In 1991 Perma Thuha, a certified public accountant, was added to the Business Office staff as the assistant business manager. The On-line Student Accounts Receivable System was implemented in 1989, giving students immediate feedback on account balances. The Financial Aid Office and the Business Office were also computerized. This computerization greatly improved the selection of classes, advisement, and payment of fees. The on-line system in the Financial Aid Office has made it possible to have direct access to College Scholarship Service (CSS) files for updating as well as correcting students files. In 1989, the university had to make the decision to require the payment of all fees for student tuition and other costs during registration because installment plans were putting the university in debt. Some students owed the university huge sums of money.

Services made available through fiscal affairs in 1989 included cable television, telephones in each dormitory room, and security cameras. In 1992 a comprehensive manual was developed to govern the operations of all services and to be used as a training tool for first-time staff members. A new laundromat was constructed for students in 1988.

The cost of receiving an education has varied from one academic year to another. In 1969, the cost of attending Alcorn was approximately $750 per semester. In 1992–1993, sample expenses per semester were as follows: for an undergraduate Mississippi resident boarding and taking twelve or more hours, $2,237, for a nonresident, $3,216.50; for a commuting undergraduate resident taking nine hours, $891, for a nonresident, $1,870.50; for a resident graduate student boarding and taking twelve hours, $1,953.50, for a nonresident, $2,933; for a commuting resident graduate student taking nine hours, $1,072, for a nonresident, $2,051.50. Amounts differ for those who are practice teaching.

In an effort to ensure that the students receive the best services, the Follett Bookstore Company of Chicago, Illinois, was contracted in 1992 to operate the university bookstore, with Classie Johnson, who succeeded John Dennis, managing it. The bookstore, which meets both academic and nonacademic needs, is spacious, neat, and quiet. It is usually open for a period of time during special events such as football games so that graduates and others can purchase Alcorn items. Faculty and students utilize the bookstore's services on a continuous basis.

Each fiscal affairs unit must thoroughly understand the policies and procedures that are appropriate in performing the duties required of that particular financial area and know how they affect the mission of the university. Upon receiving funds, the university must ensure through this office that such monies are properly used and monitored so that there will not be excess expenditures. The office must also ensure that receipts and expenditures are properly documented, so that there will be nothing to hinder planning the budget for the next year.

The process of budget planning starts when the university receives notice from the Board of Trustees of State Institutions of Higher Learning. The preliminary budget process takes place about a year ahead of the year under consideration. Funds from capital improvement and special labeled purposes are appropriated by the legislature for the institution to use directly; however, these are still under the board's control. Funds are received from federal government sources for land-grant purposes, research, and special programs, as well as for student aid. The board must also approve the acceptance of these funds. State law requires that agencies operate with a balanced budget and that no more than one-half of appropriated funds be spent during the first six months of the fiscal year. Alcorn's budget control system conforms to all of the requirements of the state as well as to those of federal agencies. Walter Washington has ensured this through his accountability system. Annual audits are conducted, and during these years Alcorn has always been found to be in excellent financial order.

The Personnel Office, directed by Oliver Taylor, is one of the major units housed in the Office of Fiscal Affairs. It serves as the coordinating office for planning, implementing, and administering the policies and activities related to university personnel and counsels university employees on personnel-related matters. This office maintains files on university employees and orients new employees concerning all aspects of the university's operations. Leave forms for business, vacation, or sick leave are channeled through this office, and it also provides Certification of Immigration and Naturalization Service documents and assists state agencies in obtaining pertinent personnel information.

ELEVEN

Determining the Mission

Institutional Advancement, Planning, and Research

The office of institutional advancement, planning, and research at the university is headed by Dr. Franklin Jackson and serves several functions in the university's overall operations. It oversees alumni relations; placement services; development (fundraising); public information services; Title III program, including administration and coordination (the Strengthening Grant Project, a funded project for the purpose of enhancing or strengthening academic programs and all other areas of university operations); planning, management, research and evaluation; and admissions and recruiting. It monitors the effective implementation of institutional long-range plans and serves to identify areas that need modification. Institutional annual priorities are reviewed and updated to ensure that other unit plans are congruent with those priorities.

Since state appropriations have never been sufficient, the Title III program has been a major help to Alcorn in fulfilling its mission. Implemented in 1967 during the Boyd administration, it has continued to flourish during the presidency of Walter Washington. Funds are received under Title III of the Higher Education Act of 1965 and fall under the auspices of the Institutional Aid Programs of the United States Department of Education. Projects are funded in critical areas of a university where dire need for external financial assistance exists. These funds have proven beneficial to Alcorn in the areas of administrative and fiscal management, student services, and curriculum and faculty development. Two twenty-year endowment programs established by the university that resulted from Title III support have contributed to the continued fiscal stability of Alcorn. The endowments serve to support financial assistance for deserving students.

During the 1982–83 academic year, twenty-three activities were funded by Title III. Through this program, significant progress has been made in implementing computer-assisted instructional programs in several departments. The long-range plan is to computerize the entire university.

During the 1988–89 academic year, the Title III grant totaled $760,892 for the purpose of strengthening academic programs in the areas of science programs and laboratories, the honors curriculum, basic education, teacher education, international studies, communications, and cultural literacy. By 1991 Title III funds had increased to $1,050,000. These funds provided for continuous improvement in existing programs, such as the addition of institutional marketing and advancement and computer-assisted student advisement (including financial aid management and registration). In 1987, the office coordinated a twenty-four-month outreach project on historically black colleges and universities, a Job Training Partnership Program directed by John Bennett.

The Office of Institutional Advancement, Planning, and Research has assisted in the preparation of many proposals and has sponsored grantsmanship workshops for faculty and staff. During the 1983–84 academic year, a total of $1,026,729 was raised from private sources such as industry, foundations, and organizations. Approximately $95,884 of that amount represented alumni contributions. During the 1987–88 term there were 542 donors from 26 states and the District of Columbia. Including income from the federal government, the total for that year was $8,461,763.

During the 1989–1990 year, a one-year grant in the amount of $1,050,000 was received from the U.S. Department of Education to assist in strengthening academics, academic support services, and administrative programs university wide. Non-state funds secured during that year amounted to $10,280,094.

By 1993, much of the implementation of development activities was done by departments and individual faculty and staff so as to get more involvement at these levels. Collaboration continues to take place on a continuous basis with other state universities in an effort to generate funds and establish programs.

The planning, management, and evaluation process (PME) consists of strategic planning, long-range and short-range planning, management, and evaluation. The first committee for this purpose was formed in 1969. It coordinated the revision of the mission and goals of the university and recommended policies to the president. By 1992 the committee concerned itself with establishing five-year goals and annual priorities, identifying implementation strategies, allocating and monitoring the use of resources, and developing and implementing the system of evaluation.

Strategic planning is also a significant component of the Office of Institutional Advancement, Planning, and Research. This process contributed greatly to the completion of the university's self-study for reaffirmation of accreditation by the Southern Association of Colleges and Schools in 1991. In 1990–91 the institution's strategic goals were to accomplish the following:

> Achieve national, regional, and professional accreditation for all applicable programs
> Maintain financial stability
> Expand the endowment program
> Acquire adequate science facilities
> Acquire adequate student housing on the main campus and the Natchez campus and improve the cleanliness and maintenance of existing ones
> Improve communication and services to alumni
> Improve faculty and staff salaries and assure competent and committed faculty and staff
> Acquire an adequate physical plant
> Improve the retention rate and the graduation rate of students
> Maintain strong academic and fiscal integrity of the university

A number of assumptions were made by the university in developing this comprehensive plan having to do with demographic trends in enrollment, finance and economy, societal demands, continuation of the trend toward a more technically oriented society, and community opportunities. It is obvious that emphasis was placed on external environmental factors over which the institution has little or no direct control but which could affect the institution's growth. Strategic planning has become a major tool for achieving and maintaining excellence in programs, services, students, and personnel.

The management component of the university ensures that all established plans are implemented. This responsibility belongs to appropriate unit heads who are governed by prepared position descriptions. Faculty and staff members are, however, responsible for the accomplishment of their individual objectives. All of these areas of planning resulted from the total comprehensive study initiated in 1969 to reevaluate every component of the university. The committee formed for this purpose implemented a five-phase process to carry out its task: (1) review of documents involving in-depth study of any historical information relating to the mission and goals of the university; (2) use of a series of instruments designed with consultant assistance to determine perceptions of what the university's mission should be and to determine the goals necessary to achieve said mission; (3) downflow of information, which involved Washington calling a faculty and staff conference and explaining the entire process, and, as follow-up, the holding of divisional and departmental meetings for further explanation and to encourage involvement; (4) upward flow, in which faculty and staff returned the completed instruments (opinionnaires) to the immediate supervisor for review. These were then submitted to the division directors. Students submitted their opinionnaires to the Dean of Student Affairs, who was then James Bolden. Once these instruments had been carefully analyzed and edited, they were submitted to the Long-Range Planning Committee for review before their presentation to President Washington. The fifth and final phase was interaction and exchange. After the statement of mission of the university was approved by President Washington, another faculty/staff conference was held to discuss the results of the committee's work, its relationship to the mission, and the new thrust of the university.

During the 1978-79 academic year, planning was expanded to include systematic and formalized management and evaluation procedures, which led to the formation of the aforementioned PME committee.

The Office of Institutional Research, a component of the larger institutional advancement, planning and research unit, provides coordination for a comprehensive assessment of the university's effectiveness, a requirement for continued accreditation from the Southern Association of Colleges and Schools. This office became active in 1989-90 under the direction of Thelma Spencer, who had been preceded by Dr. Robert Johnson, and is under the direction of Dr. Sidney McLaurin in 1993. An alumni survey sent to graduates showed that they were positive toward their educational experiences at Alcorn. The office sought to strengthen the university by supporting its efforts in strategic planning, decision-making, and program evaluation to develop and maintain a comprehensive program in the area of research and assessment. This office, which is responsible for the implementation of an institutional data base to ensure a centralized focus for certain significant data, also monitors and administers assessment and institutional effectiveness and coordinates external reporting while working closely with departments in assessing their performance. The students' evaluation of instruction and the graduating seniors' survey were two major instruments used in determining effectiveness. This office, in addition, plays a major role in preparing reports to be submitted to the Board of Trustees of State Institutions of Higher Learning and any other external agency or organization.

The Office of Institutional Advancement, Planning and Research has succeeded in coordinating institution-wide activities while involving individuals outside the unit and the university. Dr. Franklin Jackson, in addition to directing this unit, carries out various other tasks as required of him as a special assistant to President Washington. He prepares and disseminates minutes of the Administrative Council, reviews documents, prepares special reports, conducts hearings, serves on special committees, drafts university policies and drafts and updates position descriptions.

All of the components discussed in this chapter stem from the Office of Institutional Advancement, Planning, and Assessment, though Institutional Research is located in a different area. (The responsibilities of these entities may sometimes overlap.) Because planning, whether short-range, long-range, five-year, ten-year, or strategic, is a major concern, this office has been successful in contributing to departmental, divisional, and overall effectiveness in the university.

TWELVE

From Greek Revival to Modern

Physical Facilities

By 1993, Alcorn had seventy-nine buildings. Some of these structures are modern; others are historic. Some are used by more than one academic or administrative unit, while others provide space for classroom and/or laboratory instruction as well as for faculty offices.

The most impressive modern structure on the campus is the new administration-classroom building, which was completed in 1977. It is six stories high and encompasses sixty thousand square feet. The offices of the president, vice president, academic dean, and the director of Institutional Advancement, Planning, and Research are housed in this magnificent facility. Other units located here are the divisions of graduate studies, agriculture, education and psychology, the Office of the Registrar, the Office of Public Relations, the Business Office, the Institutional Assessment Office, the Personnel Office, and the Cooperative Extension Service. Two other significant entities housed in the building are the Computing Center, under the auspices of Dr. Jonathan Turner, and the Printing and Duplicating Center, headed by Harry

Steward. The classroom side of the new administration building covers two floors and is twenty thousand square feet in area. It houses the offices of the Department of Education, eleven classrooms and/or laboratories, and the Curriculum Resource Center.

The agricultural science building was constructed in 1974. It houses offices, classrooms, and laboratories for the agriculture department, and the assembly room and classrooms are often used by other departments. The facility was recently named the Jesse A. Morris, Sr./W. C. Boykin Agricultural Science Building.

Eunice D. Powell Hall, the home economics building, was constructed in 1955. It is a two-story brick building that houses offices, classrooms, and laboratories for the home economics department and the nursery-kindergarten. Its classroom space is also utilized by other departments. It has recently undergone some much-needed renovation.

The health, physical education, and recreation complex was completed in 1975. In addition to the offices of the department, it contains offices for coaches of intercollegiate athletic teams. The complex has classrooms, including an audio-visual room, and a gymnasium with seating for 7,500, with more on the floor when needed. Other features of this building are an Olympic-size swimming pool, two handball courts, a dance studio, and rooms for gymnastics, weight lifting, wrestling, and other physical exercises. In 1992 this facility was named in honor of the "Wizard," former basketball coach Dave Whitney.

The library and science building, in 1993 named in honor of E. Albert Dumas, an Alcornite of the Year, was erected in 1959 and renovated in 1962 and again in 1989. It is a two-story brick building that provides classrooms, laboratories and offices for the chemistry and physics, mathematical sciences, and business departments.

The Fine Arts Building, which was constructed in 1964 during the presidency of J. D. Boyd, houses classrooms, laboratories, and offices for music, art, speech, and theatre. It also has a band room, practice studios for music students, an art laboratory, a language laboratory, and a twenty-one-thousand-square-foot Little Theatre. The theatre and the classrooms are used by other departments as well.

The Industrial Technology Building was erected in 1981 to provide classrooms, laboratories, offices, workshops, and a conference room for the department. This facility also houses the communications department, Alcorn's radio station (WPRL-FM), a television studio, a media office, and an institutional management laboratory.

The Mechanical Arts Building, constructed in 1959, now contains offices, classrooms, and drill space for the military science department.

Harmon Hall was erected in 1929 as a dormitory during the presidency of Levi J. Rowan. It is a two-story building and in 1993 provided office space for the departments of English, foreign languages, and social sciences.

Bowles Hall, also completed in 1929, has been renovated twice since 1969. This building contains classrooms and offices for the Department of Biological Sciences, teaching and research laboratories for biology and physics, a reading laboratory, and offices for the Upward Bound program.

The J. D. Boyd Library was constructed in 1969 and renovated in 1989. It is a two-story facility, with fifty-four thousand square feet of space and a seating capacity of nine hundred. Reading and study areas are available on each floor, while administrative offices and circulation, technical, and reference services are located on the main floor.

The nursing complex in Natchez, built in 1984 and recently named the Cora S. Balmat School of Nursing, is a forty-seven-thousand-square-foot building that accommodates four hundred students, necessary support staff, and services. It has classrooms, conference rooms, laboratories for biology, chemistry, and nursing skills, a learning resource center, a computer-assisted instruction laboratory, a bookstore, an auditorium, student locker space and lounge, faculty library and lounge, a word-processing center, and building management. This facility, located on ten acres donated by Adams County to Alcorn, is convenient to in-town clinical facilities. An additional eighteen-hundred-square-foot-building, the Nursing Center for the Family-Centered Adolescent Health Promotion Project, is part of the complex. It was funded by a $1.2 million grant from the W. K. Kellogg Foundation. The facility also includes a mobile nursing unit.

The president's home, dormitories II and III, the Belle Lettres Hall, and Oakland Memorial Chapel are among the major historic buildings on the campus that were constructed in 1830. They are unique in architectural design.

Oakland Chapel, which is listed in the National Register of Historic Places, was one of the first buildings to be constructed for Oakland College in 1830. It was restored in 1959 after being damaged by a tornado. The iron steps leading to the main floor of the chapel came from the elegant Windsor Castle, the building destroyed by a fire in 1890 except for its columns, which still stand.

A three-story building with six large columns, Oakland Chapel has been a campus landmark for two institutions, first serving as a prayer hall for Oakland College and now providing Alcorn with a prayer hall, religious center, and laboratory and classroom space. The chapel was built by slaves of the Presbyterian founding fathers and has served generations as the nucleus of an educational tradition for the slaves' children, grandchildren, great-grandchildren and great-great-grandchildren. It was the custom of the slaves to sit in the balcony of the chapel during worship services while the whites had the main floor. They could scarcely have imagined that their descendants would be students in that same building.

Although the chapel was completely renovated in 1959, its appearance remains virtually unchanged. The pews are original; the chandelier is a replica of the original, hung during the renovation. Officially entered on the National Register of Historic Places in 1975, the building is considered to be one of the best examples of Greek Revival architecture in America. Beulah Turner Robinson, the first black woman in the nation to graduate from a state-supported school, received her degree in Oakland Chapel in 1888.

Today the upper level of the building is used for religious services, while the lower level houses offices, classrooms, and computer-assisted instruction laboratories for the General College for Excellence.

The buildings, grounds, and university equipment are maintained according to a detailed plan, which includes preventive maintenance, minute record keeping, and a weekly program schedule. The Superintendent of Buildings and Grounds, James Martin, aided by his assistants James Robinson and Q. T. Cameron and thirty-five to forty staff members, supervises maintenance. The staff includes mechanics, electricians, carpenters, plumbers, grounds keepers, and janitorial workers. Service consists of overseeing repairs, renewals, and replacements in the areas of carpentry and painting; minor automotive repairs; plumbing, heating and air-conditioning; water plant; pest control; custodial services; garbage collection; care and maintenance of campus grounds including recreational areas and agricultural lots; use of heavy equipment; and supplementary checks on utility equipment.

Alcorn has an excellent physical plant covering more than seventeen hundred acres. The campus is a pleasing blend of the old and the new, including up-to-date towering structures and several original buildings from Oakland College. (In 1979 the building commission authorized a study of the feasibility of constructing a new president's home. Because the cost would have been about two hundred thousand dollars, the present one was updated instead.) The horseshoe-shaped campus is considered to be the most well-groomed in the state. The giant moss-draped oak trees contribute to the overall beauty of the campus. Having heard about Alcorn's location in the "woods," first-time visitors to the campus are generally surprised. They love what they see. The outdoor recreation park was recently named the Willie Mae Latham Taylor Park.

The drive to the campus in 1993 is quite different from what it was before 1981. Groundbreaking ceremonies took place at that time for the construction of Highway 552 between Alcorn and Lorman. It was an occasion that Alcorn had long hoped for. In 1993, Walter Washington lobbied diligently for a four-lane highway to the campus.

(For a complete list of university buildings, see Appendix 2. Note that many have been renamed in honor of outstanding individuals who have made significant contributions to the university.)

THIRTEEN

Preparing to Win

Athletics

During the past twenty-five years, Alcorn has participated in numerous athletic arenas: varsity football, basketball, cross country, track and field, golf, volleyball, and tennis. In football, the Braves have won or shared seven Southwestern Athletic Conference (SWAC) titles since 1968, the latest being in 1992. The Braves have appeared on television many times both locally and nationally. As a National Collegiate Athletic Association (NCAA) member of Division 1-A (1-AA in football) and the SWAC, the football team in 1980 became the first predominantly black college athletic team to participate in an NCAA championship. In 1984 it was the first SWAC school to finish the season as number one in the NCAA, Division 1-AA. Marino Casem, referred to as the Godfather of the SWAC, was the man behind the football team's success until 1986 when he left Alcorn to become athletic director at Southern University in Baton Rouge, Louisiana. Casem gave three decades of service to Alcorn and was very much responsible for building Alcorn's reputation in the football arena. He led the way to upgrading the school's athletic facilities and led the conference into Division I competition. He gained six SWAC Coach-of-the-Year honors and won 139 games including 7 Southwestern Athletic Conference titles.

Casem accepted no shortcuts or half-hearted efforts from his coaches or his players. He described Alcorn's way as making do with less and succeeding. In 1979, Casem reached his 100th college game win when the Braves beat Mississippi Valley State University 24–3. He is considered to be Alcorn's living legend in football.

Theophilus Danzy replaced Casem as athletic director and head football coach. In 1989, the two positions were split, and James Brooks became athletic director. Danzy remained as head coach until 1990 when Cardell Jones, an assistant at Jackson State University, replaced him in this position. Brooks remained athletic director until he was released from these duties in 1991. Because of budget restraints, the university could no longer staff both positions, head football coach and athletic director. (Board policy was not to spend more than $500,000 of state funds for the support of athletics.) Jones then became athletic director and also remained head football coach. He was determined to return Alcorn to its winning tradition. An Alcorn alumnus (1965), he led the university to finish in a tie for the SWAC championship position in 1991, the first time that the team had tied for the SWAC in twenty-eight years. In 1992, he won the SWAC championship. Jones believes in starting the best players and backing them up with talented reserves so that the starters reach their highest capacity. Despite the handicap of playing the most games in one season since 1982 and playing more off-campus games than ever in the history of football dating back to 1922, Jones has produced a winning team. In his role as athletic director, he stresses the same system of order for all sports that he does with his football team.

During Jones's first year, the Braves finished second in the SWAC under the motto "Next Year Is Now." During his second season, 1992, the motto became "99½ just won't do" and the Braves won the SWAC championship. Offensive Player of the Year Steve "Air II" McNair provided important leadership as quarterback. Air II, whose brother, Fred McNair (known as Air I), is a former Alcorn quarterback, broke a host of passing records by completing in one year 189 out of 338 attempted passes for 2895 yards and 24 touchdowns. He was named SWAC Offensive Player of the Week four times in eight games, a remarkable achievement for a freshman, and in 1993 has been nominated for the Heisman Trophy, the highest honor to be received by an athlete in the SWAC.

Jones's offensive staff is called the "Brave War Council." In 1993 it consisted of Ocie Brown, a twenty-season veteran who works with running backs and also coaches golf, and Alonzo Stevens, a second-year veteran who works with the offensive line and also heads the men's track and field. The staff is led by offensive coordinator Rickey Taylor. Taylor is a second-year veteran with the team but had previous college-level experience at Jackson State and West Virginia State. The "Defensive Mind Trust" consists of Mario Kirksey, a three-year Alcorn veteran with previous college experience at Mississippi Valley State University, who works with the linebackers; Anthony Woolfolk, with previous college experience at South Carolina State and Albany State, who works with the defensive backs; and Louis Jones, Jr., who also works with the linebackers and is the chief recruiter, as well as being the volleyball coach. He is in his twenty-third season at Alcorn. Willie McGowan is the defensive coordinator. A twenty-four-year veteran of Alcorn, he also serves as head baseball coach. In 1988 McGowan and his assistants produced the number-one defense in the entire nation.

Dr. Norris Edney has long served as the athletic faculty representative and is a past president of the Southwestern Athletic Conference. Augustus George "Gus" Howard has served as sports information director since 1988 and received the *Jackson Advocate* Promotion Award in 1990. John Burrell is athletic trainer and serves in various capacities.

Until 1992, the Braves played in Henderson Stadium, built in 1952 and named in honor of Octavious Henderson, an assistant professor of math during the 1920s who chaired the athletic committee and was baseball coach. The new stadium that opened forty years later is named the Jack Spinks Stadium in honor of an Alcorn alumnus who was the first black player from the state of Mississippi to play professional football in the National Football League. The new stadium's seating capacity is twenty thousand, double that of the old one. The field itself honors Dwight Fisher, the second winningest football coach in the history of Alcorn, who served from 1948 to 1956.

Dave Whitney put Alcorn on the basketball map during his 1969–1989 coaching career at the university. He compiled a 395-199 career record, leading the Braves to nine Southwestern Athletic Conference regular season championships and eleven postseason tournaments. Alcorn appeared in four NCAA basketball tournaments in the eighties (1980, 1982, 1983, and 1984). Whitney, whose nickname was "the Wizard," believed in hard work and discipline. "Preparing to win was more important than the willingness to win," he insisted.

Alcorn claimed the number-one spot in the SWAC quite often during this period and represented the state for three consecutive years in the NAIA basketball playoffs. In 1979 Whitney was SWAC's Coach of the Year. He headed the Venezuelan national basketball team during the summer of 1981. By 1980, Alcorn was beginning to be recognized statewide and nationally as a basketball powerhouse and that year gained 20 straight wins. When the Braves finished the 1988–89 season 5-23 after a series of losing years, however, Whitney was relieved of his duties as men's head basketball coach. Since that time he has been assistant coach with Wichita of the Continental Basketball League and assistant for the Gulf Coast Sharks of the Global Basketball Association.

Lonnie Walker, an Alcorn player during the 1960s and later an assistant to Whitney, became the head coach for men's basketball in 1989. In 1991–92, aided by his assistant Anthony Woody, he led the Braves to their first winning season since the mid-eighties. Walker had hopes of further progress but his fourth year was a disappointment, and he was released in 1993 after posting a 7-20 record. Sam Weaver, a former assistant basketball coach at Southern Illinois University in Carbondale, Illinois, took over as head coach.

Shirley Walker, who is married to Lonnie Walker, has coached the women's basketball team for fifteen years, winning five SWAC titles in the last nine years and being named SWAC Coach of the Year for two consecutive seasons (1990–91 and 1991–92). In 1993 her overall coaching record stands at 215 wins and 167 losses. Walker, a 1968 graduate of Alcorn, is assisted by Coach Nathaniel Kilbert.

One of the best years ever in baseball was 1979, with Willie McGowan leading the Braves. McGowan was selected SWAC Coach of the Year in 1976, 1978, 1981, and 1988. An assistant baseball coach under Dave Whitney, McGowan assumed the role as head coach in 1973, adding that job to his football duties. As a student football player at Alcorn he lettered four years and was voted Most Valuable Player in 1959.

Casem, Whitney, Walker, and McGowan have all been successful even though their budgets have always been much smaller than those of their opponents. In the 1984–85 school term, for example, the Braves won SWAC Championships in men's and women's basketball, in football, and in baseball. Skill and dedication have frequently allowed Alcorn athletics to overcome a lack of funding.

In order to stay in NCAA Division I, Alcorn had to add women's volleyball and women's tennis. Golf is also now available at Alcorn. In

1993 Alcorn belonged to the National Collegiate Athletic Association Division I, National Association of Intercollegiate Athletics, Mississippi Association Intercollegiate Association for Women, Large College Division, National Association of Women Sports and the Southwestern Athletic Conference.

In the world of track and field, Alcorn's women set Olympic competition as a goal and made a good showing at the Gulf AAU championship meet in June 1972. Mildrette Netter placed first in the 100-yard dash with a time of 10.5, while her teammates Helen Williams and Mollie Hence came in second and third with times of 10.6 and 10.9. Another record was set in the long jump when Helen Williams leaped 19'3.4 and Leanna Sams surpassed the old record with a 18.5 jump. Edmonia Veals placed second in the 220- and 100-meter hurdles, clocking 29.0 and 14.6. Netter, Williams, and Hence finished third, fourth, and fifth in the 220-yard dash. Netter was an Olympic gold medal winner in 1968, becoming the first one in the history of the college. A native of Rosedale, Mississippi, she was also the only Mississippian on the team in 1969 and was named Outstanding Athlete of the AAU Southern Region. There were also success stories in men's track. Jerry Sims was an all-American track star, and Willie Magee was recognized as one of the fastest human beings alive.

By 1993 Alonzo Stevens had done much toward regaining the success in the track and field program that it once had. In addition to track, Braves baseball is on the upswing. With golf, tennis, and volleyball being implemented in recent years, the athletic program at Alcorn is well-rounded.

A $37,000 grant from the National Collegiate Athletic Association and the Community Service Association has made it possible for Alcorn to sponsor a National Youth Sports Program (NYSP) during recent summers. In this program, sports instruction is available in basketball, volleyball, dance, swimming, tennis, flag football, gymnastics, racquet ball, and weight training. The program accommodates from four hundred to five hundred students from nearby schools in southwest Mississippi with disadvantaged backgrounds. Free meals are provided, and opportunities are also available for health education and counseling in career opportunities.

In 1983, NCAA delegates adopted Proposition 48, which went into effect in 1986. This involved the incorporation of a required core curriculum of high school classes, a 2.0 grade point average, and a minimum score on standardized tests. In order to be eligible to play as freshmen, athletes had to achieve 700 on the SAT or 15 on the ACT. Proposition 48 survived in spite of a furor that involved charging lawmakers with racism. In 1987, as the uproar over the proposition began to settle down, the delegates adopted Proposition 42 in an effort to close the loopholes of Proposition 48. The new ruling stated that partial qualifiers—those who passed the core courses or the standardized tests but not both—could not receive academic aid. This ruling was not looked upon favorably either.

Involvement with athletics at Alcorn means demonstrating stamina, courage, and a sincere determination to win. Since Alcorn thrives on challenges in all aspects of its operations, the athletics programs play a significant symbolic role in university life. Happily, these programs have had a history of success. (For a listing of the achievements of individuals and teams, see Appendix 3.)

FOURTEEN

THE ALCORN SPIRIT

Alumni Relations

THE ALUMNI RELATIONS OFFICE, since 1981 directed by Henry Houze, Jr., serves as the official liaison between the university and its many alumni scattered throughout the world. The office plays an instrumental role in maintaining correspondence with alumni and promoting an annual giving campaign, is involved with student recruitment, and coordinates alumni activities for local chapters all over the nation.

The Alumni Relations Office, centrally located on the main campus, works directly with the Alcorn State University National Alumni Association, which was organized in 1890 and incorporated in 1952. Dr. A. D. Snodgrass, member of the first graduating class of 1882, was the first alumni president.

Initially, the club was mainly social in nature, perhaps occasionally giving a coach a small token for an outstanding season. The 1940 effort to raise money for band uniforms was probably the only other activity spearheaded by the club. Activities that prodded the alumni into coming alive in the 1960s included the Olympics gold medal performance of Mildrette Netter on the track team, the emergence of Jerry Sims as an all-American track star, the success of basketball and football teams, and the emergence of Willie Magee, who ran 100 yards in

9.1 seconds, as one of the fastest humans alive. By 1969, the greatest single financial effort that the alumni had made was buying retiring President J. D. Boyd a jeep and a camper at a cost of $5,200. Walter Washington brought new direction to this area of college affairs when he took over in 1969. He employed a full-time director, Dr. Robert W. Bowles, who served as an official liaison between the college and the alumni. The office's major goals have been stimulating alumni interest and promoting collaboration for the common purpose of advancing the university. Recruitment—giving students assistance and acquainting them with opportunities available at Alcorn—became a major focus.

Alumni programs were not limited just to alumni. Alcorn has had one of the top university fund-raising programs in the country. The Annual Giving Program and special projects such as challenge grants from the Department of Education are means through which funds have been generated. Other fund-raisers have included the Alumni Endowment Program, the Alumni Centennial Fund, and the Revolving Student Loan Fund. Many alumni chapters throughout the world provide academic scholarships for prospective students. Donations are also made by private corporations and businesses. Annual giving has increased through the years. Over the past twenty years, annual donations have ranged between $25,000 and $150,000.

Alumni and others who have had close affiliations with Alcorn have shown their affection for the school by donating to the university through endowed scholarships, memorial scholarships, awards, educational trust funds, and other scholarship funds. Additionally, the B-Real Project, through which alumni give whatever they can, however small or large, has made a significant contribution. The project was initiated by Rev. Joseph Bartee, along with the Utica Alumni Chapter.

Alcorn has awarded more than twenty thousand degrees since 1871. Alcornites have succeeded in business, industry, government, education, and public and foreign service. Alcornites throughout the world are affiliated with an Alcorn alumni chapter in or near the vicinity in which they live. The simple fact of having at any time been a part of the campus provides the opportunity for shared friendship, dedication, and respect for Alcorn. A chapter may be organized in any location if there are at least five alumni willing to belong. Local chapters hold monthly meetings. The National Alumni Association holds two conferences annually, the mid-winter conference in February, rotated from one state to another, and the alumni weekend meeting held the weekend of graduation on the main campus.

National alumni presidents who have served since the beginning of the association are as follows: A. D. Snodgrass, 1890–1929; J. H. Moseley, 1929–1950; W. S. Demby, 1950–1957; Ruby S. Lyells, 1957–1959; E. T. Hawkins, 1959–1970; Thomas Moman, 1970–1972; Frank Dobbins, 1972–1974; Jim Stirgus, 1974–1978; Luther Alexander, 1978–1986; Matthew Thomas, 1986–1990; John Rigsby, 1990–1992; John Walls, 1992–present (1993).

The 1993 National Alumni Board includes John Walls, president; Freddie Owens, vice president; Mary Greenwood, first vice president; Dr. Josephine Posey, executive secretary; Zelmarine Murphy, recording secretary; Angie Roberson, assistant secretary; Rev. Joseph Bartee, chaplain; D. W. Wilburn, parliamentarian; Jewell Lockhart, treasurer; and Henry Houze, director of alumni affairs. John, Freddie, and Mary run a tight ship; Zelmarine, assisted by Angie Roberson, is said to be a rare sort of recording secretary, one who can make minutes interesting. Josephine, who succeeded Shirley Washington, may be the only executive secretary in the world who instead of a report gives a speech. Rev. Bartee gave the invocation at the 1992 Alcorn-Jackson State football game, and fans continue to believe that it was this prayer that gave Alcorn the victory. D. W. keeps it all in order. Murphy and Lockhart have been recording secretary and treasurer longer than anyone else has held those positions.

The National Alumni Association, through its local chapters, acquaints high school and junior college graduates with programs, facilities, and the many opportunities awaiting them at Alcorn. Members of the association work with legislators in soliciting their continuous support for general support in capital outlay, repair, renovations, and any other aspect of effective university operations. Walter Washington has always encouraged the alumni to be leading spokesmen for the value of an Alcorn education. To involve alumni in all Mississippi counties in recruiting quality students, staff hold alumni liaison recruitment workshops in various sections of the state.

The *Alcorn Report*, which was initiated in 1981 in an effort to summarize important developments at the university for alumni, is sent all over the world. This publication results from the joint efforts of the offices of public relations and alumni affairs. Alumni also receive newsletters, brochures, and the *Alumnus Magazine*.

The Athletic Endowment Fund received its initial boost during a February 16, 1983, reception in the campus union. Jimmy Giles, a 1981 graduate of Alcorn and a tight end for the Tampa Bay Buccaneers, and

Lawrence Pillars, who also attended Alcorn and became a defensive lineman for the San Francisco 49ers, were in attendance to support the endowment plan. In a press conference the next day, Luther Alexander, then president of the National Alumni Association, expressed to the media that the school's goal was to raise at least one million dollars in two years. Alexander stressed that Alcornites from everywhere should participate in this vital effort. Dave Washington, former all-pro in the NFL, and Willie Alexander, former pro with the Houston Oilers, both Alcornites, cochaired the Athletic Endowment Program. They encouraged alumni to share their enthusiasm and to join in making the project a reality. Willie Alexander and Dave Washington recalled that when they played football at Alcorn they had no idea how expensive it was to maintain a competitive athletic program, only becoming aware of the situation after having played professional football. They encouraged alumni to consider what Alcorn had meant to them and then make the largest contribution possible. The campaign began in July 1982 and ended on June 30, 1984. Though the goal was not met, more than $100,000 was raised to support Alcorn athletics.

The first annual Alumni Hall of Honor affair, initiated by Dr. Robert Bowles, who himself in 1993 was named Alcornite of the Year, was held in Vicksburg, Mississippi, during Alumni Weekend in 1990. The Hall of Honor recognizes outstanding individuals in the areas of service, alumni relations, and athletics. Twenty-seven individuals were inducted as charter members of the Hall of Honor. Several of these will also be listed with the Alcornites of the Year later in this chapter. A brief description of each follows, beginning with the area of alumni relations.

Luther Alexander, a member of the class of 1955, is described in the Alcornites of the Year section of this chapter.

William Smith Demby, who graduated from Alcorn in 1926, is included with the Alcornites of the Year section of this chapter.

Cleveland J. Duckworth graduated from Alcorn in 1948. He is a retired associate executive secretary of the Mississippi Association of Educators. Born in Smith County, he received the Distinguished Alumni of the Year award in 1962. His membership affiliations included the National Education Association and Phi Delta Kappa.

Medgar Wiley Evers was a civil rights leader and NAACP field secretary in the state of Mississippi. He was born in Decatur, Mississippi. At Alcorn he majored in business administration, was a member of the football and track teams, served as editor of the *Alcorn Herald*, and was president of the junior class and vice president of the Student Forum. He graduated in 1952. An outstanding spokesman for the cause of civil rights and human dignity, he was assassinated in June 1963. He is buried in Arlington National Cemetery.

Andrew Graves, who was a member of the class of 1934, is featured in the Alcornites of the Year section.

Leon Griffith graduated from Alcorn in 1959. Born in Simpson County, he is employed in the Jefferson Davis school system as assistant principal of Bassfield High School. He served as president of the Jefferson Davis County Alcorn alumni chapter and held leadership roles in other organizations. He is a life member of the Alcorn State National Alumni Association. He is the recipient of many awards including Outstanding Leader in American Secondary Education, Meritorious Service to Cooperative Extension, and Outstanding Service Award from the Mississippi Association of Educators.

T. L. Jordan was inducted posthumously.

Lillian Cade Lane was born in Jackson and graduated from Alcorn in 1940. She was an assistant professor of reading at Jackson State University. Her many membership affiliations include Who's Who in American Women in 1976. Among honors she received are the Meritorious Service Award from the Student National Education Association and the Dedicated Service Award from the Jackson State University Laboratory School.

Jewell Lockhart, a member of the class of 1956, is described with other Alcornites of the Year.

Grady McMillion, Jr., was a graduate in the class of 1965. He was born in Drewry, Alabama. In 1983 he was the Alumnus of the Year in his local chapter and in 1976 received the National Alumni Loyal Alumnus Award. He was employed as a chemist at Ingalls Shipbuilding in Pascagoula, Mississippi.

Alpha Lockhart Morris, also an Alcornite of the Year, graduated in 1952.

Arthur Bennett Peyton, Sr., is a 1951 graduate of Alcorn. He served as assistant superintendent of schools in Greenville, Mississippi, and chaired the state's lay board of education. He is past president of the Mississippi Teachers Association and a member of Phi Delta Kappa. Among his many awards are the 1983 Outstanding Community Service Award from the Community Service Administrative regional office and the 1989 Service Award from Washington County Opportunities, Inc.

Willie Mimms Powell graduated from Alcorn in 1949. She was an educator and program coordinator of an adult literacy program in the Leland school system. She served as president of the Washington County Alcorn State University Alumni Association and holds membership in many other organizations. She received the Meritorious Award from the Alcorn National Alumni Association in 1987, as well as several outstanding service awards from other organizations.

Calvin Rhodes, a member of the class of 1935, appears in the Alcornites of Year section.

David E. Thomas, Sr., was a 1935 graduate of Alcorn. Born in Warren County, he was an administrator in the Warren County schools system. He received many honors and awards including the Volunteer Selective Service Award for twenty-five years presented by Richard Nixon when he was president of the United States, the Award of Excellence from the Mississippi Education Association, and the Loyal Support Award from the Vicksburg chapter of Alcorn Alumni.

Cleopatra D. Thompson, who graduated from Alcorn in 1932, is featured with other Alcornites of the Year.

David Wilson Wilburn, a 1933 graduate of Alcorn, also appears with the Alcornites of the Year.

The following people were inducted in 1990 in the area of athletics.

Clifton Osborne Davis, Jr., was born in Birmingham, Alabama. In 1974, he received the Outstanding Achievement Award in the Field of Sports from Alcorn. He was also given the Tri-Lake Conference Coach of the Year Citation in 1987 and 1989 and named Star Teacher in 1987.

Felix H. Dunn, who was born in Biloxi, graduated from Alcorn in 1949 and became a physician. He is a life member of the NAACP, which he served as local president for twelve years. He was founder of Emergency Chapter of the Urban League as well as founder and president of other associations and corporations. He belonged to the state medical association, American Medical Association, and National Medical Association and to the Gulf Coast Medical and Pharmaceutical Association. He was the developer of the concept of Saraland Health Care Center. The infirmary was recently named in his honor.

James Ford graduated from Alcorn in 1951. From Clarksdale, he served as a law enforcement officer and received many honors and awards including the Recognition Award from the Los Angeles Police Commission and the National Organization of Black Enforcement Executives. He was correspondence secretary for the Los Angeles chapter of the Alcorn State University Alumni Association, president of the

South West College Foundation, and president of the Baldwin Hills Boys Football Association.

William "Bill" Foster, a 1931 graduate of Alcorn, was born in Rodney, Mississippi. He served as baseball coach at Alcorn and was a professional baseball player in the Negro League. He was honored by the Negro Baseball Organization in many states including Louisiana, Illinois, and Missouri. He was inducted into the Hall of Honor posthumously.

Glover C. "Gus" Gardner was a 1925 graduate of Alcorn and worked for the U. S. Army Corps of Engineers, Department of Reproduction. He was a four-year letterman in sports and the first life-time honorary member of the Port City Kiwanis Club. He was a life member of the Alcorn State National Alumni Association and of the Vicksburg-Warren chapter of the alumni association.

John Allen Jackson graduated from Alcorn in 1926. Born in Bolton, Mississippi, he was an entrepreneur and an educator. He served as president and executive secretary of SCAC, later known as SWAC (Southwestern Athletic Conference) and as president of the 5th District Teachers Association. He was a member of the South Central Board of Athletic Officials and the Alcorn State University National Alumni Association.

Robert Pickett, born in Brookhaven, Mississippi, serves as deputy superintendent of the Vicksburg-Warren school district. He was an outstanding athlete and was co-captain of the basketball teams while a student at Alcorn. He is a member of many organizations, including the Mississippi Association of School Administrators, the National Association of Secondary School Principals, and the American Association of Secondary School Principals. He is a life member of the Alcorn State University National Alumni Association.

Johnny "Jack" Spinks, a 1952 graduate of Alcorn, was elected to the Mississippi Hall of Fame in 1986 and has been honored by the Mississippi House of Representatives and Senate. He was a Pittsburgh Courier All-American from 1949 to 1952 and was Mississippi's first black professional football player in the National Football League, becoming in 1952 the first black to play for the Pittsburgh Steelers. A retired football coach of the Alcorn Braves, he received an Outstanding Service Award from the Alcorn State University National Alumni Association. The present Alcorn Stadium is named in his honor.

Claude E. Watson was born in Fernwood, Mississippi, and graduated from Alcorn in 1937. He served as president of the Cleveland, Ohio, chapter of the Alcorn State University Alumni Association and was district representative of the NAACP. He was the first black All-American football player from Mississippi. Also an educator, he served on the Cleveland, Ohio, board of education and as recreation director in Cleveland.

The 1991 inductees in the alumni area were as follows:

Barbara D. Bacon was a 1961 graduate of Alcorn State University. A native of St. Louis, Missouri, she served as president of the Washington County and Mississippi Delta chapters of the Alcorn Alumni Association and spearheaded the recruitment committee. She received a Meritorious Award from the Greenville public school system, Woman of the Year Award in Education from the Elite, Social and Civic Club, and the Loyal Service and Financial Support Award from the Alcorn State University National Alumni Association. She was an educator in the Greenville school district.

Robert W. Bowles graduated from Alcorn in 1966 and is described with other Alcornites of the Year.

George Hull, Jr., a 1943 graduate of Alcorn, was born in Indianola, Mississippi. He served as director of the Division of Natural Science and Mathematics at Fisk University. He received numerous honors and awards, including the NAFEO Distinguished Alumni Award and the Distinguished Service Award from the Nashville, Tennessee, alumni chapter. He was affiliated with the American Association for the Advancement of Science, the American Institute of Biological Science, and the American Physiological Society and served as president of Optimist International.

Carl E. Jones graduated from Alcorn in 1963. Born in Mason, Tennessee, he serves as president and co-owner of Jones and Jones Contractors, Inc., in Nashville, Tennessee. He was a member of the board of directors of the Chicago chapter of the Alcorn State University Alumni Association, chairman of the board of directors of the Tidewater Area Business and Contractors Inc., and is a life member of the NAACP. Among his honors and awards were the Recognition Award from the Chicago chapter of the Alcorn State University Alumni Association and several community service awards.

Thomas Madison Moman II graduated magna cum laude from Alcorn in 1940. He was born in Magnolia, Mississippi. He was a survivor and worked with the Neighborhood Youth Corps Program and the Mississippi Cooperative Extension Service. His honors and awards include the Recognition Award for Leadership and Service to the Cooperative

Extension Service, the Meritorious Service Award from Jackson Redevelopment Authority and the Distinguished Service Award from state associations of county agricultural agents. He also served as president of the Alcorn State University National Alumni Association.

Gertrude Payton, who was born in Crystal Springs, Mississippi, graduated from Alcorn in 1950. She was director of guidance at Milwaukee High School of Fine Arts. She received many honors and awards including the Outstanding Service Award from the Wisconsin State Department, the Prince Hall Masonic Foundation Board Award, several community service awards from various organizations and the Alcorn State University presidential award.

Mack W. Payton, a 1950 graduate of Alcorn, is featured in the Alcornites of the Year section.

John Rigsby graduated cum laude from Alcorn in 1954. Born in Forest, Mississippi, he was director of the Division of Compensation and Records in the Jackson public schools. Among his many honors and awards is the Distinguished Alumni Citation Award from NAFEO. He served as president of the Alcorn State University National Alumni Association and president of the Jackson chapter of Alcorn alumni.

Kenneth Laverne Simmons, Sr., was a 1956 graduate of Alcorn. He is described with other Alcornites of the Year.

Ann Johnson Stepney, a 1951 graduate and a Miss Alcorn, was born in Claiborne County. She served as vice-president of the Alcorn State University National Alumni Association and belongs to the Gulf Coast Alcorn alumni chapter and the Gulfport Teachers Association. Her honors and awards include the Loyal Alumnus and Meritorious Award from the Alcorn State University National Alumni Association and Outstanding Woman of the NAACP. She has been featured in outstanding publications and appeared on the television show "Good Morning, South Mississippi." She was an educator. She organized the first club for all former "Miss Alcorns" in 1992.

In the area of service, the following people were inducted in 1991:

Walter Downs, a 1941 graduate of Alcorn, was born in McComb, Mississippi. He served as president of the Detroit chapter of the Alcorn State University Alumni Association where he received the Outstanding Service Award. He received certificates of recognition and appreciation from many organizations, including the United States Air Force Academy.

Leander T. Ellis, Sr., was a 1925 graduate of Alcorn. Born in Claiborne County, he was organizer, president, and treasurer of the Jones

County Educational Federal Credit Union and president of the Sixth District Teachers Association. He also served on the board of directors of the Mississippi Teachers Association and was the principal of Oak Park High School in Laurel, Mississippi. His honors and awards were many, including the twenty-five-year citation for valuable service in vocational agriculture and Certificate of Merit for significant contributions to the betterment of humanity from Alcorn College. He was also chosen Alcornite of the Year by the Jones County alumni chapter. He was inducted posthumously.

George Jones, Sr., a 1931 graduate of Alcorn, is described in the Alcornites of the Year section.

James D. Martin, who graduated from Alcorn in 1975, was born in Coffeeville, Mississippi. He was "Teacher of the Year" in the Sharkey-Issaquena school district. He also received the Young Educator Achievement Award among Educators, the Faithful Service Award from the Alcorn State University National Alumni Association and the Recognition Award and Presidential Citation for Financial Support to the Alcorn Foundation. He was vice president of the Vicksburg alumni chapter and served in the United States Army Reserves.

William B. Nelson graduated from Alcorn in 1919. He was director of the Division of Trade and Industrial Technology at Savannah State College in Savannah, Georgia. Membership affiliations included board of directors of the American Cancer Society and the Georgia Community Improvement Association. He was inducted posthumously.

Sidney L. Redmond graduated in 1950 from Alcorn. Born in Prentiss, Mississippi, he was an educator and a manager of the Washington Funeral Home, Inc., in Tylertown, Mississippi. He received many honors and awards including recognitions for outstanding service by several organizations and groups. He served as a member of former Governor Bill Waller's advisory board and was vice-president of the Mississippi Funeral Directors and Morticians Association.

Emmett James Stringer, who was born in Yazoo City, graduated from Alcorn in 1941. A dentist in Columbus, Mississippi, he served as president of the Columbus-Lowndes County Alcorn alumni chapter, president emeritus of the Mississippi State Conference of NAACP Branches, and chaplain of the Mississippi Dental Society. He was given the Dentist of the Decade Award from Meharry Dental School in 1950 and the Humanitarian Award from the Mississippi Dental Society and the National Dental Association.

In the area of athletics, the 1991 inductee into the Hall of Honor was

Lonnie Moore. Born in Philadelphia, Mississippi, he graduated from Alcorn in 1951. He was a vocational counselor with the state department of education's Division of Rehabilitation. He was president of the Jackson Alcorn alumni chapter. His honors and awards included Coach of the Year for five years at the Highland Conference and Outstanding Coach of Neshoba County. He was one of the original five Alcorn A. & M. College Athletes of the 1948 SCAC Conference, now known as SWAC.

The 1992 inductees into the Hall of Honor in the area of alumni relations were as follows:

William C. Boykin, Sr., was a 1942 graduate of Alcorn. A native of Sylvarena, Mississippi, he was an outstanding leader in education. He was included in Who's Who in the South and Southwest and held membership in many organizations, including the American Vocational Association and the Southern Association of Teacher Educators in Agriculture. He worked in agricultural extension and research at Alcorn until his retirement after which he was named president of Natchez Junior College in Natchez, Mississippi. The agriculture science building was recently named in his honor. He was inducted posthumously.

LaPlose T. Jackson, who graduated from Alcorn in 1954, was born in Hattiesburg. He received the Faculty and Staff Alumnus of the Year Award from the Alcorn National Alumni Association, as well as a Certificate of Appreciation from the Upward Bound program and the Centennial Award for loyal support to the Alcorn National Alumni Association. He was secretary of the Mississippi Association of Financial Aid Administrators and a member of the American Association for Counseling and Development and the Association for Adult Development and Aging. He served as Director of Financial Aid at Alcorn and later Director of Counseling and Testing.

James Earl Miller, a 1932 Alcorn graduate, is featured with the Alcornites of the Year.

James Minor graduated from Alcorn in 1966. Born in Starkville, he is a county agent with the Mississippi Cooperative Extension Service in Laurel, Mississippi. He holds membership in many organizations, including the Mississippi Association of County Agricultural Agents, the National Association of County Agricultural Agents and the Jones County Forestry Association. He was president of both the Jasper County Alcorn alumni chapter and the Jones County chapter. He was named Outstanding Future Farmers of America advisor, Jasper County Alcornite of the Year and the Most Outstanding Alumnus. He also received the Public Information Award from the National Association of County Agriculture Agents.

Jessie A. Morris, Sr., a 1950 graduate of Alcorn, is described with other Alcornites of the Year. He was inducted posthumously.

Esther Martin Rigsby, who was born in Port Gibson, Mississippi, graduated from Alcorn in 1954. Included in Who's Who Among Black Americans, she also received the Outstanding Family Award from the Urban League, the Activist Award from Women for Progress, and several achievement and service awards from Alpha Kappa Alpha Sorority. She was president of the Jackson Council of English Teachers and was a member of the National Council of English Teachers, which honored her with the Leadership Award.

Henry R. Smith, a 1940 Alcorn graduate, is described in the Alcornites of the Year section.

Issac Thomas, who graduated from Alcorn in 1942, is featured with other Alcornites of the Year.

Shelby R. Wilkes, born in Crystal Springs, Mississippi, graduated in 1971. He was a recipient of the Distinguished Alumni Award from the National Association of Equal Opportunity in Higher Education. An ophthalmologist and vitreoretinal surgeon, he is president of the Atlanta Eye Consultants, a member of the Association of Research in Vision and Ophthalmology, and vice chairman of the Diabetes Advisory Committee. He is a life member of the NAACP.

Clementine A. Williams graduated from Alcorn in 1962. She was born in New Orleans, Louisiana. Her honors and awards include being named Outstanding Personality of the Gulf Coast and Administrator of the Year by the Bay St. Louis Rotary Club, and receiving the Citizenship Award from the Hancock NAACP Chapter. A member of the Hancock County chapter of the NAACP, she was chairman of the Hancock County Library Board of Trustees and president of the Gulf Coast alumni chapter. She is a school administrator in the Charles B. Murphy Elementary School in Pearlington, Mississippi.

In the area of service, the following people were inducted in 1992:

Willie Burton is a 1974 graduate of Alcorn. He served as project leader for Dow Chemical, USA, in Plaquemine, Louisiana. He received many honors and awards including certificates of service and appreciation from the Baton Rouge Bar Association and other groups. He received the NAFEO Distinguished Alumni Award and the Faithful Service Award from the Alcorn National Alumni Association. He served on the board of directors of the Brookhaven Outreach Ministries.

Melissa Louise Demby is a 1956 magna cum laude graduate of Alcorn. Born in Davenport, Mississippi, she was an elementary teacher in Vicksburg. She received many citations for outstanding service from many organizations and was named the Links and Mississippi State Federation of Colored Women's Club Woman of the Year. She was a member of the Mississippi Teachers Association, president of the Vicksburg Teachers Association, and a life member of the Alcorn National Alumni Association.

Benjamin F. Harper, Jr., graduated from Alcorn in 1956. He was born in Forest, Mississippi. He served as academic coordinator and chairperson of the Division of Natural Science at Hinds Community College on the Utica campus in Utica, Mississippi. He was honored as an outstanding academic instructor at Hinds Community College and received the Distinguished Service Award from Phi Delta Kappa. He was president of the Hinds County Teachers Association.

Laura Hart Hearn received the B.S. degree from Alcorn in 1937. She was an educator in the Clarksdale public schools. Born in Anding, Mississippi, she received the Faithful Service Award from the Alcorn National Alumni Association and the Dedicated Service Award from the North Delta Alcorn alumni chapter. She received the award for dedication to education from the Clarksdale Association of Educators and the Outstanding Service Award from the March of Dimes.

Waldo M. James, who was born in Columbia, Mississippi, graduated from Alcorn in 1952. He was an educator in the Marion County schools. A varsity letterman in basketball at Alcorn, he received the East Marion School Service Award, the Loyal and Dedicated Service Award in athletics from the Marion County school district, and the Service Award from the East Marion County Association of Educators, and he was named Marion County's basketball Coach of the Year. Listed in the Centennial History of Alcorn, he is a dedicated member of the National Education Association and the Alcorn National Alumni Association.

Leon Limbric Knowles graduated from Alcorn in 1931. From Fayette, Mississippi, he was an educator in the Jackson public schools. He was named Outstanding Teacher in Leflore County, and in the Jackson city schools and received the Alumni Service Award from the Jackson Alcorn alumni chapter, the Community Service Award from the Jackson City Council, and many awards for outstanding service with the Boy Scouts of America. He served as treasurer of the Jackson chapter and is a life member of the Alcorn National Alumni Association.

Aretta Esterling Moore, a 1942 graduate of Alcorn, was born in Mt. Olive, Mississippi. An educator and community volunteer, she was given the Outstanding and Dedicated Service Award from the Washington, D.C., Alcorn alumni chapter. She received many other outstanding service awards from various organizations, including the David Silberman Memorial Award for Outstanding Staff Performance and the Outstanding Service Award from Help for Retarded Citizens, Inc.

Patricia Anderson Segrest graduated from Alcorn in 1967. She was born in Vicksburg and served as a school administrator at the Beechwood Elementary School in that city. She is on the board of supervisors for the Vicksburg Bridge Commission and is a member of Young Adults for Positive Action, Inc. She served as president of the Vicksburg Alcorn alumni chapter. She received the Alumni Service Award from the Alcorn National Alumni Association and the Dedicated Service Award from the Vicksburg alumni chapter. She is listed in the United States Achievement Academy and received the Leadership Award from the Southeastern Region of Alpha Kappa Alpha Sorority.

Christine Simmons graduated summa cum laude from Alcorn in 1961. Born in Madison, Florida, she served as secretary/office manager for the Office of Alumni Affairs at Alcorn. She is a member of the Claiborne County Alcorn alumni chapter. She worked with Boy Scouts and Girl Scouts of America. Her honors and awards include the Silver Star Award for twenty-five years of service to Alpha Kappa Alpha Sorority and the Founders Club plaque from the Alcorn Foundation, Inc.

Lutille Stepney, who graduated from Alcorn in 1953, was born in Montrose, Mississippi, and was a coach and a teacher in the Gulfport public schools. A life member of the Alcorn National Alumni Association, he served as business manager for the Gulfport Alcorn Alumni chapter. He served on the board of directors of the Gulf Coast Community Action Agency and was a member of the Mississippi Association of Coaches. His awards include the Alcorn State University Alumni Faithful Service Award, the Alcorn State University Loyal Alumnus Award, and the Gulfport city schools Dedicated Service Award, among others.

Mabel Thomas, a 1909 graduate of Alcorn who was born on the college campus, was a county extension home demonstration agent. She held membership in the North Delta Chapter of the Alcorn State University National Alumni Association. She received the Centennial Service Award from the Alcorn State University Alumni Association and was recognized by the Alcorn Foundation for her monetary contributions. New Women's dormitory was recently named in her honor.

Rosa Brent Wynn graduated from Alcorn in 1942. Born in Jackson, Mississippi, she was a school administrator in the Detroit, Michigan, public school system. Her professional memberships included the Michigan Cancer Foundation and the Michigan Foundation for the Blind. She received the Outstanding Service Award from the Detroit Alcorn alumni chapter and the Distinguished Service Award from the National Alumni Association. She also received the Service Award from Delta Sigma Theta Sorority, Inc.

In the area of athletics, the 1992 Hall of Honor inductees were as follows:

Harry G. Brown received the B.S. degree from Alcorn in 1964. He was born in Vicksburg and served as an equal opportunity specialist with the U.S. Army Corps of Engineers there. He was a four-year letterman who made all-conference in 1961, 1962, and 1964 and was team captain in baseball from 1962 to 1964. He received the Outstanding Performance and Achievement Award as an engineering technician and the Director's Award for Outstanding Achievement in Equal Employment Opportunity. He served as president of the Vicksburg chapter of the Alcorn State University Alumni Association and chairman of the scholarship committee. He is a university recruiter for the Vicksburg Alcorn alumni chapter.

Davis Weathersby, who was born in Liberty, Mississippi, graduated from Alcorn in 1955. He was athletic director and head football coach at Mississippi Valley State University in Itta Bena, Mississippi. He received the Four-Year Letterman Award in football and track at Alcorn and was named Coach of the Year by the Southwest Board of Athletic Officials and by Mississippi Valley State University. Other awards included the SWAC Dedicated Service Award.

The fourth annual Hall of Honor induction ceremony (1993) featured twelve inductees. For the first time, individuals were eligible who were not Alcornites. Honorees in the area of alumni relations were as follows:

James "Bo" Clark graduated in 1962 from Alcorn, where he was a letterman in football and baseball. Born in Forest, Mississippi, he was a coach/athletic director in the Forest Separate School District and was alderman of the city of Forest. He received the Twenty-Five Year Service Award from the Mississippi Association of Coaches, the Dedicated Service Award from Alcorn State University National Alumni, and the Leadership Award from Phi Beta Sigma Fraternity. He served twelve years on the Forest City Council and held memberships in the Mississippi Association of Coaches, the Forest Chamber of Commerce, Optimist International, of which he was president, and the Alcorn State University National Alumni Association.

Warren E. Cox, a 1957 graduate of Alcorn, was born in Brookhaven, Mississippi. He served as attorney-at-law and manager of the U.S. Department of Labor Office of Federal Contract Compliance Programs in Jackson, Mississippi. He received the Officer of the Year Award from the Federal Contract Compliance program in 1989 and 1990. He was also the recipient of the Meritorious and Foundation Founder's Club Award from Alcorn State University National Alumni Association as well as the Outstanding Service Award. He was a member of the Mississippi Bar Association, the Magnolia Bar Association and the National Bar Association. He was president of the Jackson Alcorn alumni chapter and a member of the national alumni association.

Ella Watson Robinson graduated from Alcorn in 1953. She was born in Learned, Mississippi. A teacher in the Jackson public schools, she served as fundraising chairman of the Jackson Alcorn alumni chapter. She received the Outstanding Service Award from the national alumni association, the Alcorn State University Distinguished Service Award from the Jackson Alcorn alumni chapter, a Certificate of Appreciation from the Jackson public schools, and the Mississippi Federation of Colored Women's Clubs Service Award. She was a member of the Coalition of 100 Black Women.

Joseph W. Reese, who graduated magna cum laude from Alcorn in 1968, was born in Bassfield, Mississippi. He was supervisor of the Shipping Department of the Georgia Pacific Corporation in Monticello, Mississippi. His honors and awards included the Alcorn State University Faithful Service Award, the Alcorn State University Alumni Outstanding Service Award, the Jefferson Davis County Alcorn Alumni Appreciation Award, and the NAFEO Distinguished Alumni Citation Award. He served as president of the Jefferson Davis County Alcorn alumni chapter and is a life member of the Alcorn State University National Alumni Association. He is a member of the Inter-Alumni Council of Mississippi.

Albert L. Lott, a 1941 graduate of Alcorn, was born in Brookhaven, Mississippi, and is a medical doctor. He was a charter member and chairman of the Alcorn State University Foundation and a charter member of the Lincoln County Alumni Chapter. A member and president of the Brookhaven Public School Board, a member of the Meharry Medical College Alumni Association, and a member of the Mississippi Medical and Dental Association, he was honored with a "Dr. A. L. Lott Appreciation Day" by the citizens of Lincoln County. He received numerous awards from the Alcorn State University National Alumni Association. New men's dormitory was recently named in his honor.

In the area of service, the following were honored in 1993:

Alma Brent Edwards, who graduated from Alcorn in 1944, was born in Jackson, Mississippi, and was an administrator in the Detroit, Michigan, public school system. She is a charter member of the Detroit Alcorn alumni chapter and a life member of the Alcorn State University National Alumni Association. She served on the board of trustees at Adrian College and was director of the Wayne State Wesley Foundation. She received the Service Award from the Detroit Alcorn alumni chapter and the Special Service Award from Brooks Middle School. She also received the Spirit of Detroit Award and served as director of the General Board of Global Ministries.

Johnnie Greenwood, a 1970 magna cum laude graduate of Alcorn, was born in Canton, Mississippi. He was director of the contracts division of the United States Department of Energy in Argonne, Illinois. He was a member of the community advisory panel of Dow Chemical USA in Joliet, Illinois, and president of the Easter Seal board of directors in Will and Grundy counties. He was a charter member of the Will County Area Alcorn State University alumni chapter and a life member of Alcorn State University National Alumni Association. He received the Alcorn State University Outstanding Service Award, the Distinguished Alumni Citation Award from NAFEO, and the Founder's Award from Alcorn State University. He also received a Certificate of Merit from the United States Department of Energy and an Appreciation Award from Village Shorewood, Illinois.

Walter Washington received his B.S. degree from Tougaloo College and served as Alcorn's president for twenty-five years. He is further described in Chapter 5 of this book.

Inductees in athletics in 1993 were as follows:

Marino Casem was born in Memphis, Tennessee. He served as athletic director and head football coach at Alcorn State University for twenty-two years. He was also athletic director at Southern University in Baton Rouge, Louisiana. He is further described in Chapter 13 in this book.

Davey Whitney, Jr., received his B.S. degree from Kentucky State University in 1953 and in 1989 received the M.S. degree from Alcorn State University. He served as head basketball coach at Alcorn for twenty years. He was inducted into the Mississippi Sports Hall of Fame and the Kentucky State University Athletic Hall of Fame. He is further described in Chapter 13. The health, physical education and recreation complex was recently named in his honor.

Two honorees were inducted posthumously in 1993:

E. T. Hawkins graduated from Alcorn in 1930. Born in Church Hill, Mississippi, he was principal of E. T. Hawkins High School in Forest, Mississippi. He was a member of the Mississippi Teachers Association and president of the Alcorn State University National Alumni Association. He received the Outstanding Service Award from the Department of Agriculture and the Citation Award for educational leadership in public education from Alcorn A. & M. College. The high school where he served as principal was built in 1951 and named in his honor.

Charles R. Humphrey, who was from Egypt, Mississippi, was a 1953 cum laude graduate of Alcorn. He was director and founder of the Medgar Evers Comprehensive Health Center in Fayette, Mississippi. He was an All-American on Alcorn State University's football team and was named Coach of the Year by the North Central Mississippi Athletic Conference. He was in Personalities of the South and Community Leaders of America. He was a member of the Urban League, the NAACP, the American Medical Association and National Medical Association, and was chairman of the Central District Council of Boy Scouts of America.

Alumni who come to Alcorn as young students need polishing. When they leave the school as mature graduates, they go into the work force to be of service to mankind. The outstanding accomplishments of the university's alumni rise beyond documented records and reside in the minds of many who have passed this way. Alcornites' commitment to serving the people is seen in the huge numbers who have gone into the fields of education, industry, medicine, research, social services, politics, religion, and many other service-oriented areas. Alcornites have, through the years, made the slogan "Serving the People" a living reality.

The "old Alcorn spirit" rings all over the land in the hearts of Alcornites who have walked beneath the shade of the giant oak trees. Its true meaning comes out in the words that have warmed the hearts of so many when they sing "I'm so glad I went to the 'Mighty Corn'" and "Give me that old Alcorn spirit." This spirit has been carried on through the years and passed from one generation to another. Alumni have acquired good jobs, received high honors, and succeeded in life.

Numerous Alcornites have received the National Association for Equal Opportunity in Higher Education Distinguished Alumni of the Year Citation (NAFEO). Founded in 1969, NAFEO is a nonprofit, voluntary, independent association composed of 114 historically black colleges and universities. (For a list of Alcorn's recipients, see Appendix 4.)

In 1988, the National Association of State Universities and Land-Grant Colleges Distinguished Alumni (NASULGC) gave seven Alcornites awards. The awards went to Herman Coleman, Wright Lassiter, Jr., Montague S. Lawrence, Nebraska Mays, Cleopatra Thompson, Shelby Wilkes, and Louise Lawson.

The 1990 Alcorn's Distinguished Centennial Alumnus Award went to Cleopatra D. Thompson, a 1932 graduate of Alcorn, who represented the alumni with distinction.

Alcornites have worked untiringly for the livelihood of their alma mater. Each year since 1948, an Alcornite who has distinguished himself or herself through service and support of Alcorn is elected as Alcornite of the Year by the Alcorn State University National Alumni Association. Since being named Alcornite of the Year is the highest honor for an alumnus, a brief profile of each of the honorees is presented here.

George Cox, the 1948 Alcornite of the Year, was a Sunflower County native. He was a 1914 graduate and became an insurance executive. He served as vice president of the North Carolina Mutual Life Insurance Company in Durham, North Carolina, the largest black-operated insurance company in the nation. He also chaired the board of directors of a building-and-loan association in Durham. Not only a successful businessman, he was also a leader in civic and religious activities.

Richard Sylvester Grossley, selected in 1949, was a native of Gloster, Mississippi. He graduated from Alcorn in 1911 and chose teaching as a career. He taught in Delaware, Louisiana, and Mississippi and was also a school supervisor. In 1923 he became president of the State College for Colored Students in Dover, Delaware. He served as president of several associations including the Conference of Presidents of Negro Land-Grant Colleges and the National Association of Teachers in Colored Schools. He always gave Alcorn the credit for building the foundation that allowed him to succeed in his professional career.

Milan W. Davis, a native of Jonestown, Mississippi, was Alcornite of the Year in 1950. He attended both high school and college at Alcorn, graduating in 1932. He wrote *Pushing Forward*, a brief Alcorn history covering the first sixty-seven years of the institution's existence. He later served as president of Okolona Junior College in Mississippi.

Daniel W. Ambrose, the 1951 Alcornite of the Year, was from Holmes County. A 1918 graduate, he became a successful lawyer after receiving the Bachelor of Laws degree from Howard University. A member of Kappa Alpha Psi Fraternity, he was named Man of the Year by the Pan Hellenic Council. Ambrose was also a nationally known civic worker.

George W. Lee, chosen in 1952, was from Memphis, Tennessee, and was a member of the class of 1918. He was one of three Alcornites nominated for the national centennial honor roll. A World War I veteran, he was known by some as Lieutenant Lee. He assisted in initiating the Elks Scholarship Fund.

Robert Hunter, a real scholar and educator, became Alcornite of the Year in 1953. A 1940 graduate, he worked at Alcorn from 1940 to 1954. His other college-level teaching experiences included years at Southern University and Grambling State University in Louisiana. His articles, published widely in the professional journals of his time, included "The Teaching Function," "Some Often-Overlooked Issues that Affect Educational Practice," and "The Educational Practitioner."

Ruby Elizabeth Cowan Stutts Lyells, the 1954 Alcornite of the Year, was from Yazoo County in Mississippi. Valedictorian of her class in 1929, she became librarian at Alcorn in 1930 and was the first black professionally trained librarian in the state of Mississippi. She worked at Alcorn from 1930 to 1945 as a library administrator and student counselor and was instrumental in the origin and development of the Library Division of the Mississippi Teachers Association. From 1945 to 1947 she was head librarian at Jackson State College and was later employed by the city of Jackson as director of the Carver and College Park branches of the Jackson Public Library. In 1968 the Ruby E. Stutts Lyells Library at Prentiss Institute was named in her honor for her library work and her efforts to desegregate the Jackson public schools.

Hampton P. Wilburn, a native of Yazoo City, Mississippi, was the 1955 Alcornite of the Year. A 1942 graduate, he later served as president of Campbell College in Jackson, Mississippi, and Okolona College in Okolona, Mississippi.

John D. Boyd, honored in 1957, was one of four alumni to serve the university as president. Before his tenure at Alcorn, he had served as president of Utica Junior College in Utica, Mississippi. He was also an outstanding artist, educator, farmer, financer, and sportsman. He was a 1931 graduate of Alcorn. For more information about Boyd, see Chapter 4 of this book.

W. S. Demby, born in Rodney, Mississippi, was the 1959 Alcornite of the Year. He acquired the title "Mr. Alcorn" because of his total commitment to the school. He was responsible for recruiting hundreds of students and was one of the pioneers of the Alumni Association, serving as its president for two terms. A 1926 graduate of Alcorn, he held the position of county agent in Warren County for twenty-four years. Mr. Demby's daughter, Dr. Allene Demby Gayles, presents an annual scholarship in his honor to the Alcorn student from Warren County with the highest cumulative average. He has accompanied her to the university each year to make the presentation on Honors Day. New men's tower was recently named in his honor.

Cleopatra D. Thompson, a 1932 graduate, was selected in 1961. She was a leader in educational curriculum development, elementary and secondary education, administration, supervision, and educational psychology. Among her many publications was an article in the *Mississippi Educational Journal* (1967) entitled "The Educational Responsibility of the Mississippi Teachers Association in World Affairs." She taught at Alcorn, Rust, Okolona, Tougaloo, the University of Liberia, and Jackson State University, where she served as dean of the School of Education and as distinguished professor.

Chester L. Marcus, the 1962 Alcornite of the Year, was the secretary of the United Church Board for World Ministries. He is credited with taking a tour of the Board of Missions Stations in Africa. He was a 1941 graduate of Alcorn.

Jessie A. Morris, the 1963 honoree, was a native of Leake County, Mississippi and received his degree from Alcorn in 1950. He served in the navy during World War II and later became a disabled veteran of the Korean War. A teacher of vocational guidance, he also directed the Division of Vocational Education at Alcorn and received the Mississippi Association of New Farmers of America Honorary Modern Farmers degree in 1959. He once served as executive secretary to the Alcorn State University National Alumni Association. The agriculture science building was recently named in his honor.

Delors E. Magee, chosen in 1964, had previously received the Man of the Year Award from St. Matthews A.M.E. Church in Greenville, Mississippi. He was the first Mississippian to be honored for outstanding service to farmers and rural people in the state. Born in Walthall County, Mississippi, Magee graduated from Alcorn in 1935. His many professional experiences included being a high school principal, an agriculture teacher, and a staff assistant for the Office of the State Director of the Farmers Home Administration in the State of Mississippi.

Benjamin Franklin McLaurin, from Covington County, was the 1965 Alcornite of the Year. A 1935 graduate, he was a vocational agriculture teacher in the Coahoma County Agricultural High School. When it later became the first public black junior college in the state, he served as president.

Rube Harrington, Jr., the 1966 Alcornite of the Year, was from Winston County and received his B.S. degree from Alcorn in 1951. He served in the U.S. Air Force from 1951 to 1952. In 1961 he was employed by the Animal Eradication Division of the U.S. Department of Agriculture as an area veterinarian in Nebraska, where he was assigned seven counties for two and a half years. Having received the degree of Doctor of Veterinary Medicine at Tuskegee Institute in 1961, he published a paper in 1965 in the *Journal of Applied Microbiology* related to his extensive research on bacilli and serological tests for tuberculosis.

George J. Bacon, the 1967 Alcornite of the Year, was a Natchez, Mississippi, native who graduated in 1938 and taught at Alcorn during World War II. He was very active in religious and civic activities at the local, state, and national levels. The first elected Taborian Man of the Year, he was the founder of Delta Memorial Gardens in Greenville, Mississippi.

Evans T. Hawkins, born in Jefferson County, received the award in 1968. He graduated from Alcorn in 1930 and taught school in Tennessee. He later served as principal, coach, and vocational agricultural teacher in Forest, Mississippi, where a high school was named in his honor in 1951. He is a past president of the National Alumni Association.

William Earthy Ammons, from Holmes County, was chosen in 1969. He graduated from Alcorn in 1933 and spent his whole career, more than thirty-six years of service, in the field of agriculture. He was assistant supervisor of Negro Extension Work in Mississippi from 1947 to 1952 and was a staff assistant of the Cooperative Extension Service at Mississippi State University. He received a Certificate of Merit from Alcorn in 1961. Eight of the twelve siblings in the family were Alcorn graduates.

James Charles Evers was the 1970 Alcornite of the Year. A native of

Decatur, Mississippi, he was very active in politics at all levels and twice served as mayor of Fayette. A World War II veteran, Evers served as State Field Secretary of the NAACP and ran for the Senate and the governor's office in Mississippi. He graduated from Alcorn in 1951.

James C. Gilliam, the 1971 Alcornite of the Year, was from Coahoma County and was a mail carrier. He was a grandmaster of the Stringer Grand Lodge beginning in 1946. During his twenty-five years as Grand Master he made it possible for over two hundred young men and women to attend the colleges of their choice. He was very active in civil rights and involved in every movement that appeared to enhance the citizenship of black people. He was the forerunner in the fight to get blacks to register and vote. He was one of the organizers of the largest black businesses in the state, the State Mutual Federal Savings and Loan Association. He helped organize the Mississippi Action for Progress (MAP), giving needy children a chance to attend school. He was also among the first to help organize Boy Scouts for blacks in Coahoma County.

Charles Humphrey, a native of Oxford, Mississippi, was honored in 1972. Having graduated from Alcorn in 1953, he was employed at Alcorn as the college physician in 1962. He was also a physician at Methodist Hospital and Forrest General Hospital in Hattiesburg, Mississippi. In 1970 he served as project director of the Comprehensive Health Care Program in Fayette, Mississippi, directed the Medgar Evers Health Clinic there, and served on the staff of Jefferson County Hospital.

James E. Miller was the 1973 Alcornite of the Year. He was a native of Yazoo County, Mississippi. He finished high school and college at Alcorn, taught school in Leake, Sunflower, and Greenwood, and later went from being a classroom teacher at Coahoma Junior College to being its president. He graduated from Alcorn in 1932. He was the initiator and the first editor of the *Greater Alcorn Herald*. He was a member of the board of trustees of Coahoma Opportunities, Inc., the board of directors of the Mississippi Teachers Association, and president of the Third District Teachers Association. He supports and promotes the activities of the local alumni chapter and is a loyal contributor to the Alcorn National Alumni Association.

Calvin Rhodes, the 1974 Alcornite of the Year, is a native of Edwards, Mississippi. He is thought of as "the Alcorn Father" in the Detroit, Michigan, area. A 1935 graduate, he has been one of Alcorn's greatest alumni supporters. He taught math and science at the Lampton County Training School in Marion County and became assistant principal at Globe Academy in Hub, Mississippi. He also served as basketball coach in both of these positions. In 1939, he became principal of Jones County Training School at Summerland, Mississippi. When he left Mississippi and went to Detroit, he became very involved with many significant aspects of the city's overall operations. He started his new life as an industrial worker. In 1976, he received the service award from the Alcorn State University Alumni Chapter in Detroit, and he has been given numerous other awards from various community and service-oriented organizations. He is a life member of the Alcorn Alumni Association.

David Wilson Wilburn, selected in 1975, was born in Yazoo County and attended high school and college at Alcorn, graduating in 1933. He taught in the public schools in Monticello, Mississippi, and served fifteen years as registrar at Alcorn. He also served as executive secretary and parliamentarian of the Alcorn National Alumni Association.

Luther Alexander, a native of McComb, Mississippi, was the 1976 Alcornite of the Year. He graduated from Alcorn in 1953 after having left in 1951 to join the armed forces. He served with the Cooperative Extension Service for thirty-two years, becoming Washington County's first black Cooperative Extension county agent. He also became the first black person elected as president of the Greenville Park Commission as well as the first black to be elected supervisor in Washington County and the first black to be elected vice president of the Delta Council. Highly involved with the Washington County Alcorn Alumni Chapter, he also served as president of the National Alumni Association, holding that position longer than anyone else. His success in recruiting students was recognized when he received a "Certificate of Excellence" in 1967. He was inducted into the Alcorn State University Hall of Honor in 1990, becoming one of its charter members. The poultry facility was recently named in his honor.

Robert Jordan, selected in 1977, graduated from Alcorn in 1954. He was from Waynesboro, Mississippi, and served in the United States Army as a medical aidman for two years after leaving Alcorn. He was a teacher, counselor, and administrator with the Chicago Board of Education. Actively involved in the alumni association at the local and national levels, he served as president of the Chicago chapter for five years.

Henry R. Smith, who graduated from Alcorn in 1940, was the 1978 Alcornite of the Year. He served as principal of Ruleville Central

High School for more than twenty years and was actively involved in many public organizations including the Ruleville Board of Aldermen of which he was a member. He has recruited many students to Alcorn.

Andrew Graves received the honor in 1979. Born in Port Gibson, Mississippi, he received the B.S. degree from Alcorn in 1934. The recipient of numerous service awards, including that of outstanding county agent, he served as classroom teacher and coach at the Pike County Training School in Magnolia, Mississippi, and as a vocational agriculture teacher in Leflore County. For thirty-seven years, he worked with the Cooperative Extension Service as Negro county agent, associate county agent, and area horticulture agent. During Alcorn's centennial celebration, he was awarded the "Loyal Alumnus" plaque for outstanding contributions to Alcorn State University. He served as chairman of the Scott County Alumni Recruiting Committee and is a life member of the Alcorn National Alumni Association.

E. A. Dumas was named Alcornite of the Year in 1980. A 1923 graduate of Alcorn, he was a charter member of the Chicago alumni chapter, serving as secretary, president and chairman of the board of directors. He was very active in the Alumni Association as well as in the medical profession. He was a delegate to the National Medical Association for twenty-five years and was a member of the board of trustees for six years. Though he did not receive a letter as an outstanding baseball pitcher while attending Alcorn, athletic director Marino Casem and baseball coach Willie "Rat" McGowan presented him with a letter and an Alcorn T-shirt in later years. The library-science building was recently named in his honor.

Fred Cunningham, selected in 1981, graduated from Alcorn in 1949. Prior to becoming employed at Jackson State University, he was a director of Alcorn's plant operations. He served many Mississippi counties as instructor of institutional-on-farm training and was director of farm operations at Oakley Training School in Raymond, Mississippi. He served as a lecturer in physical plant administration and operation and directed several interns in physical plant management for many colleges. He was a member of several evaluation teams for the Southern Association of Colleges and Schools. He volunteered much of his time in service to Alcorn's physical plant.

Jewell C. Lockhart, the 1982 Alcornite of the Year, was born in Taylor, Mississippi. After graduating with honors in the class of 1956, he served for two years in Korea and later for six years in the United States Army Reserve. He was a science teacher at the Smith County High

School and assistant principal at Turner Chapel High School in Raleigh, Mississippi. He worked in Newton County with the Cooperative Extension Service and was later employed with the Farmers Home Administration and the National FHA Office in Washington, D.C. He also served as district commissioner for the Mississippi District Boy Scouts of America and as scoutmaster in Greenville. His many honors include an outstanding accomplishment certificate from the Farmers Home Administration. He was instrumental in securing a rural water system for residents in Metcalfe, Winterville, and Elizabeth communities in Washington County. He has served as treasurer of the Alcorn National Alumni Association since 1963.

Vera H. Bryant, the 1983 honoree, received the B.S. degree from Alcorn in 1957. One of the top ten students in her class, she held the title of Miss Alcorn in 1956. She taught in the elementary schools of Stone, Marion, and Pike counties and served as a reading supervisor in the South Pike School District in Magnolia, Mississippi. She has received numerous honors throughout her career including Pike County Alcornite of the Year in 1978 and the Certificate of Merit from the Alcorn State University National Alumni Association in 1982. She is a past recording secretary of the National Alumni Association. A native of Columbia, Mississippi, she has been involved in many civic, educational, social, and religious organizations.

Issac L. Thomas, the 1984 recipient, graduated from Alcorn in 1942 and was a registered pharmacist until he retired in 1979. Having served in the United States Army during World War II, he later worked for one year in Covington County, Mississippi. In 1951 he completed requirements for the Louisiana State Board of Pharmacy from Xavier University in New Orleans. Thomas's drugstore in Laurel, Mississippi, Thomas Professional Pharmacy, has been successful for more than forty years. "Doc Thomas," as he was affectionately known, was honored as the Jones County Alcornite of the Year in 1969, and also received the Outstanding Leadership Award, the Loyal Alumnus Award, and the Most Outstanding Service Award in Financial Support from the Jones County Alumni Chapter. He was the first black to be appointed to the biracial committee of the Laurel City School District, to the board of trustees of Jones County Community Hospital, and to the fifteen-county Pat Harrison Waterway District. He is credited with having been the person behind the building of a modern highway from Highway 61 to the Alcorn campus.

Kenneth L. Simmons, honored in 1985, was a 1956 graduate of Alcorn. A native of Madison County, he received his degree in industrial education and served as instructor and assistant director of the Cooperative Education Program at Texas Southern University in Houston, Texas, before returning to Alcorn in 1972 as the department chairman of Industrial Education and Technology. He was instrumental in Alcorn's receiving a federal grant in 1973 that set up the school's first Cooperative Education Program. A widely published writer, he received his doctorate in 1977 and resumed a leadership role at Alcorn by planning the new industrial technology building, which was occupied in 1982. He has made significant contributions to civic, educational, and religious organizations and has received many honors, including the National Alumni Association's Faculty-Staff Alumnus of the Year Award.

Lottie H. Powell, a native of Gary, Indiana, was the 1986 Alcornite of the Year. She received her B.S. degree from Alcorn in 1915. She taught school in Mound Bayou, Mississippi, and in Gary, Indiana. A volunteer worker in a local public library, she was actively involved in community service and was chosen Senior Citizen of the Year three times. In 1986 she was founder and the only president of the Bishops' Wives Hall of Fame in Cassapolis, Michigan. She spent most of her life helping the poor and the needy.

Alyce G. Clark, the first black woman to be elected to the Mississippi House of Representatives, was named the 1987 Alcornite of the Year. She graduated from Alcorn in 1961 and was the director of the Nutrition/WIC Services at the Jackson-Hinds Comprehensive Health Center. Active in many service-oriented activities, she served on the Mayor's Advisory Committee and the Hinds County Democratic Executive Committee. She has received many awards and special recognitions, including Alcorn's Meritorious Award in 1984, the Faithful Service Award in 1983 and the Alpha Kappa Alpha Leadership and Community Service Award.

Alpha L. Morris received the 1988 award. A native of Taylor, Mississippi, she received the B.S. degree in 1952. In addition to being a social, civic, and religious leader, she is an educator and scholar, having served as a teacher of home economics and adult education. She is an associate professor of sociology and social sciences at Alcorn where, in 1993, she serves as department chairperson. Her services to the National Alumni Association and Alcorn State University have included serving as an active member of the board of directors of the Alcorn State University Foundation. She has received many awards, honors, and citations including Faculty-Staff Alumnus of the Year in 1987. She is a founding member of the Alcorn Alumnae Chapter of Delta Sigma Theta Sorority from which she received the Delta Woman of the Year Award in 1982. She was appointed by former governor Bill Allain to the Mississippi Bicentennial Commission on the United States Constitution, on which she served from 1987 to 1988. In 1992, she was chosen Alcorn's Outstanding Faculty Member and was recognized by the foundation as the university's Outstanding Teacher. In 1993, she was honored by the Mississippi Legislature as outstanding Faculty at Alcorn.

Mack Willie Payton, the 1989 Alcornite of the Year, is a 1950 graduate of Alcorn. He has worked as a supervisor of juvenile probation officers at Children's Court Center, as a teacher in Pike County, and as an employee with the Milwaukee County Civil Service Commission. His honors include a listing in *Who's Who in the Midwest Field of Humanities*, certificates of appreciation from the Milwaukee Boys Club and other community-service organizations, and certificates and plaques from Alcorn State University for service and financial donations. His professional memberships include the National Association of Social Workers, the National Probation and Parole Association, the Wisconsin Public Welfare Association, and the Juvenile Court Workers Association. He is an active recruiter for Alcorn State University and an annual financial contributor to the Alcorn Foundation.

Mary P. Demby, a 1956 graduate, was named Alcornite of the Year in 1990. After graduation, she worked at the Sadie V. Thompson High School in Natchez, at Coahoma Junior College in Clarksdale, at Rosa A. Temple High School in Vicksburg, and at the University of Southern California in Los Angeles. In 1990, she had worked in the Compton Unified School District in Compton, California, for twenty-three years. She has to her credit many community and professional involvements and honors, among them the Faithful Service Award from the National Alumni Association in 1987. She also serves on the Education Task Force of the Black Women's Forum in Compton. A life member of the Alcorn State University National Alumni, she is president of the Los Angeles chapter.

Matthew W. Thomas, Jr., the 1991 Alcornite of the Year, is a native of Pinola, Mississippi, and received the B.S. degree in 1964. He has been an accountant, comptroller, and businessman, as well as a civic and religious leader. He is the president and owner of Statewide General Insurance Agency, Inc., and was president of the Alcorn State University National Alumni Association for two terms. Thomas served as chairman of the board of directors of the Alcorn State University Foundation, Inc. He has received numerous awards and honors, including being chosen Black Businessman of the Year by the Jackson YMCA in 1978. He was also a representative to the White House Conference on Small Businesses in 1978 and chaired the Inter-Alumni Council of Mississippi Institutions of Higher Learning. Faculty garden apartments were recently named in his honor.

George Jones, Jr., a native of Hermanville, Mississippi, was honored by Alcorn in 1992. A 1931 graduate, he spent forty years as a classroom teacher. In 1992 he had been a member of the Jackson-Alcorn Alumni Chapter for forty years. Cofounder of the Jackson Metropolitan Retired Teachers Association, he has received many honors and citations including the National Alumni Outstanding Service Award and Meritorious Award. He also served as an assistant to the pastor of the Hope Springs Missionary Baptist Church. His career spans six decades of public and community service. He was the first chaplain of the Alcorn National Alumni Association.

Robert Wayne Bowles, selected in 1993, is a native of Lumberton, Mississippi, and received the B.S. degree in 1966. In 1970 he became the first Director of Alumni Affairs at Alcorn. During this time he established the Alumni Annual Giving Program and the Alumni Endowed Scholarship Fund. He also helped to establish the Alcorn Business and Industry Cluster and is one of the original charter members of the Alcorn State University Foundation, Inc., which he served as the first secretary. He served as cochairman of Alcorn's first Alumni Centennial Fund Drive and created the Alcorn Hall of Honor. His many awards include Faculty-Staff Alumnus of the Year in 1986, the Alumni Meritorious Award in 1981 and the Faithful Service Award in 1992. As president of the Gulf Coast Alcorn Alumni Chapter, Bowles was instrumental in building the largest chapter membership in the nation. After serving eighteen years in various capacities at Alcorn, he became assistant superintendent for the Biloxi school district where in 1993 he was named deputy superintendent.

The designation of Alcornite of the Year is the highest honor that can be received by any Alcornite. Other distinguished alumni who were cited and described in one or both of the previous published histories of Alcorn became a part of the Alcorn Centennial Roll. (For a listing of these and also of 1993 presidents of local alumni chapters, see Appendixes 5 and 6.)

Alcornites are known throughout the world. School districts make special efforts to hire Alcorn graduates; businesses look for Alcorn products. Leaders of various firms have said that there is something unique and outstanding about Alcorn graduates: their commitment and dedication to a task, their desire to be successful, their ambition to move forward, their confidence in themselves, their feeling of quality and self-worth, their outlook on life, and their sincerity and love for their alma mater. An Alcorn graduate can successfully compete with a graduate from any other institution in the United States or the world. Vice President Rudolph Waters has always stated that an institution is great not because of its buildings or its beautiful campus, not simply because it's a Harvard or a Yale, but because of its alumni. Alcorn's alumni epitomize Alcorn's greatness and project it to all those with whom they live and work.

Information on Alcornites of the Year for the years 1956, 1958, and 1960 was not available.

FIFTEEN

A Look to the Future

Alcorn has had to struggle to receive adequate funding since the founding of the institution in 1871. In November 1981, the college board continued the tradition of weak support by moving to merge academic programs at the state's universities in an effort to reduce duplication. The legislature had appropriated $138.3 million for all schools, with only $8.2 million going to Alcorn. President Walter Washington reacted by pointing out crucial problems with the way the Board of Trustees of State Institutions of Higher Learning had handled this and other issues. University presidents had had no input and were being informed only after the decisions had already been made.

Robert Walker, then state director of the NAACP and convenor of the Black Mississippi Council for Higher Education, labeled the decision part of a scheme to hinder black people from having fair access to higher education. "Blacks without an education," he said, were "easier to control than educated black people." He also expressed a concern about black students attending white universities that at one time had refused to enroll any blacks. "Black colleges are still essential to the black community," he concluded.

Blacks protested the board's so-called "missions' plan" and, in March 1982, the board delayed action. Increasingly worrisome, however, was the proposal to downsize Alcorn State University, Mississippi Valley State University, Delta State University, and Mississippi University for Women to undergraduate programs only. This plan would freeze historically black universities at their current level of unequal development. The decision would allow expansion of doctoral programs in the three predominantly white universities, while mostly black Jackson State University would have the role of research and service as an urban university with no specific academic areas on which to concentrate.

Despite the lack of adequate funds, Alcorn has always had a clean audit under Walter Washington's administration. The 28 percent budget reduction in 1987, however, cut to the very bone of the university. Washington labeled it a veritable death blow. Rather than declare a financial emergency and fire people on the spot, however, Washington reorganized and reshuffled, hoping that the future would become brighter.

In 1989, with Alcorn still struggling, Washington and other university presidents met in the White House Rose Garden, with then-president George Bush, for an announcement of new programs for black institutions. An executive order was issued to ensure that the federal government would increase and enhance programs for black schools. The black college officials applauded this announcement but voiced concern that the plan ignored such pressing issues as the admission of blacks to colleges and the financing of their tuition bills.

The Jake Ayers Case, filed in the U.S. District Court in 1975, was an effort to address the issue of inadequate funding in Mississippi for black schools. It claimed discrimination in the funding formula for the state universities and challenged the constitutionality of the state's public university system. The suit charged that Mississippi officials have not fairly distributed money, promotions, or hirings throughout the eight universities. The suit named the governor, the state, its universities, and the state college board as defendants. In 1975, the United States Justice Department agreed that the state did support a dual system of education. The Ayers Case, in 1993 still in litigation, dealt with disparities in funding for black institutions and white ones; with transferring the operation of duplicate and competing degree-granting centers to black colleges and universities; and with ending racial discrimination in employment and recruitment practices.

Ayers simply wanted Alcorn, Jackson State, and Mississippi Valley State universities to be compensated for the obvious neglect they had suffered through the years. U.S. District Judge Neal Biggers, Jr., of Oxford, Mississippi, dismissed the suit in December 1987, but his ruling was overturned by a three-judge panel of the U.S. Fifth Circuit Court of Appeals. The United States Supreme Court upheld this ruling and sent the case back to Judge Biggers's court for action, ordering Mississippi to end segregation practices at the eight universities. The state college board then voted 8-4 to submit to Biggers a plan that would only add to the problem, not solve it. The plan would further desegregate Mississippi institutions by closing and merging some of the universities. Mississippi Valley State University, Mississippi State University's School of Veterinary Medicine, and the University of Mississippi's School of Dentistry would all close under the plan, while Delta State would become a campus of the University of Mississippi. Mississippi University for Women would become a part of the University of Southern Mississippi, and Alcorn would become a part of Mississippi State University. Students and alumni of the adversely affected schools protested the board's plan. It was Walter Washington who made the plan public, despite the board's insistence on silence, saying that when someone talked about closing his institution, he had no choice but to speak out.

Governor Kirk Fordice, along with House Speaker Tim Ford and Lt. Governor Eddie Briggs, named a task force of Mississippi citizens to restructure all eight universities rather than close some. Public hearings took place and rallies opposing the college board plan continued. The legislature adjourned April 2, 1993, without taking any major action on the litigation.

Walter Washington developed a plan for the survival and growth of Alcorn in response to the Ayers Case. He said that the requests of the plaintiffs were as follows: (1) that Mississippi continue to operate all eight universities; (2) that undergraduate admissions be revamped so that a high school diploma rather than an ACT score would be the basis for admission to any of the institutions in Mississippi; (3) that more black faculty and staff be hired at the five majority white universities; (4) that schools have a more diverse student population through improved facilities and equipment, off-campus offerings, long-range planning, and proper funding; (5) that the two-year colleges be part of the case; and (6) that more blacks be named to the state college board, which in 1993 included only three black members out of twelve.

Washington submitted the plan to the board on Alcorn's behalf. He was well aware that the Board of Trustees of State Institutions of Higher Learning had overlooked the historic mission of Alcorn by designating it as a regional university with no reference to its land-grant status. The school received no direct appropriation for agricultural research or cooperative extension. In 1993, however, Alcorn received direct appropriations for these areas without funds having to come through Mississippi State University. In 1878, the Mississippi state legislature had given Alcorn and Mississippi State identical missions, yet Alcorn had never been the beneficiary of the sort of financial support that would have allowed it to realize its potential.

Alcorn also made the following assertions with respect to the Ayers Case:

>1. Alcorn State University is against the merger, closure, downgrading or any other change in the university which would adversely affect its capacity to exist as a stand alone land-grant university. Efforts of the state to comply with the order of the Supreme Court of the United States to dismantle vestiges of a segregated university system must not be to the detriment of the "victimized" institutions such as Alcorn State University. As stated by Supreme Court Justice Clarence Thomas: "It would be ironic, to say the least, if the institutions that sustained blacks during segregation were themselves destroyed in an effort to combat its vestiges."
>
>2. Alcorn State University should maintain its status as a full-fledged independent land-grant institution as stipulated in Section 213 of the Mississippi Constitution. The university should maintain its mission as a land-grant institution as stipulated in the legislation which created the university.
>
>3. There should be one system of agriculture (academic programs, research, extension) as related to the universities in the state with Alcorn State University administering agriculture in the southern part of the state.
>
>4. In order to facilitate coordination of agricultural programs in the state, there should be an Agricultural Coordinating Council with membership approved by the Board of Trustees and chairmanship rotating between Alcorn State University and Mississippi State University.
>
>5. The legislature should support Alcorn State University as a land-grant university, and the counties in south Mississippi should support Alcorn State University similarly to their present support of Mississippi State University.
>
>6. Alcorn State University's ability to attract white students and farmers is directly related to the quality of programs the university offers. For example, about sixty percent (60%) of the nursing students enrolled at Alcorn State University are white. Programs that are in demand by students and other clients should therefore be established at Alcorn State University.
>
>7. In order for students enrolled at Alcorn State University to have richer experiences and for graduates to be competitive in the marketplace, there should be increased financial support for the university. Al-

corn State University should be recognized and validated in the public view as a quality university making significant contributions to the growth and development of the state.

This plan for the growth and survival of Alcorn, if implemented, would result in a renewed mission, one that is strengthened and enhanced; funding would be available for new academic programs, academic research, and faculty and salary catch-up. (A continuous effort on the part of the Alcorn administration over the past three years to upgrade salaries has kept Alcorn from having the lowest average on the Southern Regional Education Board.) The plan keys in specifically on the land-grant function of the university, formula funding, and capital improvements.

In spite of Ayers, Alcorn's enrollment increased to 3,317 in 1991, an illustration of the little-recognized fact that black institutions award nearly one-third of the 1.1 million undergraduate degrees granted to blacks in the nation. In Mississippi, Alcorn, Jackson State, and Mississippi Valley State educate the majority of the state's blacks who go to college. Alvin O. Chambliss, Jr., a Mississippi legal aid lawyer arguing the Ayers Case for the plaintiffs, insists that for black colleges to die on the vine would be criminal. Alcorn, however, will survive, and part of the reason will be the funds received from nonlegislative sources. Funds have been contributed to Alcorn by various donors in honor of Walter Washington, and other gifts such as memorial funds and endowed scholarships have been contributed by alumni and friends of the university. These kinds of contributions will help Alcorn remain open in spite of funding discrimination.

Alcorn has survived for many years, and it does not intend to fold now. A group of student protesters chanted during a 1993 Ayers Case rally: "We don't believe He [God] brought us this far to leave us." The beautiful university campus, built on a slope and carefully carpeted with lush green grass fanned by towering oak trees and attractive shrubbery, has long been the setting for the education of black youth. This tradition will not end even though the road ahead may be difficult. Alcorn was once described as an oasis of civilization deep in the southwest Mississippi woods where one had to cross a cattle gap to get to the campus. Thousands of alumni and friends across the land love the school, and their devotion will ensure that it will be home to thousands more young men and women who will continue to arrive at its doors looking for wisdom and knowledge in these hallowed woods and for a better life in the wider world. The new Alcorn has come too far through the years to go back now.

Alcorn College Band, latter 1960s

Alcorn State University Band, early 1990s

Governor Bill Waller signing to change name from Alcorn Agricultural and Mechanical College to Alcorn State University, 1974

Inauguration of President Walter Washington, 1971

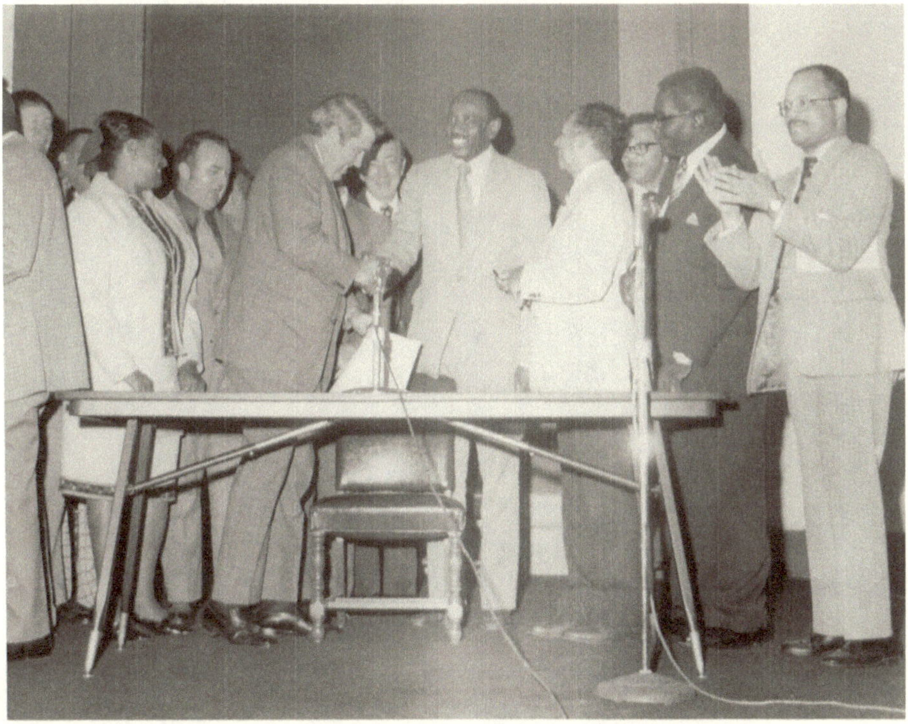

President Walter Washington receiving doctoral degree from the University of Southern Mississippi, conferred by President McCain, 1969

Kennard-Washington Hall at the University of Southern Mississippi, dedicated in 1993

Above: Walter Washington receives the Distinguished Alumni Award from Peabody-Vanderbilt. Also pictured, the President of Vanderbilt and the President of the National Alumni Association; *below:* President Washington receives an honorary doctorate of science from Purdue University, 1993; *right:* Walter and Carolyn Washington.

President Washington and Mrs. Erma Hawkins, his only executive secretary/administrative assistant during Washington's tenure as president

President Washington meeting with his administrative staff

Left and below: President George Bush delivering commencement address, 1989.

President George Bush congratulating Jerry Sims upon receiving his master's degree

Industry Cluster Conference, 1973

The Lady Braves coached by the most successful women's coach in Alcorn's history, Shirley Walker (first from left standing)

Whitney "The Wiz" receiving championship award as assistant coach Lonnie Walker, team members, and fans look on

President Washington congratulating "The Wiz" on winning the basketball championship

The Godfather of SWAC, Marino Casem

Steve McNair, Heisman Trophy candidate, 1993

Alcorn Braves pose ready to take the show on the baseball field, with Coach Willie McGowan standing on the left

Jack Spinks Stadium/Dwight Fisher Field dedicated in 1992

Above and opposite page: Alumni Relations

Above and right, respectively: President Walter Washington and Vice President Rudolph Waters at Mid-Winter Conference

Alumni Weekend on campus

Golden Diploma recipients, class of 1940 (received Golden Diplomas in 1990)

Above: President Washington congratulating Cleopatra Thompson, class of 1992, on receiving the Distinguished Centenniel Alumni Award in 1990; *right:* W. S. Demby, known to alumni as "Mr. Alcorn".

Alcornites Fred Cunningham and Jasper Davis, class of 1949, planting yucca plants near the park on campus

Board members, Alcorn Foundation, 1974

Epilogue

It is obvious that Alcorn's history is unique. Changes have taken place through the decades that have contributed greatly to Alcorn's survival and changes are still occurring today in an effort to keep Alcorn moving forward.

Since the submission of this manuscript to the press in June 1993, several updates have taken place. The academic divisions as described in the manuscript are now classified as schools. The directors of these divisions are now deans of the specific schools. The academic dean and other unit heads are now vice presidents for the first time in Alcorn's history. The Vice President of Alcorn State University is now the Executive Vice President of Alcorn State University.

The former academic divisions are now labeled as follows:

Former name	Current name
Division of Arts and Sciences	School of Arts and Sciences
Division of Business	School of Business
Division of Education and Psychology	School of Education and Psychology
Division of Agriculture and Applied Science	School of Agriculture and Applied Science
Division of Nursing	School of Nursing
Division of Graduate Studies	School of Graduate Studies
Division of General College for Excellence	General College for Excellence

Administrative officers with title changes include: Vice President Rudolph Waters to Executive Vice President; Dean of Academic Affairs Malvin Williams to Vice President for Academic Affairs; Business Manager Wiley Jones to Vice President for Business Affairs; acting Dean of Student Affairs LaPlose Jackson to acting Vice President of Student Affairs; and Director of Institutional Advancement and Planning and Research Franklin Jackson to Vice President for Institutional Advancement and Planning.

The title of each division director was changed as follows: Director of the Division of Arts and Sciences Norris Edney to Dean of the School of Arts and Sciences; Director of the Division of Business Robert Williams to Dean of the School of Business; Director of the Division of Education and Psychology John Hendricks to Dean of the School of Education and Psychology; Director of the Division of Agriculture and Applied Science to Dean of the School of Agriculture and Applied Science; Director of the Division of Nursing Frances Henderson to Dean of the School of Nursing;

Director of the Division of Graduate Studies Norris Edney to Dean of the School of Graduate Studies; and Director of the Division of General College for Excellence Newtie Boyd to the Dean of the General College of Excellence.

Alcorn continues to strive for excellence, and for decades to come commitment to excellence will continue to be the driving force toward accomplishing short-range and long-range goals of the university.

APPENDIXES

APPENDIX A   Student Organizations

APPENDIX B   University Buildings

APPENDIX C   Athletic Achievements

APPENDIX D   National Association for Equal Opportunity in Higher Education Distinguished Alumni of the Year

APPENDIX E   Centennial Roll

APPENDIX F   Presidents of Local Alumni Chapters, 1993

APPENDIX G   Catalogue of Alcorn University, 1872–1873

APPENDIX H   Mission Statement, 1993

APPENDIX I   Golden Diploma Recipients, 1933–1943

Appendix A
STUDENT ORGANIZATIONS

Educational or Departmental Organizations

Kappa Kappa Psi
Biology Club
Business Club
Chemistry Club
Council of Exceptional Children
Criminal Justice Club
Sociology Club
English Club
French Club
Collegiate Chapter of Future
    Homemakers of America
Phi Beta Lambda
Music Educators National
Professional Secretaries
    International
Army ROTC Cadet Association
Kappa Omicron Phi
Mississippi Association for
    Student Nurses

Tau Beta Sigma (Music)
Home Economics Club
Industrial Arts Club
Institutional Management Club
Math and Computer Science Club
Physical Education Majors and
    Minors Club
Pre-Med Club
Pre-Nursing Club
Psychology Club
Student National Education
    Association
Science Club
Collegiate Club
Khem
Iota Phi Lambda
National Society of Pershing
    Rifles
Agricultural Economics Club

Greek Organizations

Alpha Kappa Alpha Sorority
Delta Sigma Theta Sorority
Sigma Gamma Rho Sorority
Zeta Phi Beta Sorority

Alpha Phi Alpha Fraternity
Kappa Alpha Psi Fraternity
Omega Psi Phi Fraternity
Phi Beta Sigma Fraternity

Pan Hellenic Council

Honor Societies

Alpha Kappa Mu Honor Society
Beta Kappa Chi Honor Society
    (Science)
Alpha Mu Gamma (English)

Sigma Rho Sigma
Beta Beta Beta Honorary Society
Delta Mu Delta

Appendix A

Religious Organizations

Adventist Youth Society
Baptist Student Union
Fellowship of Christian Athletes
Gospel Choir
Heroines of Jericho
Interfaith Gospel Choir
Masons
Methodist Student Movement
Newman Club
Prayer Band
Church of God in Christ (COGIC)
Sunday School
Wesley Foundation (Wesley Campus Ministry)
Young Men's Christian Association
Young Women's Christian Association
The Usher Board

Special Interest Organizations

Alcorn Chapter of NAACP
Alpha Tau Alpha
ASU Modeling Club (Beaute Noir)
Black History Month Society
Circle-K Campus Union Board
Concert Band
Diamondnettes
The Guidons
Jazz Ensemble
Karate Team
Men's Glee Club
National Society of Guidons
Wind Ensemble
ROTC Drill Team
Pershing Rifles
Silhouette Club
The Alcorn Players
The Marching Band
The Black Cultural Society
ASU Cheering Squad
The Color Guard
The Dance Troupe
The Recondo Platoon
The University Choir
The Rifle Team
ROTC Band

Class Organizations

Freshman Class
Sophomore Class
Junior Class
Senior Class

Student Government

The Student Government Association
Inter-Residence Hall Council
Student Body Organization (SBO) for the Division of Nursing

The Student Activities Department also oversees homecoming, student government, and the selection of Miss Alcorn State University.

There have been sixty-one Miss Alcorns in the years from 1926 to 1994. Names and years of reign follow:

Appendix A

Henerine Simpkins Knaives	1926–1927
Emma Weathers Howard	1927–1928
Name Unavailable	1929–1930
Lillian O'Gwyn Palmer	1931–1932
Annie Lee Patton	1932–1933
Name Unavailable	1934–1935
Ruby Reed McDaniel	1936–1937
Lula Kelly O'Neal	1937–1938
Louise King Lawson	1938–1940
Lula Belle Stewart Robinson	1940–1941
Dorothy Hayes Overstreet	1941–1942
Mattie Bious Reed	1942–1943
Thelma Miller Owens	1943–1944
Juno Gwendolyn Nichols	1944–1945
Janice Snodgrass Waters	1945–1946
Kathryn Moore Jones	1946–1947
Catherine Anderson Taylor	1947–1948
Marjorie Funches	1948–1949
Helen Johnson Pointer	1949–1950
Annie Johnson Stepney	1950–1951
Bernice Moore Gamblin	1951–1952
Beatrice Moses Bryant	1952–1953
Erronteen Horton Evans	1953–1954
Mary Carpenter Bacon	1954–1955
Levernis Eiland Crosby	1955–1956
Vera Hendricks Bryant	1956–1957
Ethel Wilson Powe	1957–1958
Annie Stewart Flemings	1958–1959
Aneice Knight Cross	1959–1960
Dora Prater Simpson	1960–1961
Vera Mae Moore Bullock	1961–1962
Veronica Levison Richardson	1962–1963
Laura A. Brown Nelson	1963–1964
Bernette V. Dillon	1964–1965
Barbara Bacon Epps	1965–1966
Esther Jenkins	1966–1967
Lucille Smith	1967–1968
Ora Dean Marshall Powell	1968–1969
Rebecca Shaw	1969–1970
Jacqueline Barnes Cannon	1970–1971
Shirley Barnes	1971–1972
Victory Dillon Mumford	1972–1973
Carolyn Gamblin Eubanks	1973–1974

Appendix A

Hazel Connard	1974–1975
Barbara Henderson	1975–1976
Patricia Lott	1976–1977
Brenda Jackson	1977–1978
Debbie Thomas Morris	1978–1979
Ethel Bryant	1979–1980
Cynthia Dalcourt Longs	1980–1981
Betty Tucker Lockhart	1981–1982
Venita Bowie	1982–1983
Cora Graham	1983–1984
Watosa Marshall Sanders	1984–1985
Carla D. Cleveland Kirkland	1985–1986
Monique A. Jackson	1986–1987
Marilyn D. Kline	1987–1988
Guy Alice Spears	1988–1989
Lisa R. Gilmore	1989–1990
Cathy Hughes Warp	1990–1991
Wendolyn Young	1991–1992
Jessica Johnson	1992–1993
Rukeyser Shylett Thompson	1993–1994

Records list student government presidents beginning in 1957. It is believed that the office existed before then, but there is no available record of who served during certain years. The following individuals have held the position since that time:

Name	Year
Paul L. Rucker	1957–1958
Name Unavailable	1958–1959
Creevy Harness	1959–1960
James Smith, Jr.	1960–1961
Willie R. Bullock	1961–1962
Joseph Lloyd	1962–1963
Henry Warren Baker	1963–1964
Gilbert Smith	1964–1965
Joshua Hill	1965–1966
Eddie L. Tate	1966–1967
Marvin Arrington	1967–1968
Herman Thomas	1968–1969
Randolph Walker	1969–1970
Elliot Travis	1970–1971
Verba Edwards	1971–1972
Joseph Shields	1972–1973
Irvin Bullet	1973–1974

Appendix A

Ronald Hickombottom	1974–1975
Lillie Blackmon	1975–1976
Larry McMillon	1976–1977
Robert Simmons	1977–1978
Andrew Nichols	1978–1979
David Gilbert	1979–1980
Terry L. Thames	1980–1981
Jewel C. Lockhart	1981–1982
Glenn J.P. Baham	1982–1983
Glenn J.P. Baham	1983–1984
Michael Glenn	1984–1985
Dwight Manzy	1985–1986
Timothy Lewis	1986–1987
Elliott Parker	1987–1988
Karen McLaughlin	1988–1989
James McDonald	1989–1990
Valerie Carter	1990–1991
Michael Edwards	1991–1992
Willie Kennedy III	1992–1993
Tracy Dion Dace	1993–1994

Appendix B
UNIVERSITY BUILDINGS

BUILDING	YEAR CONSTRUCTED	TYPE FACILITY	CONSTRUCTION COSTS	TOTAL SQ. FT.
Administration Building	1929	Office	$ 12,000	6,535
Administration Classroom	1977	Office	3,500,000	80,001
Agricultural Science Building	1977	Classroom	1,000,000	37,430
Airstrip Building	1974	Office	3,500	144
Alice Tanner Hall	1955	Residence	225,000	18,900
Apartment "A"	1961	Residence	69,491	4,536
Apartment "B"	1961	Residence	69,401	6,720
Beef Facility (renamed Johnnie B. Collins Beef Research Facility)	1984	Supplies	152,172	1,800
Belle Lettres Hall	1830	General	75,750	3,861
Biology Lab	1976	Lab	112,119	2,452
Boar & Sow Pen	1971	Special	16,000	1,200
	1979		202,398	
	1989		130,642	
Bowles Hall	1929	Classroom	89,000	32,993
	1979		202,398	
	1989		130,642	
Burrus Hall	1968	Residence	1,019,945	52,764
Campus Union Building	1963	General	600,000	60,000
	1973		1,760,697	
Central Rec. & Storage	1961	Office	2,500	1,604
Cottage "D"	1961	Residence	13,154	1,300
Cottage D-2	1961	Residence	13,154	1,300
Cottage D-3	1961	Residence	13,154	1,300
Cottage D-4	1961	Residence	13,145	1,300
Cottage D-5	1961	Residence	13,154	1,300
Cottage D-7	1961	Residence	13,154	1,300
Cottage D-8	1961	Residence	13,154	1,300
Cottage D-9	1961	Residence	13,154	1,300

Appendix B

BUILDING	YEAR CONSTRUCTED	TYPE FACILITY	CONSTRUCTION COSTS	TOTAL SQ. FT.
Cottage D-10	1961	Residence	13,154	1,300
Cottage D-12	1965	Residence	14,500	1,218
Cottage D-13	1965	Residence	14,500	1,218
Cottage D-15	1965	Residence	14,500	1,218
Cottage D-16	1965	Residence	14,500	1,218
Cottage D-17	1965	Residence	14,500	1,997
Cottage D-21	1955	Residence	4,500	1,997
Cottage D-22	1955	Residence	4,500	1,728
Dairy (renamed David C. Carter Dairy)	1967 1978 1980	Uncertain	60,321 174,000 95,981	4,964
Dining Hall (renamed the William H. Bell Dining Hall)	1953 1976	General	162,389 250,000	32,662
Dormitory "A"	1961	Residence	68,896	5,602
Dormitory "AR"	1961	Residence	68,896	5,602
Dormitory II	1830	General	65,513	5,376
Dormitory III	1830	General	68,113	5,378
Eunice Powell Hall	1955	Classroom	213,486	33,793
Faculty Garden (renamed Matt Thomas, Jr., Garden Apartments)	1972	Residence	547,521	33,973
Farm Vehicles Building	1969	Special	9,000	6,300
Farrowing House	1971	Special	88,000	6,300
Fine Arts Building	1963	Classroom	404,749	27,286
Gym & Auditorium (renamed E. E. Simmons Gymnasium)	1959 1977	General	291,066 90,000	33,528
Harmon Hall	1929	Office	56,000	16,954
Hay Barn	1981	Supplies	81,703	9,600
Health & P. E. Complex (renamed Davey L. Whitney Health, Physical Education, and Recreation Complex	1975	Special / Classroom	3,500,000	136,170

BUILDING	YEAR CON-STRUCTED	TYPE FACILITY	CONSTRUCTION COSTS	TOTAL SQ. FT.
Home Management House (renamed Dorothy Gordon Gray Home Management House)	1956	Residence	40,227	2,696
Infirmary (renamed Felix Dunn Infirmary)	1962 1986	Health	153,632 108,076	18,832
Industrial Technology	1981	Classroom	2,900,000	66,366
Laundromat	1987	Special	49,846	1,480
Laundry	1953	Special	49,585	6,500
Lanier Hall	1939	Residence	62,000	19,320
Library, J. D. Boyd	1969 1989	Classroom	1,050,000 23,037	
Library and Science Bldg.	1959 1989	Classroom	347,111	28,167
Maintenance Building	1928	General	2,500	4,600
Mechanical Arts Bldg.	1959	Classroom	113,031	22,646
Men's Tower (renamed W. S. Demby Men's Tower)	1973	Residence	1,832,639	66,240
Microbial Poultry Lab	1974	Lab	46,000	2,346
New Men's Dormitory (renamed Albert L. Lott Hall)	1962	Residence	362,627	29,226
New Women's Dormitory (renamed Mabel Thomas Hall)	1962	Residence	392,206	34,080
Nursing School (renamed Cora S. Balmat School of Nursing)	1985	Classroom	1,706,079	47,023
Oakland Chapel	1830 1976	General	94,000 125,000	18,832
Poultry Facility (renamed Luther Alexander/E. S. Burke Poultry Research Laboratory)	1987	Special	810,631	15,623

Appendix B

BUILDING	YEAR CON-STRUCTED	TYPE FACILITY	CONSTRUCTION COSTS	TOTAL SQ. FT.
President's Home	1830	Residence	6,500	
	1984		125,101	
Pressbox	1981	Special	279,413	2,160
Quonset 20 × 96	1961	General	2,500	1,920
Quonset 20 × 96	1961	General	2,500	1,920
Quonset 20 × 96	1961	General	2,500	1,920
Revels Hall	1967	Residence	600,000	41,781
Robinson Hall	1965	Residence	588,000	38,646
Rowan Model House	1830	Residence	5,700	2,775
			17,225	
Service Station	1947	Special	7,000	987
Silo (14 × 30) S-1	1953	Special	1,000	420
Stadium Dress, Facility	1981	Supplies	588,300	9,756
Storage Bldg. (Nursing)	1986	Special	80,703	1,036
Vehicle Storage & Machine	1967	Supplies	15,186	6,444
Vegetable Shed	1971	Supplies	12,000	1,220
Water Treatment Plant	1968	Supplies	134,350	650
	1978	Supplies	575,000	
Women's Tower (renamed Cleopatra D. Thompson Women's Tower)	1973	Residence	1,854,845	92,298

Source: Bureau of Building, Grounds and Real Property Management, Annual Capital Facilities Study, 1988.

Appendix C
ATHLETIC ACHIEVEMENTS

PLAYERS DRAFTED TO THE PROFESSIONAL RANKS
1952 – 1992

Football	Year Drafted	Drafted by
Jack Spinks	1952	Pittsburgh Steelers
Frank Purnell	1956	Cleveland Browns
Williams Bailey	1963	New York Giants
Smith Reed	1965	New York Giants
Samuel Shivers	1966	Minnesota Vikings
Eddie Johnson	1966	Minnesota Vikings
Donnie G. Wallace	1966	Minnesota Vikings
Prince Borton	1967	Washington Redskins
Robert Brown	1967	St. Louis Cardinals
Raymond Brown	1967	St. Louis Cardinals
Joe Robinson	1967	Minnesota Vikings
St. Elmo Cain	1967	New Orleans Saints
Leroy Hardy	1967	Houston Oilers
Terry Lewis	1967	Los Angeles Rams
Craig Walker	1967	Montreal Beavers
Willie Banks	1968	New York Giants
James Williams	1968	Cincinnati Bengals
Joe Owens	1969	New Orleans Saints
Lawrence Watkins	1969	Detroit Lions
Dock Mosley	1969	Pittsburgh Steelers
Joe Leasy	1969	Boston Patriots
Robert Bell	1969	Ottawa Lions
Rayford Jenkins	1970	Kansas City Chiefs
David Hodley	1970	Kansas City Chiefs
Willie Peake	1970	San Francisco 49ers
Lawrence Estes	1970	New Orleans Saints
David Washington	1970	Denver Broncos
Marvin Weeks	1970	Cincinnati Bengals
Leroy Byars	1971	Miami Dolphins
Willie Young	1971	Miami Dolphins
Cleophus Johnson	1971	Denver Broncos
Floyd Rice	1971	Houston Oilers
Willie Alexander	1971	Houston Oilers
Richard Sowells	1971	New York Giants
Eddie Hackett	1971	Minnesota Vikings

Franklin Roberts	1972	Minnesota Vikings
Leon Gorror	1972	Buffalo Bills
Robert Penchion	1972	Buffalo Bills
Harry Gooden	1972	San Diego Chargers
Charles Davis	1973	New England Patriots
Clifton Davis	1973	New York Giants
Willie McGee	1973	Los Angeles Rams
Alex Price	1973	New Orleans Saints
Billy Howard	1974	Detroit Lions
Jimmy Davis	1974	Detroit Lions
Leonard Fairley	1974	Houston Oilers
Larry Cameron	1974	Denver Broncos
Bobby Huell	1974	Pittsburgh Steelers
Izell Gunner	1974	San Diego Chargers
Boyd Brown	1974	Denver Broncos
Francis Reynolds	1975	Los Angeles Rams
Willie Porter	1975	Dallas Cowboys
Adrian Capitol	1975	San Diego Chargers
Ernest Guynes	1975	Philadelphia Eagles
Jerry Dismuke	1975	New Orleans Saints
Barry Brady	1975	Chicago Bears
Lawrence Pillars	1976	New York Jets
Jimmy Giles	1977	Houston Oilers
Henry Bradley	1978	San Diego Chargers
Larry Willis	1979	Kansas City Chiefs
Roynell Young	1980	Philadelphia Eagles
Otis Wonsley	1980	New York Giants
Issiac Holt	1985	Minnesota Vikings
Wayne Dillard	1986	St. Louis Cardinals
Milton Mack	1987	New Orleans Saints
Elliott Smith	1989	San Diego Chargers
Michael Andrews	1989	Buffalo Bills
Jack Phillips	1989	Kansas City Chiefs
Gary Lewis, Jr.	1990	Los Angeles Raiders
Dwayne White	1990	New York Jets
Torrance Small	1992	New Orleans Saints
Cedric Tillman	1992	Denver Broncos

Baseball

Stanley Barker	1981	Detroit Tigers
Alfornia Jones	1981	Chicago White Sox
Keiver Campbell	1990	Toronto

Appendix C

Basketball

Willie Norwood	1969	Detroit Pistons
Julius Keyes	1969	Denver Rockets
Larry Smith	1980	Golden State Warriors
Albert Irving	1982	Golden State Warriors
Michael Phelps	1985	Seattle Supersonics

Other athletes also signed contracts as free agents in each of these sports. Sample statistics for football, basketball (men and women), and baseball follow:

FOOTBALL

CAREER LEADERS 1962 – 1991

Rank	Name	Years	At-Comp=Pct.	Int	TD	Yards
1	Richard Myles	82–85	748-366-.489	33	42	5474
2	Marvin Weeks	66–69	662-309-.497	38	55	4410
3	William Wooley	71–74	498-244-.490	34	24	3410
4	Jerone Vigne	85–87	456-223-.489	30	13	2951
5	Steve McNair	91–now	338-189-559	15	24	2895
6	Fred Davis	60–63	287-136-.474	19	27	2431
7	James McFarland	79–82	269-184-.392	31	12	2330
8	Fred "Air" McNair	88–89	261-141-.540	6	14	2311
9	Clarence Tolliver	68–70	247-91-.368	19	20	2045
10	Reginald Martin	89–now	280-134-.479	18	10	1819
11	Sherrod Green	78–81	307-121-.394	25	9	1620
12	John Steele	76–77	249-91-.365	9	19	1426
13	Willie Outlaw	74–77	301-110-.365	25	13	1418
14	Robert Raines	82–85	179-86-.480	13	10	1174
15	Larry Brown	85–87	148-74-.500	4	8	986
16	Marshall Hattix	63–66	118-77-.568	10	8	946
17	Larry Rodgers	70–73	145-51-.360	10	9	686

SINGLE SEASON HIGHS

Scoring

Most Points: 78 Perry Qualls, 1984
Most Touchdowns: 13 Perry Qualls, 1984
Most PAT's: 46 George Green, 1984
Most Field Goals: 13 Wilfredo Rosales, 1979

Rushing
Most Rushes: 218 Gregory Jones, 1980
Highest Average Rushes per Game: 21.8 Gregory Jones, 1980
Most Net Yards Gained: 1,054—Gregory Jones, 1980
Highest Average Yards Per Game: 105.4 Gregory Jones, 1980
Highest Average Gain Per Rush (Min. 5 Rushes PG): 6.7 Jarvis Jenkins, 1989

Passing
Most Attempts: 338 Steve McNair, 1991
Most Completions: 189 Steve McNair, 1991
Best Completion Percentage: 650 Robert Raines, 1984
Most Yards Gained: 2,895 Steve McNair, 1991
Most Touchdown Passes: 24 Steve McNair, 1991

Total Offense
Most Plays: 395 Steve McNair, 1991
Most Yards Rushing & Passing: 3,137 Steve McNair, 1991

Pass Receiving
Most Receptions: 63 Milton Barney, 1986
Most Yards Gained: 1068 Small, 1991
Most Touchdown Catches: 9 Oscar Martin, 1968, 1969 and 10 Small, 1989, 11 Cedric, Tillman, 1991

Interceptions
Most Interceptions: 9 David Hadley, 1968 and 9 Leslie Frazier, 1979
Most Yards Returned: 157 Leslie Frazier, 1979

Punting
Most Punts: 80 Lee Williams, 1981
Best Average: 40.8 Lee Williams, 1980

Punt Returns
vs. Most Returns: 28 Milton Barney, 1985
Best Average: 13.1 Milton Barney, 1984
Most Touchdowns: 1 Several Players

Kickoff Returns
Most Returns: 23 Eric Moon, 1982
Best Average: 28.3 Barry Robinson, 1986
Most Touchdowns: 1 Several Players

Tackles
Most Total Tackles: 134 Dennis Campbell, 1980

Appendix C

Record Since Joining the SWAC in 1962

Year	SWAC Record	Overall Record
1962	2-5-0	4-5-0
1963	0-7-0	3-7-0
1964	3-4-0	5-5-0
1965	2-4-1	3-5-1
1966	2-3-2	5-3-2
1967	3-4-0	5-4-0
*# 1968	6-1-0	9-1-0
*# 1969	6-0-1	8-0-1
1970	6-0-0	8-1-0
1971	4-2-0	6-3-0
1972	4-1-1	5-3-1
1973	3-2-1	7-2-1
*# 1974	5-1-0	9-2-0
1975	3-3-0	6-3-1
* 1976	5-1-0	8-2-0
1977	2-4-0	3-8-0
1978	2-3-1	5-4-1
* 1979	5-1-0	8-2-0
1980	3-3-0	6-4-0
1981	3-3-0	5-5-0
1982	3-3-0	5-6-0
1983	4-3-0	7-3-0
1984	7-0-0	8-1-0
1985	5-2-0	7-3-0
1986	5-2-0	5-5-0
1987	5-2-0	6-3-0
1988	4-3-0	6-4-0
1989	5-2-0	7-3-0
1990	2-4-0	2-7-0
1991	4-2-1	7-2-1

*SWAC Champions   #National Black Champions

NCAA RECORDS HELD BY ALCORN STATE (DIVISION I-AA):

Best defense in I-AA in 1988
17th in All-Time Winning Percentage as a Team (.601)
1979 Total Defense and Rushing Defense Champions
1987 Pass Defense Champions
Most Career Interceptions, Issiac Holt, 1981–84, 24 interceptions, 319 yards, 13.3 average

Lowest Team Completion Percentage Allowed, 32.3%, 1979 (76 of 235)
Most Consecutive Completed Passes: 18-Jerome Vigne vs. Florida
   A. & M. Oct. 18, 1986
Lowest Percentage of Passes Intercepted: 1.17% Richard Myles, 1985 (3 of 256)

OVERALL ALCORN COACHING LEDGER

Coach	Year	Record
O. A. Ross	1922–23	44-15-12
Morton	1934–35	1-7-10
A. A. Abraham	1936, 38, 41, 42	14-8-7
R. Alba	1946	1-8-0
Leroy Harris	1937, 39, 40, 47	19-11-1
Dwight Fisher	1948–56	56-28-7
W. Broadus	1957	1-8-0
Frank Purnell	1960–63	14-20-0
E. E. Simmons	1958–59	3-15-0
Marino Casem	1964–85	132-65-8
Theo Danzy	1986–90	26-23-0
Cardell Jones	1991–93	14-6-1

BASKETBALL
(Men)

CAREER RECORD

Total Points

1. 2,527 Richard Smith
2. 1,973 Willie Norwood
3. 1,849 Larry Smith
4. 1,740 Aaron Brandon
5. 1,727 Johnny McGill
6. 1,694 Dellie Robinson
7. 1,679 George Holloway
8. 1,664 Michael Phelps
9. 1,644 Odell Agnew
10. 1,595 Joseph Martin
11. 1,525 Charles Watkins
12. 1,512 Walter Ned
13. 1,507 Vernon Purnell
14. 1,492 Alfred Milton

15. 1,490 William Bell
16. 1,391 Alfredo Monroe
17. 1,350 Tommy Collier
18. 1,284 Eddie Archie
19. 1,240 Nathaniel Archibald
20. 1,224 Levi Wyatt
21. 1,206 James Horton
22. 1,150 Ronnie Smith
23. 1,134 Albert Irving
24. 1,130 Eddie Baker
25. 1,124 Osborne Jordon
26. 1,122 Samuel Sing
27. 1,106 Tommy Davis
28. 1,058 David Palmer
29. 1,037 Andrew Tatum
30. 1,012 Joe Jenkins

Total Rebounds

1. 1,432 Alfred Milton (71-75)
2. 1,413 Willie Norwood (65-69)
3. 1,334 Larry Smith (76-80)
4. 1,247 Walter Ned (62-66)
5. 1,134 Dellie Robinson (72-76)
6. 1,035 Levie Wyatt (67-71)
7. 1,002 Clinton Wyatt (76-80)
8. 968 Tommy Collier (81-85)
9. 968 Nathaniel Archibald (70-74)
10. 885 Alfredo Monroe (75-79)

OVERALL RECORD OF COACHES

Name	Years	Record
H. M. Thompson	1944–45	2-4
L. T. Harris	1946–48	28-9
Dwight Fisher	1948–56	190-100
W. A. Broadus	1956–59	49-49
E. E. Simmons	1959–66	123-76
Robert Hopkins	1966–69	70-12
Davey Whitney	1969–89	395-199
Lonnie Walker	1989–93	37-77

BASKETBALL
(Women)

CAREER RECORD

Total Points

1. 2,111 Ella 'Pearl' Williams
2. 1,743 Lisa 'Duck' Powell
3. 1,291 Teresa Hooker
4. 1,252 Tami Varnado
5. 1,242 Lois Watkins
6. 1,170 Regina Wells
7. 1,023 Sherlanda Lewis
8. 959 Tonya Steele
9. 938 Deloris Williams
10. 848 Valerie Rockingham
11. 752 Polly Joiner
12. 702 Venita Bowie
13. 697 Laura Carson
14. 677 Diane Fuller
15. 637 Brenda Moody
16. 552 Vernita Miller
17. 551 Robbie Powell
18. 523 Iris Floyd
19. 498 Eva Freeman
20. 430 Renee Cameron
21. 425 Juanita Reed
22. 421 Faye Minor
23. 419 Dorothy Bartee

Total Rebounds

1. 1,058 Ella 'Pearl' Williams
2. 1,001 Lisa 'Duck' Powell
3. 764 Tami Varnado
4. 709 Teresa Hooker
5. 696 Deloris Williams
6. 653 Lois Watkins
7. 512 Valerie Rockingham
8. 479 Sherlanda Lewis
9. 441 Venita Bowie
10. 345 Polly Joiner
11. 329 Robbie Powell
12. 289 Dorothy Bartee

13. 286 Renee Cameron
14. 281 Regina Wells
15. 275 Laura Carson

OVERALL RECORD OF COACH SHIRLEY WALKER

Years	Record
1978–79	16-10
1979–80	12-11
1980–81	12-16
1981–82	10-15
1982–83	18-11
1983–84	23-7
1984–85	19-9
1985–86	19-8
1986–87	5-22
1987–88	13-15
1988–89	11-16
1989–90	17-12
1990–91	20-8
1991–92	20-7

BASEBALL

SINGLE SEASON PITCHING WINS

Rank	Win	Name	Year
1	10	Richard Pickett	1981
2	9	John Owens	1982
2	9	Michael Harris	1988
3-tie	8	Ricky Morris	1986
3-tie	8	Richard Pickett	1979
5-tie	7	Alfornia Jones	1981
5-tie	7	Ronald Howard	1974
5-tie	7	Michael Harris	1987
8	6	John Harrington	1983
9-tie	5	Felix Pettaway	1974
9-tie	5	Johnny Owens	1974
9-tie	5	William Jackson	1972
9-tie	5	Ronald Howard	1972
9-tie	5	Ricky Morris	1985
9-tie	5	Delmar Sprouse	1985

9-tie	5	Ed Potts	1985
9-tie	5	Roy Hill	1987
9-tie	5	Brian Parker	1991
9-tie	5	Robert McGinty	1992

TEAM SEASON HIGHS

Most Wins: 24, 1978, 1979　　Most Losses: 25, 1990
Best Winning Pct.: .793 (23-6), 1981　　Most Games played: 44, 1992
*Most Consecutive Wins: 8, 1981　　Longest Losing Streak: 10, 1990
Longest Losing Streak: 10, 1990　　Most at Bats: 1164, 1992
Most Hits: 370　　Most Runs: 289, 1985
Best Batting Average: .368, 1985　　Most Doubles: 80, 1987
Most Triples: 24, 1979　　Most Homeruns: 20, 1981
Most RBIs: 241, 1985　　Most BB: 171, 1991
Most Stolen Bases: 103–126, 1985　　Best ERA: 2.75, 1974
Best Fielding Avg.: .967, 1977, 1981

*There was actually another ten-game winning streak in 1981, but it included three forfeits. The eight wins were actual wins on the field.

SINGLE SEASON ERA
(20 – 40 GAMES PLAYED)

Rank	Era	Name	Year
1	1.000	Aaron Jackson, RF	1983
2	1.000	Stanley Barker, LF	1981
3	1.000	Terry Fluker	1977
4	1.000	Floyd Hughes	1977
5	1.991	Willie Outlaw	1977
6	1.990	Matthew Parish	1974
7	1.988	Isiah Rounds	1990
8	1.988	Alvin Prowell	1977
9	.986	Cyrus Smith	1977
10	.984	Terrell Hunter	1976
11-tie	.981	Jimmy Giles	1974
12-tie	.981	Lionel Roberts, 1B	1983
13-tie	.980	Jerry Steele	1974
14-tie	.980	Terrell Hunter	1977
15	3.38	Michael Jackson	1984
16	3.39	Richard Pickett	1979
17	3.54	Michael Jackson	1983

18	3.54	Felix Pettaway	1974
19	3.57	Herman Randle	1975
20	3.61	Ricky Morris	1986
21	3.90	Bennie Parker	1976
22	4.03	Ricky Morris	1984
23	4.05	Larry Adams	1981
24	4.06	Michael Harris	1987
25	4.25	Ed Potts	1985

SINGLE SEASON BATTING AVERAGE
(20 – 40 GAMES PLAYED)

Rank	Batting Avg.	Name	Year	Hits-AB
1	.546	Greg Daniels	1983	55–101
2-tie	.458	Greg Daniels	1984	38–83
2-tie	.458	Jesse Jackson	1985	40–118
4	.456	Stanley Barker	1981	36–79
5	.454	Steve Brown	1985	54–119
6	.449	Dale Hughes	1983	44–98
7	.444	Terrell Hunter	1977	36–81
8	.442	Gilbert Reed	1983	42–95
9	.433	Terry Fluker	1974	18–43
10	.415	Paul Miller	1972	42–101
11	.414	Paul Miller	1974	29–76
12	.411	Willie Outlaw	1977	21–90
13	.404	Alfonzo Sumpter	1981	19–47
14-tie	.400	Aaron Watson	1974	34–85
14-tie	.400	Frank Booker	1979	28–70
16-tie	.391	James Harris	1985	45–115
18	.390	Anthony Taylor	1977	18–46
19	.385	Dale Hughes	1981	30–77
20	.384	Matthew Cain	1986	28–73
21	.382	Rodney Burnette	1992	55–144
21-tie	.381	Kevin Stackhouse	1985	37–97
21-tie	.381	Ike Williams	1983	40–105
23	.377	Eugene Spann	1972	27–98
24	.375	John Steele	1974	33–88
25	.373	Steve Brown	1986	31–83
25	.373	Michael Harris	1989	44–118

Appendix D
National Association for Equal Opportunity in Higher Education Distinguished Alumni of the Year

1979
Albert Lott
Luther Alexander
Cleopatra D. Thompson
Andrew Graves
Henry Smith

1980
Herman W. Coleman
E. Albert Dumas
Nebraska Mays

1981
William C. Boykin, Sr.
Wright L. Lassiter, Jr.
Louise Q. Lawson

1982
Lavaughn Venchael Booth
Montague S. Lawrence
Joseph T. Travillion, Jr.

1983
Douglas R. Bender
Charles Edward Christian
Verga L. Edwards
Elmer J. Moore
Jimmie L. Powell
Howard H. Robinson

1984
Marion L. Hayes
Joshua Hill
Charles E. Johnson
Clemont L. Johnson
James S. Smith, Jr.
Roy Thigpen
Willie L. Wright

Charles Beckwith
Felix Dunn
Jesse E. McGee

1985
John Rigsby
Joseph Haynes
Grady Jordan
Phillip West
Romaine L. Richards
E. J. Stringer
I. L. Thomas
Shelby R. Wilkes
William Mills
Eddie Smith

1986
Alyce Griffin Clarke
Brasco H. Coleman
Emiel Hamberlin
Charles E. Johnson
Llewellyn C. Peyton
Margaret B. Wilson

1987
Willie Charles Burton
Katie G. Dorsett
Roscoe S. Dukes, Sr.
Walter Edward Dukes
Allene Demby Gayles
Worth E. Haynes, Sr.
Jewell C. Lockhart
Handy Williamson, Jr.

1988
Charles Bridges
Martha Brooks
Ethel R. Bryant

Reginald Head
Willie Hoskin
George Hull, Jr.
Samuel Jackson
Adam Jenkins, Jr.
Mack Payton
Franklin Shelton
James Stewart

1989
Fannie Brown
James E. Brown
Robert Bowles
Robert Collier
James Langin
Walter W. Martin
Oscar Mason
Raymond Trass
Malvin A. Williams

1990
Mary Demby
James Hill, Sr.
Walter Jones
Curtis C. Bass
Marzine Green, Jr.
D. W. Wilburn
Irving Bullet
Eddie Morant

Theodore West
Randolph Walker
James Wright
Leon Ware

1991
Alpha L. Morris
Robert R. Nelson
Richard A. Polk
Melvin E. Walker, Jr.

1992
Alfred Arrington
Fannie Gee
Johnny Greenwood
Brenza Irving
Frank Jones
Thomas M. Moman, Jr.
Joseph Reese
Betty W. Sanders
Charles Tillman

1993
Linda Haynes
Clinton Hunt
Vera G. Hunter
Willie L. Simmons
Jay T. Smith, Sr.

Appendix E
Centennial Roll 1871 – 1971

A. D. Snodgrass	1882
Oliver Lewis Coleman	1886
Beulah Robinson	1888
James Frank Norwood	1891
Levi J. Rowan	1893
Preston Sewell Bowles	1895
J. E. Johnson	1902
J. H. Mosely	1882
Joseph E. Walker	1903
S. W. A. Miller	1905
A. M. Strange	1905
A. E. Perkins	1906
John H. Mitchell	1908
Z. A. Lenoir	1909
Richard Sylvester Grossley	1911
William Purvis Hill	1911
A. J. Noel, Sr.	1911
Esau Simmons	1912
George W. Cox	1914
Daniel W. Ambrose	1918
George W. Lee	1918
W. B. Nelson	1919
Zelma Patton Price	1919
J. B. Cooley	1920
E. W. Reeves	1921
L. S. Alexander	1925
Glover (Gus) Gardner	1925
W. S. Demby	1926
Walter Strotha Davis	1926
I. E. Edwards	1926
Allen D. Fobbs	1926
Ruth Rowan Sanders	1928
Joe Y. Woodard	1928
James Hall Bolden	1928
Ruby Cowan Stutts Lyells	1929
Ruth Innman Hurd	1929
J. E. Magee, Sr.	1929
E. T. Magee, Sr.	1929
Alice Laws Tanner	1930

Cullie E. Bickham, Sr.	1930
Daniel Webster Lindsey	1930
William (Bill) Foster	1931
John Dewey Boyd	1931
Hugh H. Lee	1931
Milan W. Davis	1932
Willie Mae Latham Taylor	1932
Cleopatra D. Thompson	1932
J. E. Miller	1932
David Wilson Wilburn	1933
William Earthy Ammons	1933
Thomas E. Roberson	1933
R. E. Weddington	1933
W. L. Eiland	1933
N. R. Burger	1933
A. D. Clark	1934
John Howeard	1934
I. C. Pittman	1935
Benjamin Franklin McLaurin	1935
Delores E. Magee	1935
George W. Spears	1935
George J. Bacon	1938
Clinton C. Armstrong	1938
Venchael L. Booth	1940
Robert Hunter	1940
Thomas M. Moman, Jr.	1940
Chester L. Marcus	1941
Albert L. Lott	1941
Lula Bell Stewart	1941
W. C. Boykin	1942
Hampton P. Wilburn	1942
Montiaque S. Lawrence	1943
Sonia Wilmetta Jefferson	1947
Beatrice Jordan Boose	1947
C. J. Duckworth	1948
Robert Seaborn	1948
Sidney L. Richmond	1949
Jesse A. Morris, Sr.	1950
Purvis V. McMillian	1950
Charles L. Davis	1950
Willie F. Jackson	1950
Rube Harrington, Jr.	1951
James Charles Evers	1951

Appendix E

Jesse J. Featherstone	1952
Waldo James	1952
Johnnie R. Spinks	1952
Medgar Wiley Evers	1952
Robert Prater	1953
Charles Humphrey	1953
Dorris E. Garrett	1953
E. E. Spencer	1959
George M. Tatum	1961
Willie R. Bullock	1962
Jerry Hankins	1962
Leonard E. Brown	1962
Joseph E. Lloyd	1963
James Morris Clark	1964
Earnest Antoine Minola	1965
Johnnie B. Collins	1965
Joyce Mollye Sims	1965
John W. Sims	1966
Louise Spears	1966
Charles Beckwith	1966
Julius Eric Thompson	1969

Appendix F
Presidents of Local Alumni Chapters, 1993

Location	President
Auburn, Alabama	Clifford Jones
Bassfield, Mississippi	Joseph Reese
Baton Rouge, Louisiana	Willie Burton
Bay Springs, Mississippi	Tommie Jones
Beaumont, Texas	Willie Washington
Belzoni, Mississippi	Marion Brown
Biloxi, Mississippi	Bertha Watts
Bronx, New York	Walter Crump
Brookhaven, Mississippi	Dexter Holloway
Canton, Mississippi	Julia Thigpen
Centreville, Mississippi	Alma J. Anderson
Chicago, Illinois	Joseph C. Risby
Clarksdale, Mississippi	James Miller
Cleveland, Mississippi	James Langin
Cleveland, Ohio	Theon L. Jones
Collins, Mississippi	Johnny B. Barnes
Columbus, Mississippi	Robert Jordan
Columbia, Mississippi	Larry Jenkins
Como, Mississippi	Dorothy Kerney
Dallas, Texas	Lorna Ramsey
Daly City, California	Kenneth Coleman
Edwards, Mississippi	Robert Johnson
Fayette, Mississippi	Jesse Harness
Gary, Indiana	Lorine P. Minor
Grand Blanc, Michigan	Percy Magee
Greenville, Mississippi	Jewell Lockhart
Greenwood, Mississippi	Mildred Neal
Grenada, Mississippi	Johnnie M. Shell
Hattiesburg, Mississippi	John H. Anderson
Hazlehurst, Mississippi	Curley Linson
Indianola, Mississippi	Shirley Burks
Jackson, Mississippi	Warren Cox
Lansing, Michigan	John Hearns
Laurel, Mississippi	Frankie Peyton
Lorman, Mississippi	Kenneth Simmons
Los Angeles, California	Tommie Ratcliff

Mableton, Georgia	Edna Brumfield
Macon, Georgia	Shirley Washington
Magnolia, Mississippi	Leon Sartin
Marion, Mississippi	Mitchell Howard, Jr.
McCarley, Mississippi	Laura Davis
Memphis, Tennessee	Frank Davis
Milwaukee, Wisconsin	Lemuel Killins
Minneapolis, Minnesota	Lewis Cooper
Monticello, Mississippi	James Hill
Morton, Mississippi	Freddie Owens
Moss Point, Mississippi	Grady McMillan
Nashville, Tennessee	George Hull, Jr.
Natchez, Mississippi	Michael Wynn
New Orleans, Louisiana	Eula Beckwith
Picayune, Mississippi	Gayle Bledsoe
Port Gibson, Mississippi	Gloria Liggans
Plantesville, Mississippi	Harold Arrington
Reston, Virginia	Fannie Gee
Shorewood, Illinois	Mary E. Greenwood
Savannah, Georgia	Alice C. Wright
Shreveport, Louisiana	Jerry E. Paige
Saginaw, Michigan	Willie J. Gill
Southfield, Michigan	Irma Walton
San Antonio, Texas	Brenda Jones
St. Louis, Missouri	Winston Fouche
Tchula, Mississippi	Pastella Hampton
Tupelo, Mississippi	Ira Rupect
Tylertown, Mississippi	Amos Newman, Jr.
Vicksburg, Mississippi	John Walls
Waynesboro, Mississippi	Roosevelt Staten
West Point, Mississippi	Warren Stamps
Winona, Mississippi	Annie G. Anthony
Yazoo City, Mississippi	Peter Beston
Yellowspring, Ohio	Margaret Jackson

Appendix G
Catalogue of Alcorn State University, 1872 – 1873

CATALOGUE

OF THE

OFFICERS AND STUDENTS

OF

ALCORN UNIVERSITY,

AT

OAKLAND, MISSISSIPPI,

SECOND YEAR, 1872-'73.

JACKSON, MISS.:
KIMBALL, RAYMOND & CO., BOOK AND JOB PRINTERS,
1873.

Board of Trustees.

REV. HYRAM R. REVELS, D. D., President;

HON. JAMES J. SPELMAN, Secretary;

COL. SAMUEL J. IRELAND,	REV. JESSE F. BOULDEN,
HON. AMBROSE HENDERSON,	HON. GEORGE F. BROWN,
HON. WILLIAM H. GIBBS,	GEN. WILLIAM W. DEDRICK,
HON. DOCTOR STITES;	HON. MERRIMAN HOWARD,
HON. JAMES J. SPELMAN,	HON. ROBERT GLEED.

Executive Committee.

GEORGE F. BROWN, W. W. DEDRICK, JAMES J. SPELMAN.

Treasurer.

ROBERT H. WOOD, Esq.

Academic Department.

Branches of Study.

Mathematics.

Mental Arithmetic, Higher Arithmetic, University Arithmetic, Algebra, Geometry.

English Language.

Reading, Writing, Grammar, English and American Literature, History, Elocution.

Miscellaneous.

Geography, Natural Philosophy, Chemistry, Natural History.

College Preparatory Department.

FIRST YEAR.

First Term.

LATIN—Introductory Book .... HARKNESS.
HISTORY—
MATHEMATICS—Arithmetic.................................... WHITE.

Second Term.

LATIN—Introductory Book..................................... HARKNESS.
READER AND GRAMMAR.. HARKNESS.
HISTORY—
MATHEMATICS—Arithmetic..................................... WHITE.

Third Term.

LATIN—Cæsar.. HARKNESS.
HISTORY—
MATHEMATICS—Arithmetic..................................... WHITE.

SECOND YEAR.

First Term.

LATIN—Cicero's Orations.
GREEK—First Book... HARKNESS.
    Or First Lessons...................................... WHITON.
MATHEMATICS—Algebra.. RAY.

Second Term.

LATIN—Cicero's Orations.
GREEK—First Book... HARKNESS.
    Or First Lessons...................................... WHITON.
GRAMMAR.. HADLEY.
MATHEMATICS—Algebra.. RAY.

Third Term.

LATIN—Virgil.
GREEK—First Book... HARKNESS.
    Or First Lessons...................................... WHITON.
MATHEMATICS—Algebra.. RAY.

Declamations and Compositions weekly, throughout the Course.

Classical Department.

Requisites for Admission.

Candidates for the Freshman Class are examined in the folllowing books, or their equivalents:

GREEK—Harkness' First Book, or Whiton's First Lessons.

LATIN—Latin Grammar; Harkness' Reader; Cæsar; Cicero's Orations; Virgil.

MATHEMATICS—Arithmetic; Algebra, to Quadratic Equations.

ENGLISH—English Grammar; Geography.

Candidates for Advanced Standing, in addition to the above studies, are examined in the studies that have been pursued by the class which they propose to enter, or in others equivalent to them.

Course of Study.

Freshman Class.

First Term.

LATIN—Cicero de Senectute, et de Amicitia.
    Prose Composition..HARKNESS.
GREEK—Herodotus.
MATHEMATICS—Algebra...RAY.
ENGLISH—Rhetoric..QUACKENBOS.

Second Term.

LATIN—Livy...LINCOLN.
    Prose Composition..HARKNESS.
GREEK—Anabasis..BOISE.
    Prose Composition.
MATHEMATICS—Geometry..LOOMIS.
ENGLISH—Rhetoric..QUACKENBOS.

Third Term.

LATIN—Livy...LINCOLN.
    Liddell's History of Rome.
    Prose Composition..HARKNESS.
MATHEMATICS—Geometry..LOOMIS.
ENGLISH—Rhetoric..QUACKENBOS.

Themes and Declamations During the Year.

Sophomore Class.

First Term.

LATIN—Horace's Odes.
    Prose Composition..HARKNESS.
GREEK—Homer's Iliad..OWEN.
    Smith's History of Greece.
MATHEMATICS—Trigonometry, Mensuration, Surveying,
    and Navigation...LOOMIS.

Second Term.
LATIN—Horace's Satires and Epistles.
Bojesen's Manual of Greek and Roman Antiquities.
GREEK—Homer's Iliad..OWEN.
MATHEMATICS—Analytical Geometry.........................LOOMIS.

Third Term.
LATIN—Tacitus--Histories..TYLER.
GREEK..ÆSCHINES.
MATHEMATICS—Calculus...LOOMIS.

Themes and Declamations during the Year.

Junior Class.

First Term.
LATIN—Tacitus—Germania and Agricola.......................TYLER.
GREEK—Demosthenes on the Crown...........................CHAMPLIN.
NATURAL PAILOSOPHY—

Second Term.
LATIN—Quintillian.
GREEK—Plato's Gorgias..WOOLSEY.
NATURAL PHILOSOPHY—

Third Term.
LATIN—Satires of Juvenal.
GREEK—Prometheus, of Æschylus..............................WOOLSEY.
BOTANY..GRAY.
ASTRONOMY..LOOMIS.

Original Declamations before the University during the Year.

Senior Class.

First Term.
CHEMISTRY—
HUMAN INTELLECT...PORTER.
EVIDENCES OF CHRISTIANITY.................................HOPKINS.
ANATOMY AND PHYSIOLOGY—Lectures.
RHETORIC..WHALEY.

Second Term.
HUMAN INTELLECT..................................Porter.
GEOLOGY—Mineralogy.
POLITICAL ECONOMY—
ENGLISH LITERATURE..............................Shaw.

Third Term.
MORAL PHILOSOPHY...............................Fairchild.
CONSTITUTIONAL LAW—
ZOOLOGY—Lectures.
KAMES' ELEMENTS OF CRITICISMS—

Original Declamations before the University during the Year.

Scientific Department.

Requisites for Admission.

Candidates for the First Year must be thoroughly prepared for a complete examination in Reading, Spelling, Penmanship, English Grammar, Arithmetic, Geography and Algebra, to Quadratic Equations.

Candidates for Advanced Standing must be prepared for examination in the studies which the Class have pursued, or a satisfactory equivalent.

Scientific Course.

FIRST YEAR.

First Term.
ALGEBRA .... RAY.
PHYSIOLOGY—
HISTORY—
FREE DRAWING—

Second Term.
GEOMETRY .... LOOMIS.
BOOK-KEEPING—
HISTORY—
FREE DRAWING—

Third Term.
GEOMETRY .... LOOMIS.
BOTANY .... GRAY.
HISTORY—
FREE DRAWING—

Themes and Declamations during the Year.

SECOND YEAR.

First Term.
TRIGONOMETRY, MENSURATION, SURVEYING—
NAVIGATION .... LOOMIS.
GRECIAN HISTORY .... SMITH.
FRENCH, OR GERMAN—

Second Term.
ANALYTICAL GEOMETRY .... LOOMIS.
ROMAN HISTORY .... LIDDELL.
FRENCH, OR GERMAN—

Third Term.
ANALYTICAL GEOMETRY—
DESCRIPTIVE GEOMETRY—
FRENCH, or GERMAN—

Themes and Declamations during the Year.

THIRD YEAR.

First Term.
NATURAL PHILOSOPHY—
ZOOLOGY—
CALCULUS—
FRENCH, or GERMAN—

Second Term.
NATURAL PHILOSOPHY—
LOGIC..WHATELY.
ANALYTICAL MECHANICS—
FRENCH, or GERMAN—

Third Term.
ASTRONOMY..LOOMIS.
CHEMISTRY—
RHETORIC..WHATELY.
FRENCH, or GERMAN—

Original Declamations during the Year.

FOURTH YEAR.

First Term.
CHEMISTRY—
HUMAN INTELLECT..PORTER.
EVIDENCES OF CHRISTIANITY...............................HOPKINS.

Second Term.
HUMAN INTELLECT...PORTER.
GEOLOGY—Mineralogy.
POLITICAL ECONOMY—
ENGLISH LITERATURE......................................SHAW.

Third Term.

MORAL PHILOSOPHY.................. ....FAIRCHILD.
CONSTITUTIONAL LAW—
KAMES' ELEMENTS OF CRITICISM—

Original Declamations during the Year.

Calendar.

1873.
Oct. 1.....FIRST TERM BEGINS....................WEDNESDAY MORNING.
Dec. 19.....FIRST TERM ENDS.....................FRIDAY EVENING.

Vacation During the Holidays.

1874.
Jan. 5.....SECOND TERM BEGINS.................MONDAY MORNING.
Mar. 27.....SECOND TERM ENDS..................FRIDAY EVENING.
Mar. 30.....THIRD TERM BEGINS..................MONDAY MORNING.
July 10.....THIRD TERM ENDS.....................THURSDAY.

Religious Exercises.

Students are required to attend Church once on the Sabbath, Sabbath School and daily prayers, morning and evening, in the Chapel.

There are weekly prayer meetings, on Wednesday and Sunday evenings. These prayer meetings are conducted by the students.

Alcorn University.

Location and Buildings.

THIS UNIVERSITY occupies the site of the Institution formerly known as Oakland College. It is situated in Claiborne County, Mississippi, four and one-half miles north-east from Rodney, on the Mississippi River. The location is high and healthful, and the surroundings agreeable and attractive in an eminent degree. Oakland College was the oldest Academic Institution in the State, and for more than thirty years a seat of learning and science. These refining influences still pervade the country surrounding the University, and exercise their silent but potent influence. The campus in which are situated the University buildings, is a beautiful oak grove, gently undulating and clothed in a perennial dress of green verdure pleasing to the eye and conducive to health and quietude. It is far removed from the contaminating influence of town or city life. There are no haunts of dissipation to lead the unwary astray; but in the country, in the midst of a moral and highly cultivated community, the student is continually surrounded by all those influences which tend to develope his moral character during the period of his intellectual training.

The Buildings

Were all erected for Academic purposes. They consist of a chapel, three brick dormitories, and a number of frame cottages devoted to the same purpose, two college literary society halls, a President's house, and refectory with all necessary out-buildings for an establishment complete within itself, dedicated to the purposes of the maintenance and education of youths.

The Chapel

Is a large, substantial brick building, three stories in height and of dimensions 65x112 feet. It contains rooms for recitations, philosophical apparatus, laboratory, cabinet, library, and a hall sufficiently large to seat nine hundred persons. It has been thoroughly repaired, painted and renovated throughout; the recitation rooms have been provided with new desks and furniture, the walls whitened, and every apartment presents a neat and cheerful appearance.

The Dormitories

Are two story brick buildings 45x48 feet, each capable of accomodating thirty-two students. They are comparatively new, with substantial slate roofs, hard finish ceilings, dry, airy and comfortable; these have also been thoroughly repaired, painted and renovated. The frame cottages, five in number, have also been repaired and renovated. All the dormitories are furnished with good new bedsteads and comfortable bedding, and contain grates, tables, wash-stands and chairs.

The Literary Halls

Are elegant brick structures, two stories in height, about 50x80 and well adapted for literary exercises. The lower room in each building is furnished with handsome book cases and the upper stories furnished for society halls. No institution in the country has better facilities for these purposes so indispensable to the proper education of the American student. These halls have been repainted, and such necessary repairs put upon them as would preserve, them from going to decay. One of them will, for the present be used as a dormitory, in case the necessities of the University demand it.

The Refectory,

Or boarding house, is a large two story frame building with a basement; the basement contains the dining hall, a room capable of seating two hundred students; a store room and a pantry. The upper stories are devoted to the Superintendent and family, and rooms for the employees of the Institution. This building though frame, now nicely repainted white with green blinds, and extensive balconies, presents a handsome appearance, and is well calculated for the purpose for which it was constructed. A commodious kitchen, furnished with a fine cooking range, and a capacious wash house, are among the out-buildings attached to the refectory.

The President's House

Is a handsome two story frame with basement. It has been newly painted white, with green blinds, and was comfortably furnished by the Executive Committee at the opening of the University in 1871. The furniture as well as the building, is thus the property of the Institution. This building is situated convenient to the chapel and dormitories, and enables the President at all times to keep a watchful eye over the discipline and conduct of the students.

Professors' Houses.

There are several other frame cottages belonging to the Institution, and situated on its grounds, adapted to the use of Professors and their families; several of these cottages are commodious and comfortable, having been erected for the use of the members of the faculty of Oakland College.

The Farm

Of the University consists of two hundred and thirty-five acres, which will be increased to two hundred and seventy-five acres by the addition of the "Hunt Tract," on the 1st day of January, 1874. The land is diversified in character, and well adapted to the various purposes of a model or experimental farm. It contains hill land and valley, with 25 or 30 acres of rich bottom, which can be irrigated at all seasons from an elevated lake or pond and is well adapted to grasses. The land is all of more than average richness and produces good corn, cotton and all other crops germain to the climate. A fine

Orchard

Consisting of five hundred selected trees of different varieties of peach, pear, apple, etc., has been set out, and is in a thrifty growing condition. It is the intention, as it is the duty of the Institution to make the farm a model of agricultural beauty and fertility, and to develop a high order of scientific as well as practical agriculture. Good substantial fences have been built around all the improved land, and the whole tract will be put under fence without delay.

Origin and Endowment of the University.

Alcorn University was created by the Act of the Legislature of Mississippi, approved, May 13, 1871. By the Act of incorporation "the sum of fifty thousand dollars in cash is appropriated and set apart in the Treasury for each and every year of ten successive years, beginning on the first day of July, 1871, for the establishment and management of a seminary of learning, to be styled, Alcorn University of Mississippi."

In addition thereto, by Act of the Legislature, approved, May 13, 1871; Alcorn University was granted by the State three-fifths of the proceeds of the sale of the Agricultural College Land Scrip. This fund amounted to $189 000, three-fifths of which, or $113 400 became the property of Alcorn University, the income from which, under the terms of the donation is to be devoted to the maintenance of the Agricultural and Mechanical department of of the Institution. In compliance with his duties under the Act. the Governor has deposited in the State Treasury in trust for the University, as the result of the investment of the fund, $123,150, in State bonds, exclusive of $13,000 advanced out of the fund in part payment of the University tract. These bonds draw eight per cent. interest from the State, and all of them fall due within three years from the 1st of January, 1874. If reinvested on the same advantageous terms, this fund will rapidly increase, and add materially to the available income of the University.

Alcorn University.

Rules and Regulations.

Terms of Admission.

No young man will be received unless he brings a certificate of good moral character, and if he has been a pupil of another educational institution, he must bring the certificate of the principal thereof, or some teacher or professor, as to his good deportment while connected therewith. The student must be fourteen years of age, and must be able to sustain a creditable examination in orthography, reading, writing, the fundamental rules of arithmetic, and the general outlines of the geography of the United States, before he can be admitted to the primary department. The acquirements requisite for admission to the collegiate course are set forth under the proper head.

No discrimination is recognized by the Institution on account of color, caste, religion or other class disinctions.

Tuition.

No charge is made for tuition to students coming from this State. A matriculation fee of fifteen dollars is required from students coming from other States.

Board, Washing, etc.

The University furnishes board, washing, bed-room furniture, fuel and lights to each student, at the rate of ten dollars per month—payable monthly, in advance. Each student is, however, expected to furnish his own looking-glass, lamp, bucket and broom, which the University will supply at wholesale prices.

Discipline.

Every student, on being admitted into the University, pledges himself thereby to obey all the rules and regulations of the Institution, and to use his influence in maintaining law and order.

The rules of the University require every student to observe properly the Sabbath; to pay due deference to each member of the Faculty, and to treat with respect all visitors and employes.

Students are required to be punctual in attending all the exercises of the University; in observing the hours for study, and in discharging the various other duties.

Students are not permitted to use intoxicating drinks; to chew, smoke, snuff or use tobacco in any form. They are not allowed to play cards, dice, or any game of chance.

No student is allowed to leave the college grounds without permission.

Students, whose course of conduct is detrimental to themselves and to the University, will be suspended, dismissed or expelled, as the Faculty may think proper.

Examinations.

There are monthly examinations, on the last Thursday and Friday in each month of the academic year.

The annual examination is held just before commencement.

A record of the monthly examinations, and of the deportment of each student, is kept.

A certificate of the examinations and deportment of each student is sent to his parents, or guardian, at the end of each term.

Library, Cabinet, Apparatus, etc.

The Oakland College, in its long years of successful educational labors, accumulated a fine library of several thousand choice volumes; also, a very complete collection of natural history, geology, mineralogy, botany and curiosities. By permission and request of the trustees of Oakland College, from whom the Alcorn University was purchased, these valuable accumulations were left in possession of the present Institution. While not absolutely the property of the Alcorn University, they remain in its charge, and it is not anticipated that they will ever be removed. It is hoped, that at no distant day, the University will be able to purchase them. At all events, the trustees of Oakland have indicated no disposition to deprive the University of these invaluable adjuncts to her educational advantages. They are open to the inspection of students and visitors, and are not among the least of the benefits which Alcorn is enabled to afford her students over other educational institutions of the State.

The philosophical and chemical apparatus is also very elaborate and complete.

Free Scholarships.

By section 2922 of the Revised Code of 1871, the Governor is required to "appoint, biennially, three persons in each representative district, or county, in the State, to act as a board of examiners, whose duty it shall be to examine, in an annual convocation of representatives of the common schools of the representative district or county, all candidates for free scholarships in Alcorn University, * * * who shall grant, to the best answerer, a certificate of free scholarship for a matriculation term of four years in Alcorn University."

This free scholarship entitles such successful candidate to $100 per year from the common school fund of the district or county. Examinations for these scholarships will take place this year in the various counties under the superuision of the various County School Superintendents, and the Circuit and Chancery Judges of each district. Parents or students desiring to avail themselves of the benefits of the free scholarship will look to the board of examiners in the respective counties, to convene for their examination. The University can do no more than to point out the provisions of the law on the subject. The University has heretofore received the warrants of the various counties as cash, in payment of board and washing of free scholarship students, and will continue to do so until further notice; but students are particularly enjoined to see to it that the warrants, in their case, are transmitted to the President of the University coincident with their application for admission, as the University cannot assume the responsibility of collecting from the counties.

General Resume.

Alcorn University has been in operation less than two years, and yet, during the last session, it numbered an attendance of one hundred and seventy-nine enrolled students. Such marked prosperity has rarely attended the rise of any institution of learning. Its rapid and healthy growth presages a success far exceeding the most sanguine expectations of its most hopeful friends. Its organization, founded, as it is, on the most liberal and humane principles, meets the educational wants of the whole people, and supplies a void that had not been hitherto filled by any educational institution in the South. It has been fortunate in the selection of earnest, capable and efficient teachers—devoted solely to the moral and intellectual advancement of the youths placed under their charge. The Trustees have spared no exertion in the building-up of the Institution, and commending it to the good opinion and favor of the people of the State. They feel assured that it has been founded upon a sure and lasting basis, and that it has become one of those great moral forces which, when once started, cannot fail to increase and strengthen with the coming years. The Institution enjoys the bounty of the State, and to a degree, is under its care and protection. It is also the recipient of the munificent generosity of the general government, which will take an interest in its growth and prosperity. The finances of the University, notwithstanding some unfounded rumors or groundless charges to the contrary, have been cautiously and prudently managed. The property, costing $40,000, has been paid for, except $5000, not yet due. The buildings have all been put in thorough repair. The *campus* and improved farm have been enclosed with handsome and substantial fences; a wash-house and barn have been built; cisterns dug, and many necessary improvements made. The farm has been kept in a condition of cultivation, under the management of a capable agriculturist, and the chair of the mechanic arts is filled by a competent and practical instructor, as required by law.

The building-up of a great institution of learning, and making it perfect in all its parts, is necessarily a work of time; but the

Alcorn University, for the time it has been in operation, we feel justified in saying, has made such substantial progress as cannot but be gratifying to all its friends, and to the people of the State, meriting their continued favor and support, and presaging its future prosperity and success.

CATALOGUE

OF THE

◁OFFICERS AND STUDENTS▷

OF THE

ALCORN

Agricultural and Mechanical College,

Rodney, Mississippi,

1880-'81.

NEW ORLEANS:
L. GRAHAM & SON, PRINTERS, 127 GRAVIER ST.

1881.

Appendix H
Mission Statement, 1993

Philosophy

Alcorn State University is committed to the principle of access and quality in all its programs and services. The university actively recruits and admits qualified students without regard to race, color, nationality, gender, age, or physical handicaps. The university seeks to develop among its clientele a broad knowledge and understanding of the basic principles and values necessary to perform intelligently and responsibly as effective citizens in a free and democratic society.

In performing its legislated functions as a land-grant institution, Alcorn envisions the fundamental and historical concern for preparing its students to effectively live in the mainstream of contemporary America. The institution strives to prepare graduates who are useful, proficient, efficient, of good character, scholarship and democratic living, and a program of liberal education which seeks to help each student attain his/her rightful place in society.

Mission Statement

Alcorn State University is a co-educational, land-grant, liberal arts, science and teacher education public institution offering programs leading to associate (in nursing only), baccalaureate, master's, and educational specialist degrees. The primary purpose of the university is to provide well-rounded quality educational programs to meet the needs of all students. While the university is committed to the further development of educational programs to serve the best interests, needs, and aspirations of talented students, it is also sensitive to and active in educating those students who suffer under the handicaps of socioeconomic and cultural deprivation.

The university seeks to meet the higher education needs primarily of the region and state, as well as the nation. To assume the role of a citadel of learning where scholars are freely encouraged to seek new truths and make the proper application of existing knowledge for the betterment of mankind is regarded as the primary aim and mission of Alcorn State University. The university is committed to providing the support programs and services necessary to facilitate the optimum success of each student.

Long-Range Goals

In accordance with and in support of its purposes and philosophy, the institution seeks to achieve the following long-range (continuing) goals:

Appendix H

1. To prepare students for scholarship and service in the areas of general and applied knowledge.

2. To develop leadership, in general, and in areas peculiar to the various curricular offerings for Mississipi, the United States, and the world.

3. To perform the roles and functions of a land-grant university in the areas of teaching, research, and extension services.

4. To contribute various educational services to meet the needs of the community at large.

5. To provide curricula and other services to respond to the demands of a dynamic democratic society.

6. To provide such diversification of specialized educational programs as to accommodate students with varying educational and occupational interests and levels of potential for achievement.

7. To provide an undergraduate education that will enable students to continue their work in graduate and professional schools, and to engage in teaching and other professions.

8. To provide graduate programs which enable students to obtain advanced training in specialized fields and to contribute to the advancement of knowledge and new truths through scholarly research and inquiry.

9. To strengthen and maintain a viable comprehensive planning, management, and evaluation system in order to facilitate effective decision making, resource allocation and utilization, fiscal accountability and program review, and evaluation.

10. To achieve and maintain optimum student retention by providing effective services in the areas of student advisement, counseling, tutoring, cultural activities, and instructional methodologies.

11. To secure the financial resources necessary to carry out the mission and goals of the institution.

12. To provide opportunities for students to develop as responsible citizens and scholars in a democratic society by maintaining a campus atmosphere which is safe, healthy, and conducive to cultural, personal, and social development.

Appendix I
Golden Diploma Recipients
1933 – 1943

1933
Roscoe E. Alexander
Thelma Bailey
Annie Barron
Newton Billups
Geraldine Brown
Wayne Calbert
Albert Clark
Clarence Cooper
Josephine Davis
Susetta Gibson
Estella Green
James Gresham
McCleveland Harver
Elnora Howard
Arnie James
Ulysses Johnson
Fannie Luckette
Elizabeth Majors
Sylvester Marshall
Orange McNair
John Morris
Anne Newman
Emma Newman
James Norman
Bertha Parker
Issac Pollard
Richard Randall
Thomas Robinson
Lamar Scoby
Curtis Seaberry
Aaron Thomas
J. P. Watts
Robert Weddington
Melvin Wiggins
D. W. Wilburn
Andrew Wollwans

1934
Lannyus A. Armstrong
Estus L. Barron
Harvey Lee Beale
Kenneth Charles Brooks
Mary Kate Brown
Nathaniel Burger
Albert D. Clark
Malcolm Leon Coleman
Goldie Taylor Collins
Laura Powell Gibson
Henry Leroy Graves
Leroy Percy Johnson
Tecumeseh C. McLaurin
Willis Turner Sias
Bernice Allen Stimley
Lawrence Guice Towers
Cordelia Ella Watkins
Julius Pettibone Watts
Eugene Webster

1935
Florene D. Allen
Addie N. Burger
William Camphor
Charles Coleman
Milton Dean
Charles Fletcher
Meredith Johnson
Vernie T. Magee
Benjamin McLaurin
Annie Patton
Edgar Rails
Maggie Redmond
Calvin Rhodes
Mahala Smith
Pernella Smith

George W. Spears
Rufus Stennis
David E. Thomas
Maggie L. Turner
Annie White
Hilliard P. Young

1936
Hettie Smith Cain
Julia M. A. Dillon
Edward Duncan
Velma Palmer Elliot
Rollo Fletcher
Odessa Hayes Graves
Nola J. C. Hayden
Theodric B. Hendrix
Sargent P. Jackson
Curtis Kelly
Eva Jones McCune
Lewis S. Sinclair
Ruth C. Powell Sledge
Leola B. H. Turner
Ruby L. Wheatley

1937
Jason W. Allen
Bernice Bishop
Willie Calbert
Ruby W. Coleman
Joseph Collins
Katie Collins
Joseph Davis
Edith Dickens
Bertha W. Edwards
Annie N. Gaston
Ruby Hammond
Laura H. Hearn

William Hunt
Marguerite B. Jeffries
Shirley Neal
George Russell
Ruby Jones Seymour
Alma S. Warren
Claude Watson

1938
Charles Carson
Bennie W. Cooper
C. F. Edwards
J. W. Grantham
Lillie Stutts Handy
Lela Hawkins Hardy
Joseph Henderson
John H. Hope
J. W. Keller
Inez Stutts Knowles
Robert Lee
James Miller
Lillian O. Palmer
Branch Ray
M. C. Sterling
Robert L. Stewart
Willie Mae L. Taylor
Cleopatra D. Thompson
William H. Travis

1939
Sidney Brent
Frank D. Boston
Lawrence Campbell
Hooker D. Davis
Allie V. Dunn
Arnie W. Downs
James H. Gross
Mary L. Howard
Rufus F. James
James McKay
Lula K. O'Neal
John L. Page, Sr.

Wallace C. Rials
Anna Ross
Nolan Tate

1940
Tyree J. B. Pendleton
Edward W. Barrett
Vancheal Booth
John Boston
Helen D. Coleman
Allen L. Coney
Inez G. Gray
Eugene Isaac
Millicent B. Jackson
Celeste J. Jacques
Thomas J. Jones
Lillian C. Lane
Mary H. Masters
Thomas Moman
Willy R. Patton
Elizabeth R. Pharr
Felton P. Posey
William D. Purnell
Henry R. Smith
Willa N. Smith
Alex C. Warren

1941
Syna M. Boston
Aurabelle M. Caggins
Luberta G. Caldwell
John W. Davis
Walter M. Downs
Ruth U. Hansen
Claude Higgins
Audell O'Neil Horton
Lois B. Ingram
Allene R. Leggette
Joseph D. Leggette
Dr. Albert Lott
Alphonse Marks
Willie Y. Miller

Odessai Rials
Horace D. Robinson
Elois B. Rogers
Annie B. Smith
Jessie J. Smith, Jr.
Willie D. Smith
Etheline B. Stewart
Emmett J. Stringer
Leonard Walker
Dessye M. Warren
Amos Wright
Florence N. Wright

1942
Juanita A. Adams
Mildred D. Allen
Ada B. Brown
William Brown
Alma E. Carter
Annie Clemons
Eunice Conley
M. Alberta Delgado
Helen Diamond
Pinkie L. D. Ellis
Alma Coney Evans
John Luther Frisby
John Hannah
Eva H. Harris
Isom Herron
Juanita Herron
Vera Gadsberry Hunter
Zeddie Q. Hyler
Walter J. Jones
Ireland O'Brien Kee
Hattie M. Knox
James S. Logan
Mary B. Marks
Aretta B. Moore
Cyrus H. Nero
Dorothy H. Overstreet
Frank R. Robinson
George Robinson

Charles Rowlett   Myrtle W. Wyche   Corrine B. Porter
Henry J. Sanderson   Rose B. Wynn   Mattie B. Reed
Exermenia Searcy   Flora G. Stringer
Ernestine P. Strong   *1943*   Carmen P. Walker
Issac L. Thomas   Mildred J. Armstrong   Albert Woolfolk
William Leroy Triplett   Douglas L. Conner   Loretha Woolfolk
Charles L. Varnado   Bessie Ruth Johnson
Grace Varnado   Clymathes B. King

A NOTE ON SOURCES

The following sources were used in the writing of the history of Alcorn:

University Yearbooks
University Catalogs
National Council for Accreditation of Teacher Education Documents
Southern Association of Colleges and Schools Documents
Institutional Self Studies
Departmental Self Studies
The *Alcorn Herald*
ASU Bi-weekly Bulletins
Administrative Council Minutes
Industry Cluster Minutes/Reports
Memos from Administrative Heads
Faculty Senate Minutes
Alumni Newsletters
The President's Annual Message to Alumni
Biennial Reports to the Board of Trustees of Institutions of Higher Learning
Interviews with Administrators, Faculty, Staff, Students, Alumni, and Community Leaders
Alcorn State University Long Range Plan
ASU Foundation Reports
The *Alcorn Report*
The *Alumnus*
College Handbook
The Student Guide
Alcorn State University Financial Reports
Paper on Alcorn written by Maggie Musgrove Atlas (Mississippi Department of Archives and History)

Paper on Alcorn written by R. M. Calloway, 1942 (Mississippi Department of Archives and History)
Paper on Alcorn written by Ruth D. Bates, 1951 (Alcorn State University Library, The Alcorn Room)
Alcorn State University Facilities Master Plan
Alcorn State University Fact Book

OTHER SOURCES

Conner, Douglas L. with John F. Marszalek. *A Black Physician's Story, Bringing Hope in Mississippi*. Jackson: University Press of Mississippi, 1985.

Davis, W. Milan. *Pushing Forward*. Okolona: Okolona Industrial School, 1938.

Dunbar, Rowland. *Mississippi*. Spartanburg, South Carolina: Reprint Company, Publishers, 1976.

Dunham, Merlerson Guy. *Centennial History of Alcorn A & M College*. Hattiesburg: University and College Press of Mississippi, 1971.

Jenkins, Robert L. *Black Voices in Reconstruction: The Senate Careers of Hiram R. Revels and Blanche K. Bruce*. Thesis submitted to Mississippi State University, 1975.

McMillen, Neil R. *Dark Journey—Black Mississippians in the Age of Jim Crow*. Champaign: University of Illinois Press, 1990.

Rogers, Tammy Wayne. "Oakland College, 1830–1871." *Journal of Mississippi History*, May 1974.

Sansing, David G. *Making Haste Slowly: The Troubled History of Higher Education in Mississippi*. Jackson and London: University Press of Mississippi, 1990.

Sewell, George A. "Alcorn A & M: Pioneer in Black Pride." *Crisis*, April 1972.

Smith, Jay T., Sr. *Origin and Development of Industrial Education at Alcorn Agricultural and Mechanical College*. Ann Arbor, Michigan: Dissertation Information Service, 1971.

Thompson, Cleopatra D. *The History of the Mississippi Teachers Association*. Washington: N. E. A. Teachers Rights, 1973.

INDEX

Academic Hall, 23
Administration, 31, 40, 43–47; Administrative Council members, listed, 43
Admissions and Recruitment, Office of, 74
Advisement system, 53
African Methodist Episcopal Church, 9, 12
Agriculture, Department of, 68
Agriculture, Research, Extension and Applied Sciences, Division of, 68
Alcorn, Governor James L., and founding of college, 3; term as governor, 8, 9; Senate term of, 10
Alcorn Agricultural and Mechanical College, name changed to, 11, 12; mentioned, 14
Alcorn Agricultural and Mechanical College Informer, The, 19
Alcorn Herald, 81, 113
Alcorn Lever, The, 19
Alcorn Report, 81, 112
Alcorn State University Foundation, 78
Alcorn State University National Alumni Association, 13, 113, 114, 124, 129
Alcorn State University Weekly Bulletin, 81
Alcornites of the Year (1948–1993), 128–39
Alexander, Luther, 112, 113, 133
Alexander, Willie, 113
Allen, Bettye, 63

Alumni Fund, 78
Alumni Hall of Honor, 113–27
Alumni relations, 110–39
Alumni Relations Office, 110
Alumnus Magazine, 81, 112
Ambrose, Daniel, 129
Ames, Adelbert, term as governor, 8, 11
Ammons, William Earthy, 131
Anderson, Dr. Ella, 48
Anderson, Herbert, 86
Appreciation Day, 83
Appropriations, to Alcorn, 57, 92, 140
Arnold, Jessie, 73
Arts and Sciences, Division of, 60, 70
Athletics, 24, 104–09; Athletic Endowment Fund, 113, 114
Ayers, Jake, Case, 141–44; Alcorn State University statement regarding, 143–44

Bacon, Barbara D., 117
Bacon, George J., 131
Bailey, Percy, 25
Bailey, Governor Thomas, 38
Balmat, Dr. Cora, 57
Banks, Willie, 25
Barnes, Emanuel, 43, 46, 86
Bartak, Captain Thomas J., 63
Bartee, Rev. Joseph, 112, 113
Baseball, 24–25, 108
Basketball, 25, 107–08
Bass, Phoeba, 9
Beginning Teacher Support Program, 65

Index

Bell, William H., term as Alcorn president, 24–26; letter to Board of Trustees, Institutions of Higher Learning, 26; mentioned, 30, 67
Belles Lettres Hall, 15
Biggers, Judge Neal, Jr., 141
Biological Sciences, Department of, 60
Black Executive Exchange Program, 67
Black Mississippi Council for Higher Education, 140
Black Mississippi History Makers, Sewell, 81
Black Mississippi History Makers (revised), Sewell and Dwight, 81
Blackburn, John R., 10
Board of Trustees, of colleges, consolidation of, 23
Bolden, Dr. Joyce, 62
Bolden, James L., 46, 86, 97
Bowles, Preston Sewell, term as Alcorn president, 28
Bowles, Robert W., 111, 113, 117, 138
Bowles Industrial Hall, 23
Boyd, John Dewey, term as Alcorn president, 32–36; demonstrations about, 35; mentioned, 72, 94, 100, 111, 129–30
Boyd, Dr. Newtie, 44, 54
Boykin, W. C., Agricultural Science Building, 101
Boykin, William C., Sr., 121
Boykin, Wilmetta, 86
Branch Experiment Station, 68
Braves (Alcorn football team), 105, 106
Briggs, Lieutenant Governor Eddie, 142
Brooks, James, 105
Broome, Paul, 61
Brown, Harry G., 124
Brown, Hon. George F., 10
Brown, Ocie, 106
Brown, Robert, 25
Bryant, Vera H., 135
Buie, Mary, 84
Buildings, construction of, 23, 24, 30, 34, 40–41, 57, 100–02; building expansion program, 31

Burrell, John, 106
Burrus, James, 16
Burrus, John, second president, 14–16; resignation of, 16, 17; mentioned, 22
Burton, Willie, 121
Bush, President George, 141
Business, Division of, 67
Byrne, Mayor Tony, and nursing program, 56–57

Calhoun, John C., 10, 14
Calloway, Thomas J., term as Alcorn president, 17–18, 20
Cameron, Q. T., 102
Campus Campaign Program, 78
Career Planning and Placement Services, Office of, 76
Carter, Cleopatra, 34
Casem, Marino, 104–05, 107, 126
Centennial History of Alcorn A & M College, The, Dunham, 81
Chamberlain, Rev. Jeremiah, and establishment of Oakland College, 5–6
Chamberlain, John, 6
Chamberlain Hunt Academy, establishment of, 7
Chambers, Timothy, 62
Chambliss, Alvin O., Jr., 144
Chemistry and Physics, Department of, 60
Choirs, 62
Civil War, and closing of Oakland College, 7; fighting of near college, 8
Claiborne County, 5
Clark, A. D., 25
Clark, Alyce G., 136
Clark, James "Bo," 124
Clay, Henry, 10
Coates, Milton, 10
Coleman, Bernadine, 86
Coleman, Governor J. P., 32
Coleman, Herman, 128
Commission on Colleges of the Southern Association of Colleges and Schools, 53
Communications, Department of, 61
Congress, United States, and formation

of state, 4–5; and Natchez Trace, 4; mentioned, 15
Constitution of state of Mississippi, 5
Cooley, John, 25
Cooperative Education Program, 74
Cooperative Extension Program, 80–81
Cora S. Balmat School of Nursing, 101
Cotton, 7
Cotton, Dr. Bernard, 62
Counseling and Testing, Office of, 55–56
Cox, George, 128
Cox, Warren E., 125
Crawford, Leon, 67
Crump, Samuel, 25
Cunningham, Fred, 134
Curriculum, in 1871, 12; during 1890s, 16; mentioned, 22, 24, 34, 52–71. *See also* individual departments of study
Curriculum Resource Center, 66, 100

Dalton, V. G., 62
Danzy, Theophilus, 105
Davis, Charles, 44
Davis, Clifton Osborne, Jr., 115
Davis, Jesse, 84
Davis, Milan, history of Alcorn by, 129
Day, Glenda Danette, 83
Demby, Mary P., 137
Demby, Melissa Louise, 122
Demby, William Smith, 112, 113, 130
Dennis, John, 92
Dobbins, Frank, 112
Dodge, Nancy, 57
Donald, Dr. Samuel, 43, 47
Douglass, Frederick, quoted, 10; offered Alcorn presidency, 11
Downs, Walter, 118
Duckworth, Cleveland J., 113
Dumas, E. Albert, 100, 134
Dunham, Melerson Guy, 81
Dunn, Felix H., 115
Dwight, Dr. Margaret, 81

Edney, Dr. Norris, 43, 47, 57–60, 106
Education, Department of, 100

Education and Psychology, Division of, 64–65
Edwards, Alma Brent, 126
Ellis, Leander T., Sr., 118
English and Foreign Languages, Department of, 61
Enrollment, 15, 20, 24, 35, 84
Evers, Charles, 35, 132
Evers, Medgar Wiley, 113–14
Expenditures, university, 15

Facilities, improvements to, 96; mentioned, 99–103
Faculty, administration of, 46–51; during first year, 10; organizations, 48, 70
Field Day, 80
Fiftieth anniversary, programs of, 22–23
Financial aid, 90–91
Fine Arts, Department of, 61–62; Building, 100
Fiscal Affairs, Office of, 91–93
Fiscal management, 34, 40, 46, 89–93
Fisher, Dwight, 106
Fisk University, 14, 17, 19
Follett Bookstore Company, 92
Football, 24–25, 113
Foote, Mattie, 21
Ford, James, 115
Ford, Speaker Tim, 142
Fordice, Governor Kirk, 142
Fortenberry, J. W., 55, 80
Foster, William "Bill," 25, 116
Founding of college, 3–4
Freedmen's Bureau, 9
Fundraising, 77–78, 95, 111
Furniss, W. H., 11

Gamblin, Carolyn, 59
Gardner, Glover C. "Gus," 116
Garner, Lee (Chick), 25
Gayles, Dr. Allene Demby, 130–31
General College for Excellence, 53–56
Giles, Jimmy, 112
Gill, Dr. Alice, 44

Gilliam, James C., 132
Golf, 25
Graduate Council, 58
Graduate studies, 53, 58–59
Grants, 48, 94–95
Grantsmanship, 95
Graves, Andrew, 114, 134
Greenwood, Johnnie, 126
Greenwood, Mary, 112
Griffin, Dr. Samuel, 62
Griffith, Leon, 114
Grossley, Richard Sylvester, 128

Hadley, David, 25
Hall, Robert, 25
Hamlin, William, 62
Harper, Benjamin F., 122
Harrington, Rube, Jr., 131
Harris, Fred, 46
Hawkins, E. T., 112, 127, 131
Hawkins, Erma, 45
Health, Physical Education, and Recreation, Department of, 66; Complex, 100
Hearn, Laura Hart, 122
Hence, Mollie, 25, 108
Henderson, Dr. Frances, 43, 47–48, 57
Henderson, Octavius, stadium honoring, 106
Hendricks, Dr. Epsy, 44, 73
Hendricks, Dr. John, 44, 64
Higher Education Appreciation Day Working for Academic Excellence (HEADWAE), 48
Highway 61, 25, 30
Highway 552, construction of, 103
Hinds County Agricultural High School, 39
Holmes, Dr. Verner, 56
Home Economics, Department of, 69
Honors Curriculum Program, 73-74
Hoover, President Herbert, and race relations, 23
Housing, 84–86
Houze, Henry, 112, 113
Howard, Andrew J., 17
Howard, Augustus George "Gus," 106

Hull, George, Jr., 117
Humphrey, Charles R., 127, 132
Humphrey, Dr. Willie, 60
Hunt, Clinton, 77
Hunt, Dorothy, 86
Hunter, Robert, 129

Improvements, campus, 34
Industrial education, 17–18
Industrial Technology Building, 100
Industry Cluster (National Alliance of Businessmen College/Industry Relationship), 76–77
Institutional Advancement, Planning, and Research, Office of, 95–96, 98
Ireland, Samuel J., 10

Jackson, Andrew, presidency of, 5; and removal of Indians, 7
Jackson, Dr. Franklin, 43, 47, 77, 94
Jackson, Dr. Willie Fred, 68
Jackson, Diana, 83
Jackson, John Allen, 116
Jackson, LaPlose T., 120
Jackson College, establishment of, 7
James, Waldo M., 123
Jefferson College, establishment of, 7; mentioned, 5
Johnson, Albert, 44, 74, 76
Johnson, Betty, 84
Johnson, Classie, 92
Johnson, Paul B., Jr., 35
Johnson, Postmaster Bernard, 87
Johnson, President Lyndon B., and "Cluster," 76–77
Jones, Cardell, 44, 47, 105–06
Jones, Carl E., 117
Jones, George, Jr., 138
Jones, George, Sr., 119
Jones, Louis, Jr., 106
Jones, Wiley, 43, 46
Jordan, Robert, 133
Jordan, T. L., 114

Kellogg Foundation, and nursing program, 58
Keys, Julius, 25

Index

Kilbert, Nathaniel, 107
King, Clennon, 31–33
King, Martin Luther, Jr., 41
Kirksey, Mario, 106
Knowles, Leon Limbric, 122
Konecky, Dr. Larry, 73–74

Land-grant mission, 4, 11, 25, 29, 50
Lane, Lillian Cade, 114
Lanier, William H., term as Alcorn president, 19–20
Lassiter, Wright, Jr., 128
Lawrence, Montague S., 128
Lawson, Louise, 128
Lee, Dr. Donzell, 73
Lee, George W., 129
Lee, Dr. John, 66
Lewis, Edna, 79
Library, 23, 72–73, 101
Lockhart, Jewell, 112, 114, 134
Long-Range Planning Committee, 97
Lorman, Mississippi, 6
Lott, Albert L., 125–26
Love, Clayton, 25
Love, Pamela, 83
Lyceum Association, 13
Lyells, Ruby Elizabeth Cowan Stutts, 112, 129
Lynch, John R., and establishment of Alcorn, 10

Magee, Delors E., 130–31
Magee, Willie, 25, 110–11
Manual Training Department, 22
Marcus, Chester L., 130
Martin, James, 44, 102, 120
Martin, John Adams, term as Alcorn president, 22
Martin, Oscar, 25
Masingale, Eula, 69
Mathematical Sciences, Department of, 63
Mays, Nebraska, 128
McArthur, Dr. Willie, 84
McCoy, Willie, 25
McGowan, Doris, 66
McGowan, Willie, 25, 106, 107

McLaurin, Anselm, 19
McLaurin, Benjamin Franklin, 131
McLaurin, Dr. Sidney, 44
McManus, Joyce, 57
McMillion, Grady, Jr., 114
McMurtry, Linda, 79
McNair, Fred "Air I," 105
McNair, Steve "Air II," 105
Military Science, Department of (Army ROTC), 63
Miller, James Earl, 120, 132
Minor, James, 120
Minor, Lawrence W., 10
Mississippi, capitals of, 8; organization of state, 5
Mississippi A. & M. College (later Mississippi State University), establishment of, 8
Mississippi Agricultural and Forestry Experiment Station, 80
Mississippi Association for Teachers in Colored Schools, 22
Mississippi Legislature, and Alcorn highway, 25; appropriations to University by, 15, 23, 24, 40; and founding of college, 3
Mississippi Senate, and Hiram Revels, 9
Mississippi Territory, 4
Mitchell, Isaiah, 10
Mitchell, John G., 10
Moman, Thomas Madison, II, 112, 117
Moore, Aretta Esterling, 123
Moore, Lonnie, 120
Morehouse College, 41
Morrill Act of 1862, 11; Second Morrill Act (1890), 15, 16
Morris, Dr. Alpha, 48, 62, 114, 136
Morris, Dr. Jesse, 47, 79, 100, 121, 130
Morris, George, 25
Morris/Boykin Agricultural Science Building, 100
Moseley, J. H., 112
Moses, Clynell, 86
Moses, Dr. Napoleon, 69
Moses, O. W., 46
Moses, Willie, 83

Mott, Charles Stuart, Foundation, 75
Murphy, Zelmarine, 112

Natchez Trace, 4
National Association for Equal Opportunity in Higher Education, Distinguished Alumni of the Year Citation, 128
National Association for the Advancement of Colored People, 31–32, 35, 113, 140
National Association of Industrial Technology, 70
National Association of State Universities and Land-Grant Colleges, 56
National Association of State Universitites and Land-Grant Colleges Distinguished Alumni, 128–29
National Collegiate Athletic Association, 105, 107, 108, 109
National Council for Accreditation of Teacher Education (NCATE), 59, 65, 70
National League of Nursing, 57
National Youth Sports Program, 108
Nelson, William B., 119
Netter, Mildrette, 25, 108, 110
New National Era, The, description of Alcorn in, 10–11
Norwood, Willie, 25
Nursing, Division of, 56–58, 70

Oakland College, establishment of, 6; faculty of, 6; refurbishment of, 34; mentioned, 3, 10, 11, 101–02
Odem, Octavia, 86
Otis, Dr. Jesse R., term as Alcorn president, 30–32
Owens, Freddie, 112

Pandy, Dr. Shanti, 84
Panic of 1837, 7
Parker, Dr. Henry, 79
Payne, Ralph, 44, 81
Payton, Gertrude, 118
Payton, Mack Willie, 118, 137
Personnel Office, 93
Peyton, Arthur Bennett, Sr., 114

Phillip, Antonio, 83
Physical education, 22, 24
Pickett, Robert, 116
Pillars, Lawrence, 113
Pipes, Dr. William H., term as Alcorn president, 28–30
Poindexter, George, 5
Posey, Dr. Josephine McCann, 48, 112
Powell, Eunice D., 100
Powell, Lottie H., 136
Powell, Melvin, 25
Powell, Willie Mimms, 115
Price, William, 25
Public Relations, Office of, 81
Purnell, Franklin, 25
Purnell, Vernon, 25
Purviance, Rev. James, 6–7

Redmond, Sidney L., 119
Reed, Smith, 25
Reese, Joseph W., 125
Republican government, 8, 9, 11
Revels, Hiram R., first Alcorn president, 9–11; biographical sketch of, 9; resignation of, 14; United States senator, 10
Reynolds, Wilson H., term as Alcorn president, 17
Rhodes, Calvin, 115, 132–33
Rigsby, Esther Martin, 121
Rigsby, John, 112, 118
Ritter, Dr. Gerald, 66
Roberson, Angie, 112
Robinson, Dr. Levie, 44, 65
Robinson, Ella Watson, 125
Robinson, James, 102
Rodney, Mississippi, 10
ROTC, 63. *See also* Department of Military Science
Rowan, Levi J., elected Alcorn president, 20, 21; firing of, 22; reelection of, 22; mentioned, 101
Rowan Administration Building, 23
Russell, Dr. Joseph, 60
Rust College, 12, 24

Salaries, of teachers, 24
Sampson, Kenneth, 62

Index

Sams, Leanna, 108
Sanders, Dean I. H., 46
Second Morrill Act (1890), 15, 16
Security, 86–87
Segrest, Patricia Anderson, 123
Senior Award for Excellence, winners of, 78
Sewell, Dr. George, 81
Shaw (Rust) College, establishment of, 7
Shelvy, Laura, 44, 90
Simmons, Christine, 123
Simmons, Dr. Kenneth, 48, 69, 118, 135–36
Sims, Jerry, 25, 108, 110
Slavery, and cotton culture, 7; and Civil War, 8
Smiley, William, 62
Smith, Artie, 62
Smith, Dr. Eva D., 57
Smith, Dr. Joseph, 63
Smith, Dr. Robert L., 66
Smith, Elbert, 86
Smith, Henry R., 121, 133–34
Smith, Mrs. Clarence Carter, 62
Snodgrass, Dr. A. D., 110, 112
Social Sciences, Department of, 62
South Central Athletic Conference, 24
Southern Association of Colleges and Schools, 30, 34, 40
Southwestern Athletic Conference (SWAC), 35, 105, 106, 107
Spears, Marvell, 84
Special Services Program, 54
Spinks, Johnny "Jack," 25, 106, 116
Sports. See Athletics; individual sports
Stanton, R. L., 6
State Advisory Commission, Title VI-A of the Higher Education Act of 1965, 40
State Institutions of Higher Learning, Board of Trustees, 10, 20, 26, 58, 92, 140, 142; and Clennon King, 33
Stepney, Ann Johnson, 118
Stepney, Lutille, 123
Stevens, Alonzo, 106, 108
Stevens, Ruth, 57
Steward, Harry, 99–100
Stewart, Angela, 83
Stewart, Dr. Troy, 60
Stirgus, Jim, 112
Stone, Governor John M., 17
Stringer, Emmett James, 119
Student Affairs Office, 87
Student Financial Aid, Office of, 90
Student services, 82–88; health service, 84; meals, 86; post office, 87; activities, 87–88
Students, admission requirements for, 73–76; expenses, 91–92; racial makeup of, 70–71
Support services, 72–81

Taylor, Oliver, 44, 78, 93
Taylor, Rickey, 106
Teachers, assessment of, 64; salaries of, 24
Teachers Training Department, 23
Tellis, Vivian, 79
Tennis, 25
Testing, 55–56
Thacker, Clay, 25
Thomas, David E., 115
Thomas, Issac, 121, 135
Thomas, Justice Clarence, 143
Thomas, Mabel, 123–24
Thomas, Matthew, 112, 137–38
Thomas, Shayla, 74
Thompson, Cleopatra D., 115, 128, 130
Thornton, Marietta, 86
Thuha, Perma, 91
Tillman, Dr. Charles, 68
Title III, Higher Education Act of 1965, 95
Title VI-A, Higher Education Act of 1965, 40
Tougaloo College, establishment of, 7; mentioned, 19, 39, 41
Track and field, 25, 108
Training, agricultural, 25–26; mechanical, 25–26
Triplett, Rev. Edward H., term as Alcorn president, 18–19
Turner, Dr. Jonathan, 99
Turner, John, Jr., 79

Tuskegee Institute, 29
Tyndall, Dr. Rose Mary, 57

United States Supreme Court, and Ayers Case, 142
University of Mississippi, 4
University Press of Mississippi, 81
Upward Bound, 78–79
Utica Junior College, 38

Veals, Edmonia, 108
Vicksburg Consortium in Collaboration with Mississippi State University, 59

WPRL-FM, 100
Waites, Emma, 79
Walker, Craig, 25
Walker, Lonnie, 107
Walker, Robert, 140
Walker, Shirley, 107
Walls, John, 44, 112
Walls, Mary, 87
Warren County, 5
Washington, Booker T., 17, 19
Washington, Carolyn Carter, 41–42
Washington, Dave, 113
Washington, Dr. Walter, term as Alcorn president, 37–43; mentioned, 56, 67, 68, 72, 75, 80, 83, 91, 94, 97, 103, 111, 112, 126, 140, 141, 142
Washington, Elnora, 79
Washington, Shirley, 112
Waters, Dr. Rudolph, biographical sketch of, 44–45; mentioned, 81, 139

Watkins, Lawrence, 25
Watson, Claude E., 116–17
Weathersby, Davis, 124
Weaver, Sam, 107
Webster, Daniel, 10
Weeks, Marvin, 25
White, Dr. Calvin, 79
White House Conference on Education, 34
Whitney, Dave, 100, 106–07, 127
Wilburn, D. W., 113, 115, 133
Wilburn, Hampton P., 129
Wilkes, Shelby R., 121, 128
Wilkinson County, 5
Williams, Clementine A., 121
Williams, Dr. Malvin, 43
Williams, Dr. Robert, 44, 67
Williams, Governor John Bell, 40
Williams, Helen, 25, 108
Williams, Lettie, 87
Williams, Patrick F., 10
Williams, Riley, 25
Willie Mae Latham Taylor Park, 103
Womack, Ivan, 25
Women, admission of, 18, 20
Woody, Anthony, 107
Woolfolk, Anthony, 106
World War I, 15
World War II, 24, 25, 27
Wynn, Rose Brent, 124

Young Men's Christian Association, 15

www.ingramcontent.com/pod-product-compliance
Lightning Source LLC
Chambersburg PA
CBHW030339240426
43661CB00052B/1689